CHARY, Frederick B. **The Bulgarian Jews and the final solution, 1940–1944.** Pittsburgh, 1972. 246p tab bibl 72-78931. 9.95. ISBN 0-8229-3251-2

The destruction of the Jews in Europe in the Second World War resulted in many emotional and nonscholarly works. But the last generation has also seen, in more obscure places, a sizable body of impeccable critical studies by first-rate professionals. The work under review is a welcome addition to the latter body of work. Chary has done an admirable job of working over German and Bulgarian archival sources, supplemented by extensive interviewing. His presentation is well above the usual norms for lucidity and clarity in academic writing. The principal thesis is persuasively presented: that complex internal struggles, rather than sheer benevolence, were responsible for the survival of the Bulgarian Jews. The chief weakness of the book is the author's inability to use the Hebrew-language monograph by B. Arditti which was the pioneer monograph in the field. References and documents cited by Arditti are used by the author with proper acknowledgements, however. This book belongs in medium-size and large collections on World War II, on the Balkans, and on contemporary Jewry. Less specialized collections should get the large-canvas works by Gerald Reit-

Continued

CHARY

linger, *The final solution* (2nd ed., 1968); Raul Hilberg, *The destruction of the European Jews* (1961); and Isaiah Trunk, *Judenrat* (CHOICE, Apr. 1973).

The Bulgarian Jews and the Final Solution, 1940-1944

The Bulgarian Jews and the Final Solution 1940-1944

Frederick B. Chary

UNIVERSITY OF PITTSBURGH PRESS

Library of Congress Catalog Card Number 72-78931
ISBN 0-8229-3251-2
Copyright © 1972, University of Pittsburgh Press
Henry M. Snyder & Co., Inc., London
Manufactured in the United States of America

To Julie

Contents

Tables

Acknowledgments

A work of this nature involving many people and derived from many sources incurs numerous debts of gratitude, the first of which goes to James F. Clarke for his constant guidance and invaluable help.

I would also like to thank the following people and institutions for assisting my research or opening their archives to me: Robert Wolfe, Richard Bauer, and the staff at the German Records Section of the National Archives; the United States Department of State; the Jewish Institute (YIVO), New York; the Wiener Library, London; Le Centre de Documentation Juive Contemporaine, Paris; Der Institut für Zeitgeschichte, Munich; Yad WaShem, Jerusalem, with special thanks to Ora Alcalay; the Ichud Olei Bulgariyah, Tel Aviv, especially Joseph Ben; Benjamin Arditi; Haim Keshales; Norbert and Joseph Iasharoff; Natan Grinberg; the libraries of the HaShomer HaTzier kibbutz "Moreshet" and Kibbutz Lohamei HaGhetaoth, Israel; the State Archives of the People's Republic of Macedonia in Skopje, especially Angel Corpasev; the Organization of the Jewish Religious Communities in Yugoslavia; the Bulgarian Academy of Sciences, especially the Hebrew Studies section of the Institute of Balkan Studies; Solomon Israel; Strahil Gichev; Snezhka Panova; S. Kaludova; Nikolai Todorov; Zlati Zlatov; Vladislav Topalov; Malvina Nalchadzhian; and the staffs of the Bulgarian National Library—Cyril and Methodius, the library of the Bulgarian Academy of Sciences, and the library of the University of Sofia.

Additional thanks must go to Patricia Havelice and Betty Shaw, research librarians of the Indiana University Northwest library; Larry A. Fortudo of the Regional Campuses Libraries and Andrew Turchyn of the Slavic Library of Indiana University; and Christine Longstreet and the reference staff of the Harper and Regenstein libraries at the University of Chicago. At one stage or another Fred Duffel, Christine Kondilac, Florence Crane, and especially Rosalie Zak helped in the typing of my various manuscripts. Several of my colleagues, particularly Abshalom Mizrahi and Henry Knopf, have advised me on several matters concerning foreign-language translations and grammar. All translations, however, are my own. My thanks go also to Karilyn Bouson of the University of Pittsburgh Press for her suggestions in the editing of the manuscript.

There were, in addition to the people and institutions listed, many other scholars, as well as participants in the events described in this work, who extended to me the benefit of their knowledge, research, and experiences. Needless to say, all errors that may appear in this work are my own.

I would also like to express my gratitude to the Andrew Mellon Foundation for Education and Culture, the Inter-University Committee on Travel Grants, and the Bulgarian Academy of Sciences, all of which helped finance my research abroad.

Finally, I would like to express my great thanks to my wife Julie who has lived with this work as long as I have, who has contributed to every phase of its creation as research assistant, secretary, translator, proofreader, and typist, and whose love and patience throughout, more than anything else, helped bring this project to a successful conclusion.

Introduction

The justification for studying the application of the Nazi Final Solution to the Bulgarian Jews lies in the rather startling observation that more Jews were living in Bulgaria after World War II than before. In the general tragedy of the war years it would seem improbable that the Jewish community of a small nation could escape annihilation—especially in a country which was part of the Axis alliance.

The Bulgarians themselves have turned the anomaly into a source of pride by claiming to be the only nation in occupied Europe where all the Jews survived. Great political controversy has grown up over the cause and manner of the survival of the Bulgarian Jewish community. This controversy manifests itself in the question: "Who saved the Bulgarian Jews?" The current major argument concerns the role of King Boris III in the events surrounding the Jewish question in his country. One group claims that the king was responsible for saving the Jews and that he did so by preconceived plan, deliberately misrepresenting his intentions to Berlin. Some claim that the king's mysterious death in 1943 was in fact an assassination ordered by Hitler either in part or as a whole because Boris would not permit the Nazis to deport the Bulgarian Jews to the extermination camps in Poland.

On the other side, some historians and commentators believe that the Bulgarian Jews were saved despite the king. They say that Boris either wholeheartedly agreed with the Nazi anti-Semitic policies or was indifferent to them. Only pressure from groups within the country and outside it forced the king to cancel his plans for deporting the Jews to Poland.

The Bulgarian response to the Final Solution is complicated by the Bulgarian deportation of Greek and Yugoslav Jews from territories Bulgaria occupied in the Balkans. Why did Sofia deport these Jews while hesitating to do the same to Jews of Bulgarian citizenship? Did the Bulgarians have less control there? Were the non-Bulgarian Jews sacrificed to save those with Bulgarian citizenship?

This book attempts to investigate the attitude and actions of the Bulgarian government with respect to the Jews in these critical years. By examining the political pressures on Sofia as well as the response to these pressures in the enactment of anti-Semitic legislation and deportation procedures both fulfilled and canceled, I hope to uncover the reason for the paradox of the Final Solution in Germany's Balkan partner. The differences in Sofia's attitudes and reactions with respect to Bulgarian and non-Bulgarian Jews are also examined. I have described the preparations and deportation procedures at some length to show the inhumane and at the same time bizarrely mechanical and bureaucratic nature of the Final Solution in Bulgaria (and presumably elsewhere). The details of the Bulgarian deportations are also a case study for other areas in Nazi Europe. Furthermore, the behavior of the Bulgarian government under political pressures can give insight not only into the nature of Bulgarian and Axis politics in the early forties, but also into the general nature of the Jewish question on the continent.

This book examines also the relationship of the various sections of Bulgarian ruling circles and society to the Jewish question and the Final Solution. These sections include the king and court, the church, the *Subranie* ("parliament"), the political opposition, and various other groups. I also investigate the important question of the relative strength of political forces inside the country and those outside, for example, the Allies, as to their effect on the events concerning the Jews in Bulgaria. Finally, I consider the Bulgarians' claim that theirs was the only nation in Nazi Europe to save the Jews and, indeed, whether it is useful to ask: "Who saved the Bulgarian Jews?"

Transliteration Note

I have used the Library of Congress Bulgarian transliteration system except that I use *H* instead of *Kh* for the Bulgarian *X* and I have not used diacritical marks. However, familiar names like *Sofia* and *Bulgaria* are not transliterated exactly.

The Bulgarian Jews and the Final Solution, 1940-1944

Bulgaria, Germany, and the Jews

Bulgaria After 1934

The story of Bulgaria's treatment of the Jewish community within its boundaries during World War II is not just another history of horror and degradation or, for that matter, glory and humanity. It is a story which reveals the interconnections among big nations and small in the modern world. It reveals the way in which the forces of society and the power of ideology shape the destiny of individual men and separate peoples no matter how disparate or distant from the originators of those forces and ideology they may seem to be. The history of the implementation of Nazi "Jewish policy" in Bulgaria gives us an opportunity to see this interconnection between ideology and action, between great powers and small, as well as the interplay of societal confrontations.

From 1941 to 1944, Bulgaria was an ally of the Axis powers in Europe. Dragged into the war after vainly hoping to remain neutral, its government did what it could to keep the country's individuality while at the same time trying to uphold alliance requirements as Berlin relayed them to Sofia. Recognizing and dealing with a Jewish question was one of these requirements, just as was billeting of German troops outside of Sofia, allowing gestapo agents to help the king's police track down Bulgarian partisans, and permitting the German navy to take over the ports of Varna and Burgas to build the vessels that patrolled the Black Sea.

The Bulgarian Jews became a touchstone for the Berlin-Sofia alliance. Their fate rested more on the military fortunes of the Wehrmacht in Europe than on the political fortunes of the anti-Semites in Sofia. At the same time the eagerness or hesitancy with which the Bulgarian government implemented the Final Solution in the country gives us a picture of this alliance in progress. We can see here the interaction of three entities: the Third Reich, the Bulgarian government (and society), and the Bulgarian Jewish community. We shall see how historical events during the war years embraced these entities.

Since 1935 Bulgaria had been controlled by King Boris III of the house of Saxe-Coburg. Extremely shrewd and cognizant of the games of power politics, the monarch governed his state through ministers selected from his coterie of advisors and chamberlains with a disregard for the constitutional limitations upon his rule. This sort of royal dictatorship was not unique to Bulgaria in the thirties. Boris's fellow Balkan monarchs Alexander of Yugoslavia and Carol of Rumania followed the same form, but the former was assassinated by Croatian and Macedonian terrorists and the latter fled his country, pursued by Rumanian fascists. Boris's version of the royal dictatorship was more successful.

It was not the king, however, who had dissolved constitutional government in Bulgaria but a clique of left-wing army colonels. In May 1934, when the ruling Democrat party was unable to deal successfully with the multiple problems of the kingdom, especially the perennial Macedonian question, a section of the powerful Military League, led by Cols. Damian Velchev and Kimon Georgiev, seized power in a *coup d'état*.

The colonels were connected to a small political group of intellectuals —the *Zveno* (Link).[1] Writing later at a time when Marxist terminology was becoming an unquestioned frame of reference for politics in his country, one of the Zveno's prominent leaders called the group "left members of the right parties."[2] "Right" in this context meant *bourgeois*, not *fascist*, and the coup leaders were in many ways radical and progressive; some were even socialist. Some of them, including Velchev and Georgiev, appeared as ministers after the war in collaboration with the Bulgarian Communist party.

In their brief opportunity in government, the Zveno colonels attempted to solve the problems besetting the state. They halted the terrorism of the Internal Macedonian Revolutionary Organization (IMRO), whose interparty shootings had disrupted life in the country and whose raids had caused Bulgaria international embarrassment, but with which no party had dealt in the past because of political entanglement. Reflecting the widespread hostility toward the rival groups of

1. For the history of Bulgaria in the middle and late thirties, see Bulgarian Academy of Sciences, *Istoriia na Bulgariia* [History of Bulgaria], ed. D. Kosev et al. (Sofia: "Nauka i izkustvo," 1962-64), III, 279-354 (hereafter cited as BAN, *Istoriia*). See also Dimo Kazasov, *Burni godini 1918-1944* [Turbulent years 1918-1944] (Sofia: Knigaizdatelstvo "Naroden pechat," 1949), pp. 497-537, 552-649.

2. Kazasov, p. 435.

lawyers who had dominated Bulgarian political life for their own benefit since 1923, the colonels also outlawed all parties.

Georgiev's government lasted only eight months, but during that
time the king feared for his throne. Boris had heard republican sentiments expressed in Bulgaria before, and now the Zveno group did not
hesitate to speculate openly about the advantages of a republican government. However, the king was able to capitalize on divisions among
the military clique, the confusion in the country, and the lack of mass
support for the colonels to oust Georgiev in January 1935. After two
short-lived governments and a series of back-room negotiations, Boris
was able to install as his prime minister Georgi K'oseivanov, who had
served the king as his personal court chancellor.

K'oseivanov remained as the prime minister for his monarch during the
next five years through eight successive governments—the longest period
for any Bulgarian prime minister in the twentieth century until the
1950s. Boris took the opportunity presented by the May 19 coup to
continue the more effective measures of the colonels. Political parties
remained illegal and the national parliament suspended by the colonels
was not recalled until 1938. Furthermore the IMRO never regained the
influence that it had had in the early thirties.

The king earned much popularity in Bulgaria. After the war disasters
of 1913 and 1918 the prestige of the court had declined greatly; yet the
country's sympathies were generally still monarchist rather than republican. Boris was able to endear himself to his subjects, for none of
the responsibility for the tragic war years stigmatized him when he
ascended the throne in 1918. He was a consummate politician with a
charming personality. His marriage to the Italian princess Giovanna in
1930 increased his popularity in the country.

Bulgaria's constitution (written 1879) gave the king great potential
for political action, but it also contained the possibility of restraint under a forceful and popular prime minister, which had been the experience of Boris's father, Ferdinand, with Stefan Stambulov in the nineteenth century, and of Boris himself with Aleksandur Stamboliiski in
the 1920s. Boris felt threatened by political opposition, small as well as
great. He could not work comfortably in conflict; and although indeed
a skillful politician, he had a practice, whenever possible, of eliminating
anyone who might be a source of conflict or potential competition. The
king's main political goals were to preserve the royal line and follow
the best possible policies for Bulgaria as he saw them.

Boris's apprehension of opposition and republicanism became apparent in his anxious uneasiness over Velchev, the major author of the coup. He deemed it insufficient that he should be merely removed from power and certainly had a hand in the colonel's arrest and trial. At a secret court-martial in February 1936 a number of members of the Military League were tried for sedition. The league was dissolved and the court sentenced Velchev to death. Minister of War General Hristo Lukov, later a leader of the fascist Legionaires, hoped to carry out the sentence swiftly. However, public agitation at home and abroad, when the sentence was learned, called for leniency for Velchev. According to Bulgarian law the minister of justice had to approve the sentence before it was carried out. When the latter refused to do so, the king had no choice but to commute Velchev's sentence to life imprisonment. Boris's power was by no means absolute, and the most he could do to show his ire in this situation was to demand the dismissal of the errant minister of justice.

Opposition to the king and his government continued to exist in Bulgaria, although the means of expressing it constitutionally were for the time being prorogued. Even mayors and local officials were now appointed from Sofia. Nevertheless, the political parties, although in law disbanded, still remained a factor.

The most popular party in the country was the complex Bulgarian National Agrarian Union (BZNS), a coalition of various landed interests and poor peasants, which had crumbled under the weight of its irreconcilable factions and the blows of the court and bourgeoisie in the twenties. In the years of Boris's rule there were many parties calling themselves agrarian, but the organization's most radical leaders were forced to live abroad.

Furthermore, Bulgaria had a powerful Communist party (BKP), illegal since 1925. In fact, the country's most famous citizen may have been not its king, but the secretary-general of the Comintern, Georgi Dimitrov, the hero of the Reichstag fire trial in Leipzig in 1934. The BKP had demonstrated its popularity after World War I by gaining votes in the parliamentary elections second only to the BZNS. Even in 1932 under the name of Bulgarian Workers' party they were able to win municipal elections in Sofia. The Russian connection with bolshevism was an aid rather than a drawback to the party in Bulgaria, and, there being no really serious minority problem in the country, the party was distinguished in Eastern Europe because its membership included a high percentage of Bulgarian nationals rather than disgruntled members of minorities.

In general there were three major political groupings in the country during the royal dictatorship: a) the illegal opposition of Agrarian, Communist, and Zveno members in exile or under arrest; b) the court and its agents running the country but themselves divided into several quarreling factions; and c) the "legal" opposition of old bourgeois party men—distinguished lawyers, financiers, industrialists, merchants, and statesmen—whose political groups were outlawed, but who were still themselves in a position to influence affairs. Finally, in discussing the politics of any European country in the thirties, mention must be made of a fourth group—the fascists.

The extreme right wing of Bulgarian politics included for the most part a catchall of small fascist and Nazi-style parties and movements, but also several which attained a degree of prominence. There was never anything approaching a mass fascist movement in the kingdom, and these groups relied primarily upon their leaders' reputations, when this was possible, or on their connections with fascist movements abroad. The latter in the thirties were tenuous at best, and, with the exception of the Tsankovite movement, Bulgarian fascism before the last years of the decade was a collection of squabbling comic-opera groups led by would-be führers.[3]

Even the Tsankovite movement, the most pretentious of the right-wing groups, gravely suffered from a lack of support. Aleksandur Tsankov, the eponymous leader of the movement, had been a professor of economics at the University of Sofia and became his country's prime minister after leading the coup which ousted Aleksandur Stamboliiski in 1923. That event earned him the everlasting mistrust of Bulgaria's peasantry and thus limited his political future.

In the thirties he formed the National Social Movement which became known by his name. It was characterized by nationalism and fascism, but was not quite the same as Hitler's nazism. The apogee of the Tsankovite movement occurred in 1935 when King Boris negotiated with his ex-premier to enter into a black-red government of sorts including both Tsankov's followers and members of one of the legal BZNS factions. Because the man associated with the death of Aleksandur Stamboliiski was so disliked by the peasantry, the Agrarians re-

---

3. There is no adequate study of Bulgarian fascism, but a good nonscholarly description can be found in Gospodin Gochev, *Biuro "D-r Delius"* [Bureau "Dr. Delius"], 2d ed. rev. (Sofia: Narodna kultura, 1969), pp. 161-70. See also Benjamin Arditi, *Yehudi Bulgariyah bishanah hamishpat hanatzi: 1940-1944* [The Jews of Bulgaria during the years of Nazi occupation: 1940-1944] (Tel Aviv: Israel Press, 1962), pp. 24-35.

fused to agree and nothing came of it.[4] Tsankov's fortunes declined after that, but he still remained a prominent personality on the Bulgarian political scene, especially as a member of the opposition in the wartime parliament, following his personal, indeed often erratic, ideological path.

In the late thirties and during the war years, two other important fascist organizations gained prominence in Bulgaria—*Suiuz na bulgarskite natsionalni legioni* (Union of Bulgarian National Legions), called simply Legionaires, and *Ratnitsi napreduka na bulgarshtinata* (Guardians of the Advancement of the Bulgarian National Spirit), called *Ratnitsi*. The Legionaires' importance, like that of the Tsankovite movement, came from the renown of their leaders, particularly the previously mentioned Hristo Lukov, minister of war from 1935 to 1938, and Nikola Zhekov, who had been commander in chief of Bulgarian forces in World War I. In this period, the leader of the Ratnitsi was the less illustrious Professor Asen Kantardzhiev, but Petur Gabrovski, one of the organization's founders, held cabinet posts from 1939 to 1943.

The Ratnitsi and the Legionaires like Tsankov maintained connections with various Germans and German organizations, including the SS (*Schutzstaffel*). Although the exact nature of these connections is obscure, there are sufficient allusions to them in captured German records to substantiate their existence.[5] Thus what these fascist groups lacked in popular strength they managed to make up through the power of their German connections.

The inability of the Bulgarian right to create a genuine native fascist movement à la Italy or Germany gives some insight into the nature of Boris's rule in the late thirties. It was not a new government born of the twentieth century as much as another phase in the struggle between crown and Subranie that had marked Bulgaria's history since 1879. In fact the king did not align himself with either of the major members of the fascist group in Europe on coming to power, but decided on a foreign policy that kept the country close to the League of Nations.

4. For these political negotiations see Vladimir Mitev, "Utvurzhdavane na monarhofashiskata diktatura v Bulgariia prez 1935-1936 g i 'Tsankovoto dvizhenie' " [Confirmation of the monarcho-fascist dictatorship in Bulgaria during 1935-1936 and the "Tsankovite movement"], *Istoricheski pregled* [Historical review], 23, no. 6 (1967), pp. 62-81.

5. Washington, D.C., The National Archives and Records Service, General Services Administration, German Records Microfilmed at Alexandria, Va., Microcopy no. T120 (hereafter cited as T120), serial 2320H (Foreign Office, Inland II geheim, packet 92, Counterespionage and Agents in Bulgaria, January 1941 to September 1943). Roll 1305 is particularly informative on this matter.

Although Bulgaria still maintained its revisionist intentions in the Balkans, Boris tried to attain these national aspirations through peaceful methods and *rapprochement*. He supported the League on Abyssinia and Spain and sought an alliance with Yugoslavia; nonetheless, he could not bring himself to join the Balkan Entente, a mutual defense pact among Rumania, Greece, Yugoslavia, and Turkey, designed to uphold the status quo, that is, the Treaty of Neuilly, and hence directed against Bulgaria. If Bulgaria had joined, it would have been tantamount to renouncing even by peaceful means a revision of the treaty.

In 1938 Boris and K'oseivanov felt satisfied enough with the progress of their regime to restore the Subranie. The new electoral law forbade candidates to run as members of a party slate. This had been tried with success for the government in 1937 in the first local elections since the coup, but it was somewhat unrealistic to believe that the measures would prevent the parties from exhibiting some of the influence they had had in the past.

At the polls the government employed tactics associated with previous Bulgarian elections—control of ballots, blocking known opponents from voting, use of police guards, etc. Government supporters could electioneer, but opponents were frequently enjoined from doing so because of the rules against political parties. Boris and K'oseivanov hoped that these measures and restrictive qualifications on candidates would insure them a substantial majority.

Considering these harsh measures, the results were a setback. It is true that about 100 of the 160 representatives supported the government.[6] In an open election this would be a landslide, but in view of stringent control of the elections, the sizable opposition demonstrated widespread dissatisfaction with the regime. Furthermore, many of the government supporters were only mildly committed, and during the course of the Subranie meetings K'oseivanov was embarrassed several times.

The opposition in the Subranie, although it was unable to carry through many bills or stop many governmental proposals, was able to make its opinions felt. On one occasion it brought down the government. Boris was not happy with this unexpectedly vocal parliament, and in 1940 when K'oseivanov's cabinet went through a crisis, the king prorogued the body.

6. *La Parole Bulgare* (Sofia), March 13, 1938, p. 1; March 20, 1938, p. 1; and April 3, 1938, p. 1; Marin V. Pundeff, "Bulgaria's Place in Axis Policy" (Ph.D. diss., University of Southern California, 1958), pp. 79-81; BAN, *Istoriia*, III, 337.

However, politics in Bulgaria in the late thirties was not purely a domestic matter. The balance between monarchal dictatorship and parliamentary rule reflected international pressures on a continent where a contest raged among twentieth-century alternatives to classical liberalism. Bulgaria never completely gave up the principle of parliamentary government even in the days when it was most committed to the Axis alliance, but the emasculation of the parliament and the increased authority of the king in governing Bulgaria alone enhanced his ability to lead Bulgaria into a German alliance.

The Growth of a Bulgarian-German Alliance

Official Bulgarian anti-Semitism was dependent on the solidifying relations between Bulgaria and Nazi Germany throughout the late 1930s. A major turning point toward the Axis appeared in 1938 when, although contacts with the West were still strong and although elements of an embryonic German-Bulgarian alliance had been present even earlier, Bulgaria became heavily reliant on German loans, trade, and armaments.

Such economic dependence is a major part of any successful alliance commitment, but the major factors in the determination of an alliance are the position and influence of political factions and parties within the state and the power and influence of possible patron states. All the great European powers had both historical connections with Bulgaria and sympathizers within the country. Germany had many friends in the Bulgarian army, through ties of respect and traditional alliance, and in the middle class, many of whom had been educated in Berlin, Munich, or Vienna. Furthermore, economic patterns of the thirties brought Bulgaria closer to Germany. There were also small groups of Nazi ideologues who inherently admired the Third Reich more than did mere Germanophiles. Yet other countries too—France, England, the United States, Italy, and especially Russia—had their champions in the country.

Germany for its part was interested in the economic domination of Southeastern Europe. As long as the Balkans presented no strategic threat, Hitler would not need a German physical presence there and was content that Germany become the economic overlord of the whole region. This meant that, as far as was feasible, the Reich must not appear the partisan of one Balkan state over another even though in reality no one could forget the special relationship Germany had toward Bulgaria as a fellow revisionist power.

Germany's economic penetration into Eastern Europe and the Balkans in the thirties succeeded spectacularly, especially as economic ventures by the West had greatly decreased. The Danube region, which was Germany's natural field of commerce anyway, became even less attached to Western commercial interests and more closely connected to the business centers of Central Europe. Furthermore, since the Reich's economy was geared to political necessities rather than the world market, government-sponsored German business was more ready than the West to penetrate into the Balkans. Many histories of this period claim that Nazi economic penetration to the East in the thirties gave the advantage to the Germans and really swindled the smaller trading partners—that the German system forced these nations into bartering their goods for German items of poor quality or little use to their economies. However, we must remember that, despite its political orientation, the German economy was still affected by the depression and money was scarce; and the Germans were willing to trade with the countries to the east—sometimes buying their goods at prices even higher than the world market—when the rest of the world was not.[7]

The growth of Bulgarian dependence on Germany for foreign trade can be seen in table 1. The Germans and Bulgarians signed a trade treaty based on a barter and clearing system in 1934. Even before this, Germany was Bulgaria's major trade partner, but afterward it became even more important and soon handled more Bulgarian trade than all the other partners together. At the same time, Germany concluded similar trade agreements with other countries in Eastern Europe, and the German share in trade there rose accordingly, yet in Bulgaria it had a greater percentage of trade than elsewhere.[8] On the other hand, Bulgaria's share of German trade was only 2 percent. Thus trade dependence rested heavily on one side.[9] Economic subordination does not necessarily mean political subordination, but it is a major factor leading to it. Germany, moreover, although strongly favored in the trade balance, accumulated a debt to Bulgaria which reached 1,783,000,000 leva ($21,600,000) by 1939.[10] This factor bound Bulgaria to further German trade if the debt was to be liquidated.

7. C. A. Macartney and A. W. Palmer, *Independent Eastern Europe: A History* (London: Macmillan, 1962), pp. 314-15.
8. Ibid., pp. 315, 339-40; Pundeff, "Bulgaria's Place," pp. 101-04.
9. Pundeff, "Bulgaria's Place," p. 104.
10. L. B. Valev, "Ekonomika Bolgarii Nakanune Vtoroi Mirovoi Voini" [Bulgarian economics on the eve of the Second World War], *Kratkie soobshchenie* [Notes] of the Academy of Science of the USSR, Institute for Slavic Studies, no. 32 (Moscow, 1961), pp. 23-24. Valev cites the archives of the Bulgarian Ministry of Internal Affairs as his source.

TABLE 1
IMPORTS TO AND EXPORTS FROM BULGARIA
(Percentage of Total for Bulgaria)

| Year | Imports to Bulgaria | | |
	From Germany (and Austria after 1938)	From Italy	From United Kingdom, France, and United States
1929	22.2%	10.7%	20.4%
1930	23.2	13.6	19.4
1931	23.3	13.7	21.3
1932	25.9	15.6	18.7
1933	38.2	12.7	13.5
1934	40.1	7.8	12.5
1935	53.5	3.2	7.4
1936	61.0	0.6	8.0
1937	54.8	5.0	10.1
1938	52.0	7.5	13.5
1939	65.5	6.9	6.3

| Year | Exports from Bulgaria | | |
	To Germany (and Austria after 1938)	To Italy	To United Kingdom, France, and United States
1929	29.9%	10.5%	8.4%
1930	26.2	8.3	8.3
1931	29.5	5.8	5.8
1932	26.0	12.5	6.0
1933	36.0	9.1	6.2
1934	42.7	9.2	4.8
1935	48.0	8.8	7.2
1936	47.5	3.6	16.3
1937	43.1	4.2	19.2
1938	58.9	7.6	9.7
1939	67.8	6.1	7.4

SOURCE: Bulgaria, Direction Générale de la Statistique, *Annuaire Statistique du Royaume de Bulgarie*, 26 (1934), pp. 176–77; 30 (1938), pp. 486–87; 32 (1940), pp. 300–01.

Despite denials of commitment to any side and his avowed support of the League of Nations, King Boris, in September 1937, quietly asked about the possibility of buying German war matériel on a long-term basis. The Bulgarians were simultaneously considering an arms treaty with France. Hermann Göring, plenipotentiary of the Four Years' Plan, did not believe that the arms delivery and loan would be beneficial to the Reich, but the foreign office on the advice of its ambassador in Sofia brought the government to agreement. Talks were held in both capitals, and finally in March 1938 Berlin agreed to advance 30 million marks' ($12 million) worth of matériel to Bulgaria, still far short of the 100 million marks' worth that Boris had asked for. The Bulgarians agreed to pay for the arms over a period of five years beginning in 1942.[11]

A sale of war matériel is a politically significant economic venture. If a country buys its armaments and military furnishings from another state, it is almost committing itself to that state in case of war, at the risk of not being able to supply the necessary furnishings for the basic matériel, such as ammunition and replacement parts. English statesmen were alarmed at the rumors of the secret arms agreement. The onrush of Germany into the southeast (the Anschluss with Austria occurred in March 1938), accompanied by its new cooperation with Italy (which had thwarted German ambitions in Austria in 1934), gave the British pause, and they joined the French in their efforts to make the entire Balkan peninsula a "defensive bloc" against the Nazis.

Bulgaria remained uncommitted. Boris wooed London and Paris as well as Berlin, and conversations in regard to loans continued with all three. In August 1938 French banking houses extended 375 million francs ($10,900,000) credit for buying railroad equipment and arms in France and later further broadened the agreement.[12] In November the minister of finance, Dobri Bozhilov, went to London to arrange a moratorium on English loans to Bulgaria. Now the Germans became alarmed. They had earlier insisted that they did not wish to monopolize Bulgaria's economy, but they also did not want Bulgaria to "enter into . . . [the British and French] game [of] trying to curb Germany's trade with countries of southeast Europe." Boris reassured the Nazis, Germany promised an additional credit to the kingdom of 22 million marks, and the British agreements fell through.[13]

After Munich, in the fall of 1938, the Reich was clearly the dominant

11. Pundeff, "Bulgaria's Place," pp. 107-09.
12. BAN, Istoriia, III, 342; Pundeff, "Bulgaria's Place," pp. 109-10; New York Times, August 6, 1938, p. 5. See both the BAN history, vol. III, pp. 309-418, and Pundeff for details of this entire period.
13. Karl Clodius, deputy director of the economic policy department of the German foreign office, Berlin, August 10, 1938, memorandum, in Germany, Foreign Office, Akten zur Deutschen Auswärtigen Politik 1918-1945 (Baden-Baden: Imprimerie Nationale, 1953), ser. D, V, 249-50. In English translation, Documents on German Foreign Policy 1918-1945 (Washington, D.C.: Department of State, 1953), ser. D, V, 296-97.

force in international affairs. Bulgaria's ability and desire to side with Britain or France diminished. The same opinion moved most of Eastern Europe. Munich demonstrated the fate of small nations who trusted the passive West of the thirties. Paradoxically the agreement at first presented an opportunity to improve relations with all the great powers of Western and Central Europe. If some spirit of Munich was to be the destiny of Europe, as the anxious and naïve wished to believe, then there would be no need to align with one bloc against some other. More important for Bulgaria, the Czech settlement gave revisionists something to hope for. Their claims as well as Germany's might be considered by the diplomats. Both the government faction in the Subranie and the West-leaning opposition sent congratulations to the architects of the Munich agreement.

In a few short months the Nazis' march into Czechoslovakia shattered the dreams of peaceful cooperation in Europe. The Germans retained the position of power, and friendship to the Reich became a necessity for the countries of the Balkans. Boris had to make a difficult choice. If the road ahead led to the Axis camp, he would have to follow it, and Germany could perhaps help him attain national ends.

For the time being, Sofia put off Berlin's repeated hints to join the Anti-Comintern Pact but sought closer relations and concessions from Germany throughout 1939. Besides still more credits, Boris wanted Chancellor Adolf Hitler's intervention in the return of Dobrudzha from Rumania. Despite Göring's desire to offer more aid in return for Bulgaria's joining the pact, the German foreign office extended all the desired credits to the kingdom in exchange for German exploitation of Bulgarian mines without a commitment to the pact. Furthermore, the Reich enjoined Bulgaria from accepting British "anti-German" overtures, no matter what the offer. Since Boris desired territory in Dobrudzha and Thrace, he was put off by British and French guarantees to Rumania and Greece after the German annexation of Czechoslovakia and accepted this limitation.[14]

In the summer of 1939 Prime Minister K'oseivanov made a much publicized friendship visit to Berlin. In expectation of the trip both Berlin and Sofia were preparing new political requests. The Reich wanted a definitive adherence to the Anti-Comintern Pact, and Bulgaria wanted even further extension of credits and assurance on its irredenta questions. K'oseivanov agreed in fact not to bring up any claims against Yugoslavia, whose leaders the Nazis were also trying to

14. Pundeff, "Bulgaria's Place," pp. 136-38.

accommodate. However, these matters never came up when the prime minister was in Berlin, for the secret negotiations at that time between the Soviet Union and Germany determined that the latter pursue other political questions cautiously, and the agreements made during the visit concerned only cultural matters. Nevertheless, Karl Clodius, of the German foreign office's economic division, did go to Sofia while K'oseivanov was in Germany, in order to arrange the details of Boris's new aid request.

Shortly after K'oseivanov's visit to Berlin, Stoicho Moshanov, the president of the Subranie, journeyed to Paris and London, thus creating a scandal.[15] Moshanov was a nephew of the Democrat leader, Nikola Mushanov, and a staunch supporter of the West. Apparently Moshanov had told the king of his plans and received his consent. In England and France, where he visited the heads of state and government, he announced that Boris approved his visit.[16] The Bulgarian government, however, as well as Moshanov himself when he returned, claimed the trip was only private. K'oseivanov was disturbed and angry. News of the proposed trip reached Berlin while the prime minister was there, and he asked the German press to ignore it. The government press in Sofia hardly mentioned it but gave full coverage to the prime minister's Berlin journey.

After the signing of the German-Soviet nonaggression treaty (August 1939), Bulgaria moved even further away from the West and into Germany's camp. German-Russian *rapprochement* was in many ways even more profitable for Bulgaria than the German-Western *rapprochement* vainly promised by Munich. Reliance on German strength could be buttressed by the popularity of Russia within the country. Although Boris distrusted the Communists and Germany was far and away the chief patron of Bulgaria, relations with the Soviet Union greatly improved—communication and trade treaties were signed and exhibitions exchanged. The Bulgarian Communist party enjoyed a period of freedom unknown since the early twenties. Its press published freely and the police surveillance and harassment of its members, widespread in July, was relaxed.[17]

15. Ibid., p. 170. Von Bülow, German *chargé d'affaires* in Bulgaria, report, July 13, 1939, T120, serial 585 (Office of the Staatssekretär [Ernst Von Weizsäcker], bundle 2, Bulgaria, May 1939 to January 31, 1941), roll 329, frame 242446.

16. Herbert von Dirksen, German ambassador to England, report, July 26, 1939, T120, serial 585, roll 329, frame 242462.

17. Nissan Oren, "The Bulgarian Communist Party, 1934-1944" (Ph.D. diss., Columbia University, 1960), pp. 175-80. See Oren for information on the Bulgarian Communist party during the entire period.

On the other hand, Sofia now had to contend with new pressure from the West. In particular, the government feared a British ultimatum demanding that it adhere definitively to the Balkan Entente. The previous year K'oseivanov had willingly made concessions to such pressures by signing the Salonika Accord with the countries in the Entente, renouncing the use of force for territorial revision. Now, however, as world alignments changed and international diplomacy forced the kingdom a little further away from London and Paris, Sofia appealed to Berlin for help in resisting English pressure. Unwilling to cause trouble with his newfound eastern ally, Hitler hesitated to interfere in the Balkans. The foreign office instructed Colonel Bruckmann, the military attaché in Sofia, not to promise anything concrete except that the Bulgarians might invite a German general there for advice.

When the Second World War began, K'oseivanov immediately declared that Bulgaria would follow a policy of peace and neutrality.[18] The changes since Munich and the German-Soviet pact, as we have already seen, made this neutrality more friendly to the Reich than to England. Even so there was no reason why K'oseivanov could not head a pro-German government. Despite his French leanings, he showed himself faithfully following the king's changing policy toward the Reich. In a short time, however, political affairs forced the prime minister from the scene. K'oseivanov was not a little dismayed over the treatment he had received at the hands of his monarch (the affair of Moshanov's trip comes readily to mind). Boris had indeed chosen K'oseivanov for his personal loyalty—as prime minister he had proven a capable politician and by October 1939 had led seven consecutive cabinets for four years—nonetheless K'oseivanov was not satisfied to be a pawn, subject to the king's inconsideration. Besides, the prime minister was dissatisfied with his own cabinet, particularly Minister of Agriculture Ivan Bagrianov.

Bagrianov, a conservative Agrarian and personal friend of the king and royal family, had won a seat as a government candidate in the twenty-fourth Subranie. Yet once in the legislature, he began to champion the popular causes of the poor and middle-income peasants, and he tried to gain personal support throughout the country. In October 1938 he had led thirty dissident government representatives to side with the opposition on a government-sponsored bill appropriating funds for a semiofficial newspaper. The measure was defeated and K'oseivanov

18. *La Parole Bulgare* (Sofia), September 17, 1939, p. 1; *New York Times*, September 17, 1939, sec. 1, p. 44.

resigned. Boris at that time asked his prime minister once again to form a cabinet, this time with Bagrianov as minister of agriculture. He also brought several other representatives into the cabinet in order to harmonize relationships among the government supporters in the Subranie, but this plan did not succeed. K'oseivanov and Bagrianov could not work together, and the Subranie was no more amenable than before. After the war started in Europe, Boris wanted a government and a parliament which he could firmly control, and K'oseivanov was disgruntled over not being allowed to run his own cabinet.

On October 22, 1939, K'oseivanov again resigned, but Boris asked him to form an interim government for a few months. The minor post changes had no apparent immediate significance, but there was more here than a superficial glance would reveal. The new minister of railroads, Petur Gabrovski, was an ideological fascist and a champion of nazism. As mentioned above, he had been a founder of the Nazi-style Ratnitsi, although he resigned on entering the government.

The day after he announced his new cabinet, K'oseivanov dissolved the Subranie. New elections were held in December and January under the same system as before, with changes in the order of regional balloting—areas of heavy opposition voting last. Furthermore, the government maintained even stricter control of the elections. Only in Sofia, the largest opposition center, was the government unable to run up an overwhelming majority. In the new Subranie 121 out of 160 representatives supported the government.[19] (The government claimed 140, but without parties it is difficult to give precise figures. On some government-sponsored bills, considerably fewer than 140 voted yea, but only very rarely did the Subranie reject a government measure.)

After the elections, Boris announced a new government. K'oseivanov stepped down, and Bogdan Filov became the new prime minister. Filov had been minister of education since November 1938. He was an art historian of international renown, had been German-educated, and belonged to several German learned academies. K'oseivanov left his portfolio as well as the chair, but his replacement as minister of foreign affairs was a close friend and associate, Ivan Popov. General Ned'o Nedev, minister of internal affairs since November 1938, was now in disgrace because of election irregularities, and Petur Gabrovski re-

---

19. Kazasov, p. 652 (Kazasov estimated the opposition from the vote for the Subranie's chairman); BAN, *Istoriia*, III, 362; Pundeff, "Bulgaria's Place," pp. 202-04; *La Parole Bulgare* (Sofia), December 30, 1939, p. 3; January 21, 1940, p. 1; January 28, 1940, p. 3; February 4, 1940, p. 3.

placed him. Needless to say, ex-Ratnik Gabrovski's appointment created a sensation.

Some speculation abroad claimed that in a few months Bagrianov would replace Filov. Yet Filov, not Bagrianov, was the real man of the hour—Boris's designated head of government. The colorless Germanophile professor was to be prime minister for almost three years, and after that the major regent. Bulgaria's wartime government would be Filov's government. As prime minister, Boris wanted someone he could control. Ivan Bagrianov would hardly do, just as K'oseivanov would no longer do, although both were Boris's personal friends. In fact, Bagrianov was forced from the cabinet a year later because of his insatiable ambition.

Even more than the new pro-German government and the more malleable parliament, the nature of the war itself limited Boris's ability to remain neutral. On the crossroads of Central Europe, Russia, and the Near East, it was almost inevitable that the tiny Balkan kingdom would be brought into the war. The war gave commitment a more substantial meaning than it had had in the thirties, when Boris could play his game of walking the neutral ground between opposing camps. Now he had to move to one side and the pull was more powerful from the Axis. Furthermore, as he moved deeper into the Axis camp, the king and his country requested more favors from the Reich, effectively closing the ways of escape behind them.

In particular, the Bulgarian hope for border revision intensified. The war seemed to be a war for readjusting frontiers, not only for Germany, but also for the USSR, who without participating retrieved the possessions lost by the tsar in Poland and on the Baltic. Bulgaria hoped for similar retrieval at equally low cost. Its attention remained fixed on lands it had lost to Greece and Rumania after the Second Balkan War and World War I. The cry for an Aegean port (Kavala or Dede Agach, i.e., Alexandroupolis) and for Dobrudzha resounded in the press, the Subranie, and the streets. Of these claims, the government pursued Dobrudzha with the greatest ardor.

The Germans hesitated to commit themselves to aid in regaining Dobrudzha, but in the meantime the Balkan kingdom had become a source of tension disturbing the August accord between the Reich and the Soviet Union. The two countries had not successfully dealt with the question of influence in the Balkans, and neither was willing to let the other gain supremacy there. The overtures which the Soviet Union made to Sofia, especially the hint that it might ask the Bulgarians to sign a mutual defense and friendship pact, alarmed Berlin.[20] For their part the Bulgarians professed loyalty to the Reich, and in the spring of 1940 the ministers of the new government made it quite clear that although they were officially neutral, they were in fact pro-German.[21]

On June 26, 1940, four days after the fall of France, the Soviet Union delivered an ultimatum to Rumania demanding the cession of Bessarabia and northern Bukovina. King Carol had no choice but to acquiesce as Berlin, where the ultimatum was known in advance, advised; and two days later Soviet troops occupied these regions. Moscow also publicly supported Bulgaria's claim to southern Dobrudzha, and Berlin feared that if the Kremlin offered to help Sofia take the province, King Boris and Filov would not be able to resist public pressure to agree.[22] Under these circumstances the Germans decided to act and themselves arrange the cession of southern Dobrudzha to the Bulgarians. Rumania and Bulgaria held talks at Craiova through the summer of 1940, and Rumania settled with both Bulgaria and Hungary (which claimed Transylvania) under German auspices at Vienna on September 7, 1940.[23] In Bulgaria the Vienna Award was a signal for national jubilation. Streets in Dobrich and Sofia were named after Hitler, Benito Mussolini, and Victor Emmanuel II. Bulgaria's commitment to Germany now became irrevocable. The kingdom was indebted to the Axis, and if Hitler called in the debt, Boris would not default.

Meanwhile by summer of 1940 Hitler had become the master of the continent. Only England and its colonies remained in the field against him. Nevertheless, the possibility that the Soviet Union might enter the war disturbed Hitler, and by the end of the summer he decided to take care of this menace decisively by military means. In October 1940 the Wehrmacht entered Rumania in force, and some advisors had gone to Bulgaria to help support defenses there.

20.   Herbert von Richthofen, German ambassador to Bulgaria, report, December 4, 1939, T120, serial 585, roll 329, frames 242521-22; Weizsäcker to Richthofen, December 15, 1939, ibid., frames 242525-27.

21.   Clodius and Richthofen, report, May 5, 1940, Sofia, ibid., frames 242571-75; Pundeff, "Bulgaria's Place," pp. 221-22.

22.   Ernst Wörmann, Unterstaatssekretär for political affairs, Berlin, report, June 27, 1940, T120, serial 585, roll 329, frames 242595-96; Richthofen, report, June 29, 1940, ibid., frames 242598-99.

23.   For German involvement in the Dobrudzha question, see T120, serial 585, roll 329. See especially Weizsäcker, report on talks with Bulgarian ambassador to Germany, June 18, 1940, ibid., frames 242590-91; Ribbentrop to Richthofen, July 1, 1940, ibid., frame 242606; Paul Otto Schmidt, minister of the foreign office's secretariat—Büro RAM, report, July 28, 1940, ibid., frames 242646-48; and Richt-

In September, Germany, Italy, and Japan had signed a Three-Power Pact, and the Axis invited other countries, including Bulgaria, to join. German Foreign Minister Joachim von Ribbentrop even offered the USSR an opportunity to sign the pact; but the conditions, which included Moscow's recognition of the Balkans as a German sphere of interest, were so detrimental to Soviet interests that this overture was not taken seriously. In December 1940 Hitler issued the directives for Operation Barbarossa—the invasion and quick defeat of the Soviet Union to begin in the spring of 1941.

The Soviet Union in November had once again pressured the Bulgarian government to sign a mutual defense pact. Stalin had sent Arkadi Sobolev, the secretary-general of the Commissariat of Foreign Affairs, to Sofia late in the month with an offer guaranteeing the kingdom against Turkey and promising aid in obtaining territory in Turkish Thrace. Part of the proposal had granted permission for Sofia to join the Three-Power Pact, and Sobolev had even suggested that if the kingdom signed the agreement with Moscow, the Soviets might accept Hitler's offer to join the Three-Power Pact themselves. Popov had politely turned the offer down, despite public pressure from the Bulgarian Communist party (even though the offer was supposed to be secret!). The Bulgarian foreign minister had argued, however, that the Soviets' offer demonstrated that Bulgaria's negotiations with the Germans, taking place at that time, were not hostile to Moscow.[24]

Even when Germany planned to invade the Soviet Union, it was not necessary that the hot war reach into the Balkans. In fact, it was more advantageous for Hitler to have trans-Danubian Europe under his influence but technically neutral. Since the war's beginning the Germans had shown no desire to annex or even physically occupy the countries of the Balkans. In contrast, Great Britain hoped to form an anti-Nazi bloc in that region or even open a second front there. These overtures, along with the obvious power of the Third Reich, persuaded not only Bulgaria but the other countries of the region to come to terms with Berlin. Even Turkey, Britain's most likely ally in the area, assured Hitler of its neutrality.[25]

---

hofen, reports, September 5, 1940, and September 6, 1940, ibid., frames 242724-25.

24. Marin Pundeff, "Two Documents on Soviet-Bulgarian Relations in November, 1940," *Journal of Central European Affairs*, 4, no. 5 (January 1956), 375-78; Richthofen, reports, November 26 and 30, 1940, T120, serial 585, roll 329, frames 242786, 242796-97; unsigned report, Sofia, November 28, 1940, ibid., frames 242793-94.

25. Dzhengis Zhakov, "Osnovno nasoki na vunshnata politika na Turtsiia prez

The war in the Balkans did not originate with Hitler, but with his Italian ally. After the German leader had put off Mussolini's overtures for a joint venture against Greece, the Duce decided to invade that country himself and did so at the end of October. He invited King Boris to participate, but the Bulgarian monarch declined.

Mussolini's failure to achieve his objective was disastrous not only for himself but for Hitler's plan to allow the Balkan countries to remain neutral. In the first week of December, the Greek army broke through the Italian lines and advanced into Albania. Hitler was obliged to come to the aid of his ally, and the German general staff announced Operation Marita—the defeat of Greece—also in December 1940, even before the directives of Operation Barbarossa.

Operation Marita required the cooperation of both Bulgaria and Yugoslavia. German troops would pass through the one (Bulgaria) while the other would remain neutral. When Berlin asked Sofia for its participation, Boris readily complied. He had already offered aid if needed at a meeting with Hitler in November.

The first week of 1941 Filov journeyed to Vienna under the pretext of consulting a physician but actually to meet with Hitler and Ribbentrop. The Reich's foreign minister requested passage through Bulgaria for German troops. On January seventh Filov wrote in his diary: "War is unavoidable. If, however, we realize this, it is best that we follow it under conditions that are the least complicated for us. If we allow the Germans simply to pass through our country, they will treat us as an occupied land, like Rumania, and this will be much worse than if we ally with them. We cannot gain anything from an English victory, for a failure of German arms inevitably means we shall be 'Bolshevized'."[26]

On January 20 the cabinet unanimously approved the German passage through the country. Filov, realizing the gravity of the situation, wrote: "This was without doubt the most important meeting which we have had to date."[27]

The decision to aid the Germans caused a great many problems for Boris and Filov. They were worried about the reaction of Turkey and

Vtorata svetovna voina" [Fundamental directions of the foreign policy of Turkey during the Second World War], *Istoricheski pregled*, 23, no. 6 (1967), pp. 14-15; Bogdan Filov, "Diary," entry for March 1, 1941, published in *Naroden Sud*, no. 1, p. 10. (The *Naroden Sud* consists of a total of eight issues, published December 1944 to April 1945.)

26. Bogdan Filov, "Diary," entry for January 7, 1941, *Naroden Sud* (Sofia) no. 1, p. 14.

27. Filov, "Diary," entry for January 20, 1941, ibid.

the Soviet Union. Hitler was eager that Sofia and Ankara sign a friendship treaty and was instrumental in persuading President Ismet Inönü to agree. Ribbentrop also assured Filov that the "Russians [would] . . . put up with the situation and not react."[28] The foreign minister further promised the Bulgarian premier that the Yugoslavs, despite some hesitation, would come around. The government faced some protests from the members of the legal opposition in Bulgaria itself, who in February heard rumors of the upcoming agreement with the Germans.

Also in February preparation for a German advance into Bulgaria became obvious. Bridges appeared across the Danube. There was an influx of German "tourists" and technicians into Sofia and other cities, military boots conspicuous under their civilian trench coats. The attention of the Western press on Bulgaria increased phenomenally in these weeks. American and British diplomats became extremely concerned, and President Franklin Roosevelt's special envoy Col. William Donovan badgered Minister Popov with what Filov described as an anti-German tirade, causing the Bulgarian foreign minister to have second thoughts about the alliance.[29]

Inside the kingdom anti-German propaganda was suppressed and several prominent anti-Nazis were arrested. There was also a renewed crackdown on Communists and radical Agrarians. German economic experts came to Sofia to work on details of the alliance, and on February 1 a preliminary economic agreement was approved in Sofia arranging for the expenses of the German march through the country.

The major political negotiations, handled for the Bulgarians by a special emissary of the cabinet, were held in Berlin, and a delegation of the Bulgarian general staff met with Field Marshal List in Rumania to discuss the military treaty.[30] According to the final agreement Sofia would join the Three-Power Pact on the same day that German troops crossed the Danube. The Germans would be stationed not in the city of Sofia, but in the suburbs; however, the Bulgarians did not get their wish to declare the capital an open city. Bulgarian troops were to be stationed on the Turkish border as reserves in case of an invasion from that quarter, the friendship treaty with Ankara notwithstanding. Only

28. Filov, "Diary," entry for March 1, 1941, ibid., p. 10.
29. Filov, "Diary," entry for January 21, 1941, published in *Otechestven Front* (Sofia), December 3, 1944, p. 1.
30. Richthofen, report, February 6, 1941, T120, serial 274 (Office of the Staatssekretär, Bulgaria, vol. 2, February 1 to June 30, 1941), roll 238, frame 177644; Filov, "Diary," entry for January 16, 1941, *Otechestven Front*, December 20, 1944, p. 1.

German forces were expected to take part in frontline operations against Greece and, if necessary, Turkey.[31]

On March 1 Filov went to Vienna to sign the Three-Power Pact on behalf of his government. Simultaneously the government announced the German passage to begin March 2. Sir George Rendel, the British ambassador, left the country.[32]

Berlin put pressure on the Yugoslav government to join the Three-Power Pact as well, and on March 25 Belgrade's prime minister and foreign minister went to Vienna and signed. The next day a group of officers overthrew the government, deposed Prince Paul as regent, and declared that the young King Peter II had reached his majority. Hitler regarded the coup as a personal insult and the new government as anti-Nazi. The population of Belgrade was openly anti-Nazi, but the government assured Hitler that it would not abrogate the recent treaties and that it would remain neutral in the Greek campaign. Nevertheless, the führer resolved to attack Yugoslavia along with Greece.

On April 6, the German army invaded Yugoslavia and Greece and within a matter of weeks subdued both states. Bulgarian troops did not participate on the fronts but entered into western Thrace, Macedonia, and the district of Pirot behind the Wehrmacht to serve as an occupation force.

Bulgaria's agreement to the passage of German troops through its country and its participation in the occupation of Greece and Yugoslavia made it a combatant in the war on the side of the Germans. It did not declare war on England until December 1941. Then the government declared "symbolic" war against both England and the United States. Sofia never did declare war on the USSR. Only on September 5, 1944, a few days before a government friendly to Moscow took power in the country, did the Kremlin for political reasons declare war on the kingdom.

Germany and the Jews

Because of the Third Reich's anti-Semitic attitudes, the Bulgarian-German alliance, of course, brought especially anxious circumstances to the kingdom's Jewish community. The Nazi Final Solution to the

31. Richthofen, reports, February 4 and 15, 1941, T120, serial 274, roll 238, frames 177644, 177697-98; Filov, "Diary," entry for February 27, 1941, *Naroden Sud*, no. 1, p. 10; Pundeff, "Bulgaria's Place," pp. 372-73.

32. Filov, "Diary," entries for February 28 and March 1, 1941, *Naroden Sud*, no. 1, pp. 10-11.

Jewish question is well known, but its development came only after a number of years.[33] Indeed, the Final Solution was not reached until 1942. Since the Jewish policy developed by the Bulgarians after September 1939 was inherently dependent upon the German, it is worthwhile here to trace the initial steps of the latter's development.

Nazi ideology named the Jew as the archenemy of the German state; but when the Nazis came to power, although some steps against the Jews were taken immediately, only gradually did a major anti-Semitic policy become a part of the German legal fabric. The German anti-Semitic laws and activities of the thirties centered on the isolation of the Jewish community and the expropriation of Jewish wealth. Immediately on coming to power, the Nazis initiated two anti-Semitic laws—one dismissing the Jews from government service and another limiting the number of Jews in German universities; these laws began the segregation of the Jews.

The first group of major anti-Semitic laws did not come until 1935—the Nuremberg laws. These provided the principal measure for separating the German and Jewish communities. Jews could not be citizens. The Law for the Protection of German Blood and Honor forbade marriages (as well as extramarital relations) between Jews and Germans. Jews could not employ German female servants under forty-five years of age. In addition, the Nuremberg laws dealt with the tricky problem of defining "Jew." The law of 1933 dismissing civil servants had said simply that a non-Aryan was one who had a parent or grandparent who practiced the Jewish religion. The inclusion of half Jews and quarter Jews was too broad. Germany had one of the most assimilated Jewish communities in Europe, and had measures been taken against Germans who happened to have Jewish ancestors, their application among the population would have been widespread. German theoreticians thought that extension of the definition would deprive the Reich of the service of tens of thousands of useful people, and they argued that the German influence in one's ancestry could be as great as the Jewish. A group of German racial experts devised a compromise definition which included the concept of a mixed race of part Jews—*Mischlinge* ("half-castes"). To be considered a Jew, a person had to have at least three Jewish grandparents; two if the "Jew" in question either practiced the

---

33.   This section is based on Raul Hilberg, *The Destruction of the European Jews* (Chicago: Quadrangle Books, 1961). See also Gerald Reitlinger, *The Final Solution: The Attempt to Exterminate the Jews of Europe, 1939-1945* (New York: Beechhurst Press, 1953).

Jewish religion or were married to a Jew on or after September 15, 1935, the day of the enactment of the Law for Protection of German Blood and Honor. Later on, a distinction was made between *Mischlinge* first degree (people with two Jewish grandparents, but not fulfilling the conditions above) and *Mischlinge* second degree (people who had only one Jewish grandparent).[34]

The definition was racial in the sense that it depended to a large degree on ancestry rather than actual religion, but religion was the ultimate criterion for determining whether or not grandparents were Jews and it was also the decisive factor for determining the status of half Jews as Jews or *Mischlinge*. *Mischlinge* second degree were generally treated more like Germans; *Mischlinge* first degree like Jews. By special decree from the Nazi hierarchy a person's status could be raised. A *Mischling* first degree could become a *Mischling* second degree; a *Mischling*, a German. Neither class was ever as badly treated as the Jews—each still remained part of German society—but their condition worsened as the years passed. One way of isolating the Jewish community was to eliminate this middle ground of *Mischlinge* and leave the distinction between Jews and Germans clear. Thus later the Nazi Jewish experts seriously discussed eliminating the *Mischlinge* classification by assimilating completely all second degrees into the German community and subjecting first degrees to sterilization, deportation, or reclassification as Jews. The problem was never solved.

After the Jews were legally and sufficiently defined, the Nazis' work became easier. Special restrictions isolating Jews from the German community continued in the years following the Nuremberg laws. In 1938 the Nazis passed the second major group of anti-Semitic laws. Jews were given special identity papers, special names, special markings (Stars of David) for personal wear, businesses and homes. They were more and more enjoined from participating in German society. They could not ride on public transportation, use telephones, possess radios or cars. They could shop only at certain hours in certain stores, stay at certain hotels for limited periods. Nazis prohibited Christians from contact with Jews. They could not patronize Jewish doctors or stores (the latter by an extralegal but official boycott), nor could they have friendly relations with Jews. In 1938 the Jews were forced to live in ghettos.

Besides isolating the Jews, the Nazis wished to expropriate their property, first capital property, then personal. These expropriations

34. Hilberg, pp. 43-53.

started as soon as the Nazis came to power, but during the first years they were forced by extralegal pressure rather than by decree. The pressures brought to bear on the Jews were primarily the boycott and "voluntary" Aryanization. The latter was the transfer of enterprises from Jews to Germans, theoretically by the will of the seller; actually the Jews were subjected to economic and other pressures to sell out, for example, the longer they delayed, the smaller the compensation they received. The Nazis saw to it that the Jews were paid a fraction of the value of their property, and that the benefit did not go to the new owners but to the party and government.

The legal expropriations authorized in the summer of 1938 included forced Aryanizations eliminating Jewish enterprises entirely, special property and income taxes, forced labor under strict wage control, and blockage of Jewish bank accounts. The Jews were systematically plundered and what little money they had was supervised by the Nazis. Accompanying all the oppressive laws and actions from 1933 on was the pressure to emigrate; yet the Nazis did not facilitate this emigration. They did not want the Jews to leave unless they left their wealth in Germany, and they placed a fairly high price on the permission to emigrate, not only confiscating German Jewish wealth, but also demanding foreign payments for Jews who could not afford to buy their own exit visas.

The ultimate Nazi goal was the elimination of the Jew as a force and participant in German society, but the ideology developed in the twenties gravely hinted at the complete elimination of the Jew in Germany. The policies of the thirties accomplished the former, but not the latter. One can interpret *Mein Kampf* to show that Hitler would inevitably decide to murder all the Jews of Europe, but despite the outcome, this was not necessarily predestined. No matter what Hitler had in mind from 1933 to 1942, the Nazi bureaucracy, and for the most part, even the hierarchy, saw only one move at a time in the "destructive process." True, there always existed the problem that the Germans could isolate and rob the Jews for just so long before they would finally have to determine some way to eliminate them once and for all, but the means to this end was in no way certain. Pressure for emigration could not be totally effective because of the demands for payment to leave and the reluctance of most other countries to receive masses of impoverished Jews.

German expansion complicated the Jewish question. In 1938 and 1939, Austria and Czechoslovakia became part of the Reich, bringing hundreds of thousands more Jews under its domination. When the Second World War started in September 1939, three million Polish Jews came under Nazi administration. Further conquests would bring more. The Jews who had emigrated from Germany in the thirties were now replaced by an even greater number. With the expansions after 1938 emigrations became a German aim, but since no country desired these immigrants, it could not yet be realized. After the conquest of Poland, all Jews in zones to be incorporated into the Reich were expelled into remaining Polish territory—the Generalgouvernement under Hans Frank. Some Jews from the Reich and Protektorat (Czech areas incorporated into Germany) were likewise deported to Poland. Despite German rumors and propaganda this truncated Poland was not to become a Jewish country within Europe. The Nazi problem now was making not merely Germany, but all of Europe *judenrein*. The Generalgouvernement was to be a temporary concentration area for Jews until a Final Solution to the problem could be found. In 1939 and 1940 this solution centered on thoughts first of deportation to Palestine, and later on to Madagascar; but these plans proved to be impracticable. By 1940, Poland was designated as the collection point for European Jews. The Nazis established numerous ghettos in Polish cities, and later on they built large concentration camps which became the most infamous of Europe: Auschwitz, Sobibor, Treblinka, and others.

The Nazi problems in making Europe free of Jews soon revealed themselves to be endless. Doing so was a relatively easy matter in the area of the Reich or even in the conquered territories; but in allied and neutral states, such as Bulgaria, Hungary, Slovakia, Spain, and others the dictatorial methods of the SS (which handled the Jewish problem) were inapplicable. Here the foreign office entered into the picture, and for the Bulgarian Jews, this ministry was to become even more important than the SS.

The Bulgarian Jews

Jewish communities in the Balkan Peninsula antedate the arrival of the Slavs and Bulgars.[35] Jews also had migrated to Bulgarian lands and the rest of the Balkans in the Middle Ages—Italian Jews, especially with

35. For the history of the Bulgarian Jews until the 1920s see Saul Mezan, *Les juifs espagnols en Bulgarie* (Sofia: n.p., 1925). The General Cultural-Educational Organization of Jews in the Peoples' Republic of Bulgaria began publishing a yearbook (*Godishnik*) in 1966 which contains scholarly articles also pertaining to the history of the Jews.

the establishment of the Crusader and Italian merchant colonies, and German-speaking Jews (*Ashkenazim*) from the north. In fact, in the Middle Ages the Bulgarian Jews had a distinction which those elsewhere in Europe could envy. During the Second Bulgarian Empire (1185–1389) Tsar Ivan Aleksandur (1331–1371) married a Jew, Sara, baptized in the Bulgarian church as Theodora. The queen, however, did not forget her origins, and many Jews rose to prominent positions at court and in the government. The Bulgarians were disturbed by and jealous of the importance of the Jews. Queen Theodora could not prevent a church decree of 1352 which expelled the Jews from Bulgaria for "heretical activity," but the order was not rigorously applied.

After the conquest, the Turks organized the Jewish community as they did the Christian rayas. All Jews in Turkish lands formed a single millet, headed by a chief rabbi in Constantinople. The millet was responsible for local administration and settlement of intrareligious disputes. The Jews had their own courts which ruled on secular as well as religious matters solely concerning Jews. The millet had authority for taxation and punishment.

In 1492, when the kingdoms of Spain and Portugal expelled their Jews, many of these fled to Turkey, and Salonika became their chief city. In the Balkans the old Jewish communities adopted the Sephardic ritual and custom. Some immigration of Ashkenazi Jews (especially those driven out by anti-Semitism in Hungary and Poland) occurred during the Turkish period; but many of these were also incorporated in to the Sephardic communities. At the turn of the twentieth century, only a few Ashkenazim remained in Bulgaria. Sofia, a city on the major trade route to Constantinople, held the largest Bulgarian Jewish community. At the time of liberation (1878) almost 25 percent of its 20,000 population were Jews. (Plovdiv, not Sofia, was the leading city of the Bulgarians, but the Treaty of Berlin excluded the former from the autonomous state.)

The Bulgarian liberation was a trial for the Jews, and only a few shared the native enthusiasm of the Bulgarians. While some considered that they would be better off in a free Bulgaria, run by a nation which had known the bitterness of subjugation, than as second-class citizens under the Turks, many feared that a Christian state—especially one whose patron and benefactor was tsarist Russia—would be less tolerant than the Turks. During the war of liberation some fled with the Turkish refugees, but the majority who remained were generally not treated unkindly by the Bulgarians.

By an *ukaz* ("royal order") of 1880 the Jewish community, like other religious groups in Bulgaria, legally remained in a sort of millet system. The community chose its chief rabbi through its governing body of both rabbis and laymen, the central consistory. Through this organization, the Jewish community, as it had under the Turks, established its own religious courts which dealt with intracommunal matters, both religious (e.g., marriage and divorce) and civil (e.g., lawsuits), which pertained solely to the Jewish community. The Bulgarian government paid the chief rabbi's salary. In addition, the consistory had the right to levy imposts on the entire community to meet its own expenses. The Bulgarian Ministry of Foreign Affairs and Religious Cults supervised the legal structure of all religious communities in the state.

At the time of liberation the Jews in autonomous Bulgaria numbered about 14,500 out of 2,010,000 people, or 0.72 percent. In 1885, when Eastern Rumelia joined Bulgaria, there were approximately 8,000 Jews there out of a total population of 975,000, or 0.82 percent. As table 2

TABLE 2

JEWISH POPULATION OF BULGARIA

Year	Total Population	Bulgarians	Percentage of Bulgarians	Jews	Percentage of Jews
1910	4,337,513	3,497,613	80.6%	40,133	0.92%
1920	4,846,971	3,947,657	81.4	43,209	0.89
1934a	6,077,939	5,128,890	84.4	48,398	0.80

Source: Bulgaria, Direction Générale de la Statistique, *Annuaire Statistique*, 27 (1935), pp. 14, 27; 29 (1937), pp. 14, 25.

a. The 1934 census did not count nationalities but rather religions. The Bulgarian figure includes Greeks, Serbs, and Russians.

shows, the Jews were only a minute fraction of the population at all times. The total minority population of Bulgaria represented almost 20 percent, a considerable proportion. On the other hand, if we compare the figures for Jews and Bulgarians living in villages and cities, we see that the percentage of urban Jews was much higher, since they were primarily city dwellers. Sofia's population was always about 10 percent Jewish, and by World War II half of the Jews in Bulgaria lived in the capital. The increase of population through the years was due to natural growth rather than immigration (see table 3).

The Jews living in the cities had the urban advantages of a lower mortality rate and a higher literacy rate than the national average. (Bulgaria in general had a very high literacy rate for the Balkans—

TABLE 3

JEWISH URBAN POPULATION

Year	Total Population	Urban Population	Percentage Urban	Jews in Cities (Percentage of Total)	Minorities in Cities (Percentage of Total)
1910	4,337,513	829,522	19.1%	4.65%	24.52%
1920	4,846,971	966,375	19.9	4.39	29.41
1934	6,077,939	1,302,515	21.4	—a	—a

SOURCE: Bulgaria, Direction Générale de la Statistique, *Annuaire Statistique*, 27 (1935), p. 27; 30 (1938), p. 14.

    a. Unavailable for 1934, the last census.

according to the census of 1934, 67.2 percent could read and write compared with 43 percent for Greece, 44.6 percent for Yugoslavia, and 45.7 percent for Rumania. The rate for the Jews was 71.3 percent in 1926.) The Jews also had higher average salaries than the Bulgarians. They were engaged mostly in commerce, but there were many Jewish artisans and professional men. Very few Jews attained massive fortunes, but in a small country like Bulgaria these few stood out. Only a small number of Jews in Bulgaria ever gained international renown.[36]

In the last decades of the nineteenth century the Alliance Israélite Universelle (AIU) of Paris took an interest in the Ottoman and Bulgarian Jews. From 1870 to 1900 they established a number of schools, and this French influence is largely responsible for bringing the Bulgarian Jews into the modern world. The generation of the eighties and nineties enthusiastically accepted their instruction. French became the language of the Jewish intellectual. Not only were young Jews anxious to go to these French Jewish schools, but now unlike their parents they also wanted to go to the Bulgarian schools.

The following generation turned away from French culture and became enamoured of Zionism. As a rule the Zionist movement did not make much headway in Sephardic countries, but Bulgaria was an exception. Thus, at the beginning of the twentieth century, there were three generations of Bulgarian Jews: the old Sephardim, who had grown up in Turkish obscurantism; the westernized, Francophile, AIU-

---

    36. For in-depth descriptions of Jewish life in Bulgaria before the war, including Jewish economic participation in the country, see N. M. Gelber, "Jewish Life in Bulgaria," *Jewish Social Studies*, 8 (April 1946), 103-26, and Peter Meyer, "Bulgaria," in *The Jews in the Soviet Satellites*, ed. Peter Meyer (Syracuse, N.Y.: Syracuse University Press, 1953), pp. 559-69.

educated second generation, opposed to Zionism; and the Zionist, Jewish nationalist third generation. The middle generation ruled the community, but as the younger Jews grew in power, they fought the older leaders, the "notables." The height of the clash occurred between 1914 and 1920 when the Zionists forced the resignation of Chief Rabbi Marcus Ehrenpreis, who moved to Sweden. At this juncture the Bulgarian government assumed some of the rabbi's functions. Several of the notables left the consistory, giving the body an even more Zionist character. The Zionists were also a democratic and radical influence. They advocated schools independent of the synagogues, a graduated tax instead of a poll tax for the community, and equal suffrage regardless of position or wealth.

In 1920, a general congress was convened, in which the Zionists had overwhelming control. They elected a new consistory and revised the rules for the organization of the Jewish community, stressing the national and religious unity of all Jews. They conceded that the small Ashkenazi community could have separate synagogues, but only in Sofia and Ruse. In communities with more than five hundred Jews, the scholarly committee was divorced from the synagogue committee (the Zionist goal of secular education), and the two met only for certain special meetings. The Zionists forbade rabbis to interfere in administration. They gave foreign Jews in Bulgaria equal rights. Although the government did not approve, and the Office of Religious Cults never ratified the new organizational procedures, they went into effect anyway.

The congress selected the central consistory, consisting of seven members living in Sofia and ten Jews from the provinces at plenum meetings. This consistory was to choose the chief rabbi, the minor rabbinate, and the religious tribunals. There were local consistories as well. The judicial system consisted of tribunals in Sofia, Ruse, and Plovdiv, each with five members—three rabbis and two laymen, one of whom was to be a jurist. In addition there was a high tribunal sitting in Sofia with appellate and consultative duties. The members were three laymen and four rabbis, including, the congress decreed, the chief rabbi of Bulgaria as presiding officer; however, in fact there was no official government replacement for Ehrenpreis until after World War II.

The Jewish community was an enclave within the Bulgarian state, and there was not a great amount of intermingling with Bulgarian society. However, there were Jewish-Bulgarian friendships. The AIU period heightened contact, but the Zionist movement reemphasized Jewish uniqueness. Some Jews did join Bulgarian associations—professional, cultural, and social. Some also entered the army, and several Jews even attained high military rank. Politically the community as a whole tended to vote with the government except in the years before World War II. The Bulgarian Communist party stands out among the Communist parties of Eastern Europe for the small number of Jews in its leadership. Some of the other parties—Social Democrats, Democrats, Radicals—had Jewish sections, but these were not very active. Fewer than half a dozen Jews sat in the National Assembly after 1878.

Compared to other areas in Europe, Bulgaria has never had a great amount of anti-Semitism, but it has not been unknown. As we have seen, there was some doubt on the part of the Jews as to whether they should support the Bulgarians or Turks in the war of liberation. This did cause some anti-Jewish feeling among the Bulgarians, increased by the fact that Benjamin Disraeli maintained an anti-Bulgarian policy at the Congress of Berlin. Attacks on Jews occurred in Eastern Rumelia, where Turkish sympathizers fled after 1878. However, in reality, national conflict in Rumelia was so great that the Jews really suffered less at the hands of the Bulgarians than did others, such as Greeks and Turks.[37]

In the nineteenth and early twentieth centuries, several pogroms caused by rumors of ritual Passover execution occurred in Bulgarian cities and villages. The most infamous was that in Pazardzhik in 1895, but there were others, including Sofia (1884), Vratsa (1890), Lom (1903), and Kiustendil (1904). As the years passed and the Bulgarian Jews concentrated in the cities which had become more sophisticated, these anti-Semitic acts ceased. In the late 1800s Bulgarian anti-Semitism was chiefly associated with peasant attitudes, the origins of which are found in the Middle Ages. It was unlike the violent, middle-class, modern anti-Semitism which grew up in the cities of Central Europe. Rural anti-Semitism in Bulgaria did not have an economic basis, for oppressors of the Bulgarian peasants were Bulgarian moneylenders, not Jewish as in Rumania. There is no indication that the Bulgarian peasants sympathized with Nazi plans for the Jews. Urban anti-Semitism is of greater consequence, because here there was contact between Jews and Bulgarians; and the cities, not the countryside, ruled Bulgaria in World War II. This modern anti-Semitism was insignificant in the

37. Great Britain, *Parliamentary Papers*, vol. 81 (*Accounts and Papers*, vol. 42, 1880), Commissioner Mitchell, British representative on the International Commission in Eastern Rumelia, to Lord Salisbury, foreign minister, "Correspondence Respecting the Condition of the Musulman, Greek and Jewish Populations in Eastern Rumelia," passim.

country until the late nineteen twenties. It is true that in early years there was some exclusion of Jews from Bulgarian society; for example Petur Gabe, who was elected to the Subranie in 1889, was not seated by his colleagues. Yet the Bulgarian national movement had inspired liberal principles and traditions, and these became dominant in relations between Jews and Bulgarians. There were several factors working against urban (i.e., middle-class) anti-Semitism in Bulgaria. The Jews were a very small minority. The Turks were more numerous, and the Greeks before 1920 had as sizable a population as the Jews. These traditional enemies obviated the use of the Jews as a scapegoat in Bulgaria. In fact, all minorities, even nationals of countries at odds with Bulgaria, were normally well treated. Most Bulgarians had little contact with Jews. Competition between Jews and Bulgarians in business, in the professions, and for jobs was rare in Bulgaria, and not a great cause of concern. The leading politicans did not promote anti-Semitism as an issue as was the case, for example, in Rumania and Austria.

As anti-Semitism grew up in Europe and became a problem of international concern for liberal and democratic societies, the Bulgarian intellectuals began to reflect upon their country's relations with its own Jewish communities. They emphasized the favorable relations, and a myth of the absence of anti-Semitism grew up. Although this was not strictly true, the myth became as important as the fact, for a large section of the Bulgarian intelligentsia became committed to fighting the growth (or, as they preferred to think of it, the appearance) of anti-Semitism in their country. In 1937, a Jewish journalist, Buko Piti, published a book of statements of some one hundred and fifty leaders of Bulgarian society denouncing anti-Semitism and proclaiming the reasons for its absence in Bulgaria.[38]

The appearance of some urban anti-Semitic groups at the end of the nineteenth century was an importation from the capitals of Europe just as were other modes and fashions imported from Vienna, St. Petersburg, Berlin, and Paris. It reflected an alien middle-class attitude rather than native peasant anti-Semitism. These urban groups published a rabid racist press through the years, but they made few converts until the late twenties. They copied their literature from foreign sources—Germans, Russians, even Henry Ford. The rise of the Nazis in Germany and their coming to power created the atmosphere for anti-Semitic movements all over Europe, including Bulgarian groups such as the

38.   Buko Piti, ed., *Bulgarskata obshtestvenost za rasizma i antisemitizma* [Bulgarian public opinion on racism and anti-Semitism] (Sofia: n.p., 1937).

Nazi-style organizations mentioned above. These groups attracted people who believed in the political goals and eventual victory of fascism and nazism as well as anti-Semites. The heirs and indeed the actual members of those extremist groups that had existed since the nineties found their niche in these more serious organizations.

We may conclude that Bulgarian anti-Semitism in the thirties was imported and concentrated in a few relatively small organizations. Rural native anti-Semitism lacked real political importance because it was not so deep and violent as to be of use to the Nazis, and because of differences between the people of the countryside and the rulers of the government. On the whole, Bulgaria had less anti-Semitism than other countries of the Western world; and, moreover, an important section of the Bulgarian intelligentsia had developed the idea that its country was not anti-Semitic and that this tolerance was something in which to take pride.

2

Anti-Semitic Legislation in Bulgaria

The Law for the Defense of the Nation

There was no official anti-Semitism in Bulgaria until the fall of 1939, after the war began. Before that time fascist and Nazi extremists occasionally perpetrated anti-Jewish acts and small pogroms—even the most significant of these, however, occurred in September 1939—but the government was not involved and arrested those responsible.[1]

That same September the government issued decrees ordering foreign Jews out of the country. Many Jews had left Central Europe before the advance of the Nazis and had come to Bulgaria hoping to find passage to Palestine. As Bulgaria became more friendly to the Reich, these Jews become an embarrassment, and K'oseivanov charged Director of Police Colonel Atanas Pantev with expelling the 4,000 foreign Jews from Bulgaria. Pantev easily disposed of Turkish and Greek Jews by escorting them across the border, and answering complaints from members of the central consistory by threatening them with the same treatment. However, the Greek and Turkish Jews were only a minority of the foreign Jews, and the police director had to seek more effective measures. At this time several Bulgarian Zionist organizations were seeking ships to transfer Bulgarian Jews to Palestine (a response to Bulgaria's pro-German atmosphere). Pantev ordered the foreign Jews to Varna to await deportation on these ships, but vessels were scarce

1. Haim Keshales, "Tova se sluchi v onezi dni: Belezhki za zhivota na evreite v Bulgariia prez 1939-1950 godini" [It happened in those days: notes on the life of the Jews in Bulgaria during the period 1939-1950] (unpublished manuscript deposited in Yad WaShem, Jerusalem), pp. 5-6. There is an abridged Hebrew version of Keshales's work in A. Romano, Joseph Ben, and Nisim (Buko) Levy, eds., *Yehudut Bulgariyah* [The Jews of Bulgaria] (Jerusalem: Encyclopedia of the Jewish Diaspora Co., 1968), pp. 765-890. For a contemporary account see the *New York Times*, September 28, 1939, p. 6.

and the Jewish community was wracked by dissension concerning organization and the priority of obtaining precious entry visas for Palestine. Departures were delayed, and the foreign Jews became wards of the Varna Jewish community.

A tragic aftermath to this story occurred a year later. In December 1940 Pantev forced the captain of a small ship, the *Salvator,* carrying Bulgarian Jews to Palestine to take a number of the foreign citizens along as well, dangerously overcrowding the vessel. The ship was unseaworthy and both Bulgarian and Turkish harbor authorities hesitated to allow it to set sail through the Straits. Pantev ordered the ship's departure nevertheless; and the Turks, who did not want the refugees to stop in their country, let it pass. The *Salvator* sank in the Sea of Marmora with over two hundred casualties. This affair, which occurred during the Subranie debates over the first anti-Semitic legislation in Bulgaria, was a national, indeed, an international scandal, and Jewish sailings from Bulgaria ceased. (In any case the Germans began to discourage emigration to Palestine.) Thus Pantev was unable to complete his charge concerning the foreign Jews, and many remained in the country.[2]

There were other serious forebodings for the Jews in the fall of 1939. Anti-Semitic statements and allusions appeared in the nation's press and were heard on the radio—some emanating from government officials. The Jews were most alarmed over the inclusion of the ex-Ratnik Gabrovski in the government of October 1939. Gabrovski, a lawyer, brought one of his legal associates and protégés, Aleksandur Belev, into the government with him. Since Belev was still a leading member of the Ratnitsi, his appointment violated a law of 1939 barring Ratnitsi from government positions. Belev, nevertheless, followed Gabrovski into the Ministry of Internal Affairs the next year and became a leader of the judicial section—in fact, the expert on Jewish matters. He hired other Ratnitsi as assistants and retained his own close relations with Berlin. Thus in this department, which vitally affected the Jews, the very people from whom they had most to fear had become leaders.

The Germans were interested in their allies enacting anti-Semitic

2. Keshales, pp. 13-27; Baruh Konfino, *Aliyah Bet: Mikhofi Bulgariyah 1938-1940, 1947-1948; Khesul galut Bulgariyah 1948-1949* [Aliyah bet: from the shores of Bulgaria 1938-1940, 1947-1948; the end of the Bulgarian diaspora 1948-1949] (Jerusalem: Achiasaf Publishing House, 1965), pp. 5-90; Bulgaria, Narodno Subranie, *Stenografski Dnevnitsi* [Stenographic minutes], 25th Obiknoveno [ordinary] Narodno Subranie (hereafter cited as ONS), 2d reg. session (Oct. 28, 1940, to May 28, 1941), II, 724-25.

legislation modeled on the Nuremberg laws, and despite the king's doubts about this, he agreed. Boris, in faot, told one of his closest advisors that since an anti-Jewish law had to come, the Bulgarians should initiate it themselves, rather than let the Germans dictate a harsher one.[3] In the summer of 1940 Belev visited Germany to study the Nuremberg laws,[4] and after he returned, Gabrovski announced his intention to propose a Law for the Defense of the Nation (*Zakon za zashtitata na natsiiata*, ZZN) directed against the Jews (July 1940).

The proposed law would register all the Jews in the country and limit their right to participate in Bulgaria's economic and political life, as well as in society at large. Exceptions were provided for Jews who had converted to Christianity, married Bulgarians, or served in the military.[5] The cabinet approved the project, and it was published in October. The proposal started a great controversy in Bulgaria; the entire capital engaged in a debate concerning both the Jews and the bill. After the official publication of the bill, members of the Bulgarian Writers' Union sent a letter of protest to Filov and the president of the Subranie; and soon other groups joined in protest: the Bulgarian Union of Lawyers, the Bulgarian Union of Doctors, the Holy Synod of the Bulgarian Orthodox church, student and worker groups, and others. Dimo Kazasov, a prominent member of Zveno, wrote an eloquent public letter of personal protest to the prime minister. On the other hand, there were messages in support of the bill from trade and business groups, other student groups, right-wing organizations, military organizations, and so forth.[6]

3. Diary of Liubomir Hristov Lulchev, advisor to King Boris, November 11, 1940, Central State Historical Archives (hereafter cited as CDIA), fund no. 95, t. 1, p. 118; duplicate copy in the archives of the General Cultural-Educational Organization of the Jews in the People's Republic of Bulgaria (hereafter cited as Bulgarian Jewish Organization Archives), vol. 1 (see the bibliographical note).

4. Natan Grinberg, *Hitleristkiiat natisk za unishtozhavane na evreite ot Bulgariia* [The Hitlerist pressure for destroying the Jews of Bulgaria] (Tel Aviv: "Amal," 1961), p. 34.

5. For the final text of the law see Bulgaria, *Durzhaven Vestnik* [State gazette] (hereafter cited as *DV*), no. 16 (January 23, 1941), pp. 1-5.

6. Eli Baruh, *Iz istoriiata na bulgarskoto evreistovo* [From the history of the Bulgarian Jews] (Tel Aviv: n.p., 1960), pp. 100-11; Misho Leviev, ed., *Nashata blagodarnost* [Our thanks] (Sofia: Sbornik "Kadima" [1946]), pp. 48-59; Bulgarian Academy of Sciences, *Istoriia na Bulgariia* [History of Bulgaria], ed. D. Kosev et al. (Sofia: "Nauka i izkustvo," 1962-64), III, 366 (hereafter cited as BAN, *Istoriia*). For the story of the writers' protest see Stiliian Chilingirov, *Moite suvremennitsi* [My contemporaries] (Sofia: "Bulgarski pisatel," 1955), pp. 175-76; and Frederick B. Chary, "The Bulgarian Writers' Protest of October 1940 against the Introduction of Anti-Semitic Legislation into the Kingdom of Bulgaria," *East European Quarterly,*

The government and right-wing elements in Bulgarian society conducted a propaganda war against the Jews. Many authors wrote articles to demonstrate that the Jews as a nation economically exploited the Bulgarians, led the country in crime statistics, and were disloyal to the Bulgarian state. Aleksandur N. Pudarev in his brochure "The Jew in Bulgaria and in the World" and Boris Konstantinov in an article in the Varna journal *Ekonomist* presented statistics on the relative position of the Jews and Bulgarians in the kingdom, which both Germany and Bulgaria thereafter accepted as the basis of a Jewish problem in Bulgaria. The Jews and their supporters answered these anti-Semitic articles with statements and statistics of their own.[7]

There was really no Jewish problem even in the Nazi sense in Bulgaria, but the German alliance created a need for one. Generally, in order to prove Jewish economic exploitation, the Bulgarian anti-Semites used fraudulent analysis. An illustration of one of the most regularly quoted groups of figures demonstrates this. Pudarev claimed that the Jews had an average annual income of 26,119 leva ($317) compared to 1,067 leva ($13 or $0.04 a day!) for the Bulgarians. However, Pudarev arrived at these figures in a highly unorthodox fashion. Instead of a direct computation dividing the total income of each community by the total population, he divided the Bulgarian and Jewish incomes from certain professions only (the liberal professions, industry, labor, and internal and external trade) plus income from dividends, interest, rents, etc., by the total Bulgarian and Jewish populations respectively—the total populations, not merely those participating in the occupations and revenue sources concerned. Since the income sources used encompassed almost all Jewish employment and revenue, the figure for Jewish mean income may have been valid. Pudarev did not, however, include the income from agriculture, by which over 80 percent of Bulgarians, but none of the Jews, earned their living, and the lucrative income from

4 (March 1970), pp. 88-93. The original protests are in CDIA, fund 173. Some copies are found in a special collection of photostated documents from Bulgaria in the library of HaShomer HaTzier kibbutz "Moreshet" at Givat Harira, Israel. Copies of protests against and letters in support of the ZZN can also be found in the Bulgarian Jewish Organization Archives, copies of CDIA documents, vols. I and V.

7. Boris Konstantinov, "Narodnosten sustav i uchastie na narodnostite v bulgarskoto narodno stopanstvo" [National composition and participation of nationalities in the Bulgarian national economy], *Ekonomist* (Varna), I (1939), pp. 22-44; Aleksandur N. Pudarev, *Evreite v Bulgariia i v sveta* [The Jews in Bulgaria and in the world] (Sofia: n.p., 1940); Central Consistory of Jews in Bulgaria, *Izlozhenie po Zakona za zashtitata na natsiiata* [Report on the law for the defense of the nation] (Sofia: n.p., 1940), found in the Bulgarian Academy of Sciences, Institute for Balkan Studies, Section for Hebrew Studies archives, doc. no. 137, (hereafter cited as BAN, Ebroistika).

civil service and government employment, by which only a handful of Jews, but tens of thousands of Bulgarians, earned theirs. Furthermore, the predominance of agriculture in Bulgaria disturbs the whole balance. The consistory wrote in its report refuting anti-Semitic arguments that in 1930 the average Bulgarian liquid income was 4,289 leva, but that this was only 40 percent of the real income. Despite differences from year to year, Bulgarian income averaged roughly 13,000 leva, or about half that of the Jews.[8]

Two other factors must be taken into account. First, because the Jews were city dwellers, their statistics, as the consistory incessantly pointed out, should properly be compared only with Bulgarian urban figures. A difference between city and country existed to the financial advantage of the former; poverty was not a problem of race or national origin but rather one of geography. Moreover, the geographical difference in income did not mean that all urban Bulgarians were wealthy. The average income of the city dwellers, including the Jews, appears higher, because of the rich in their midst; but in reality, the majority of even the urban Bulgarians (all Bulgarians regardless of religious or national origin) were almost as poor as their rural compatriots, even if they had a higher liquid income. This problem of rich and poor is the second factor to consider in interpreting Pudarev's figures. Since there were 40,000 Jews and 6,000,000 Bulgarians, one Jewish millionaire would raise the Jewish national average more than a hundred Bulgarian millionaires would the Bulgarian. Although there were few Jewish millionaires, they influenced statistics to a greater degree than did their Bulgarian counterparts.

Considering the controversy the bill stirred outside its halls, the Subranie rather hastily pushed the Law for the Defense of the Nation through its chambers. The delegates spent only three days debating the first reading in November, and a month later in two meetings they passed the law at the second reading, with only a few changes, mostly of a technical nature, from the original bill. The arguments on both sides were for the most part uninspiring and unprovocative. The most heated argument during the entire debate occurred between Aleksandur Tsankov and a pro-Nazi government representative, Deni Kostov; and the subject of the disturbance was not the Jewish but the anti-Masonic sections of the proposed legislation.[9]

The government's supporters read statistics which purported to prove

8. Central Consistory, *Izlozhenie*, p. 6.
9. The debate on the ZZN is in Bulgaria, Narodno Subranie, *Dnevnitsi*, 25th ONS, 2d reg. sess., I, 204-60; II, 689-732, 808-10.

Jewish exploitation of Bulgarians. They also used arguments imported entirely from Germany. Two representatives repeated a list of anti-Semitic statements attributed to famous people throughout history. The opponents to the legislation for their part emphasized the unconstitutional nature of the bill. Articles 54 and 55 of the Turnovo Constitution provided rules of citizenship which included all those born in Bulgaria, and immigrants, if they so desired, with the consent of the Subranie.[10] Article 57, the one the opposition quoted most often, stated: "All Bulgarian subjects are equal before the law. There exists no privileged class in Bulgaria."[11] However, the Bulgarian constitution was a very impracticable document, and it had been violated many times in the past, including 1934. In particular, there was no method of judicial review to determine the constitutionality of legislation, such as the U.S. Supreme Court provides. If the Subranie passed a bill and the king signed it, it was law. Thus the opposition's constitutional arguments were really exercises in legal hairsplitting.

Actually there was no way that the opposition could stop the passage of the bill. They were a handful of men within a body whose majority greeted the vacuous speeches of the government spokesmen with tumultuous applause. The names of the spokesmen for and against the bill are more revealing than the content of their speeches. Aside from Petur Gabrovski, who spoke as minister of internal affairs, and his deputy, Docho Hristov, who succeeded Gabrovski in 1943, none of the government spokesmen were leaders of the first rank. Hristov, as the reporter for the Subranie's Committee on Internal Affairs, really exceeded his authority when he turned his statement on the purpose of the bill into an anti-Semitic tirade in support of it. Two of the five remaining speakers for the government—Deni Kostov and Krum Mitakov—were quite far from the center of power. Both of these men had limited ability and little sympathy from their colleagues. Both were ideological Nazis who, in their speeches on behalf of the ZZN, spent as much time attacking the Masons as the Jews. Mitakov even proposed to register former Masons and take sanctions against them. Since, as ex-Masons,

10. For the Bulgarian Constitution see St. (Stefan) Balemezov, *Nashata Konstitutsiia i nashiiat parliamentarizum: Chast I; Turnovskata Konstitutsiia: Istoriia na purvonachalniia tekst ot 1879 god* [Our constitution and our parliamentarianism: part I; the Turnovo constitution: the history of the original text since 1879] (Sofia: n.p., 1919), pp. 51-86. An English translation is found in C. E. Black, *The Establishment of Constitutional Government in Bulgaria* (Princeton, N.J.: Princeton University Press, 1943), pp. 291-309.

11. C. Black, p. 296.

both Filov and Gabrovski as well as other ministers would have been included in such a registration, the representatives greeted Mitakov's amendment with derisive laughter.

On the other hand, the opposition spokesmen included two of their leading members in the body—Nikola Mushanov, a former premier, and Petko Stainov, a noted law professor, who after September 9, 1944, became Bulgarian minister of foreign affairs. In addition, an important member of the government's faction, Ivan V. Petrov, broke with the majority on this issue and gave a speech against the ZZN. The Communists Todor Poliakov and Liuben Diukmedzhiev were also among the representatives who argued against the bill. The lack of leading government spokesmen to match the prestige of the opposition, the rapid passage of the bill, and the anti-Masonic passages it included clearly indicate that the origin of the ZZN is not to be found primarily in internal Bulgarian politics, but rather in pressures from Berlin and its friends in the Bulgarian government.

Gabrovski sent the law to the palace on January 15, 1941. Boris ratified it, and both he and Gabrovski signed the bill. On January 23 it was published in the *Durzhaven Vestnik*, the official gazette for promulgation of laws and decrees, as *ukaz* no. 3. (The king had waited until after Bulgarian Christmas—January 7—to accept and sign the *ukaz* because of the inherent contradiction of the law with the spirit of the season.)[12]

After the ZZN

After the publication of the ZZN in the *Durzhaven Vestnik*, the government's Jewish policy focused on its application. The law contained several provisions with time limits—a month for Jews to leave their public posts, six months to liquidate forbidden property, etc. During the next few months the cabinet, especially Belev's department in the Ministry of Internal Affairs, worked out the legal procedure for applying the clauses of the ZZN and prepared the actions required by its stipulations.

There was no great desire to go beyond the law. With some exceptions the people and government looked on the law as a reflection of ties with the Reich—an abnormal situation. One example of leniency

12. Reichssicherheitshauptamt (RSHA), section VI, Foreign Intelligence (department of Walter Schellenberg), report to Martin Luther of Abteilung Deutschland in the foreign office, January 23, 1941, T120, serial 2320H, roll 1305, frames **485359-63.**

with respect to the letter of the law rather than zeal for its spirit is told by Floyd Black, who was president of the American College in Sofia at the time. The American College was a school with limited enrollment and many Bulgarian applicants; in other words, a school which under article 21 of the ZZN would be required to limit the number of Jews (in this case to 5 percent). Black asked the minister of education to allow some Jews above the quota into the school, and the chief secretary of the ministry, Dr. Boris Iotsov, readily agreed.[13] Although Iotsov then directed the department, the minister was still Bogdan Filov, and the fact that this exception was so easily obtained from his own office reveals much about the attitude toward the law. As the German policy became even more extreme, and Bulgaria became involved in the war, the sentiments of the government toward the Jews harshened; but in January 1941 they were still mild compared to those of the Nazis.

Article 25 of the ZZN—a *numerus clausus* limiting the number of Jews in various occupations—provided for a final decision by the cabinet within six months on the distribution of occupations in the professions and in trade and manufacturing throughout the country. The number permitted for the professions was extremely small, for example, twenty-one doctors, twenty lawyers, and seven dentists. Available mercantile positions were more plentiful—505—and the law did not limit push-cart operators; but the cabinet allowed only one Jewish manufacturer —the owner of a Sofia textile factory—to remain open. Occupations were distributed only among the major cities with Jewish population: Sofia, Plovdiv, Ruse, Varna, and some others.[14] Yet many Jewish professionals, businessmen, and merchants were able to keep on with their work despite the quotas, even in restricted areas. Because the need for doctors was so great, the government impressed displaced Jewish doctors into service under the Law for Civilian Mobilization, requiring them to practice in the cities or in small villages. They also mobilized key industrialists, veterinarians, dentists, and others.

    13.   Floyd H. Black, *The American College of Sofia: A Chapter in American-Bulgarian Relations* (Boston: Trustees of Sofia American Schools, 1958), pp. 70-71.
    14.   *DV*, no. 164 (July 29, 1941), pp. 4-5. According to available statistics in 1926 there were 834 Jews in the professions and civil service; 4,665 self-employed in commerce, credit, and insurance; and 1,736 self-employed in manufacturing, crafts, and transportation (Peter Meyer, "Bulgaria," in *The Jews in the Soviet Satellites*, ed. Peter Meyer [Syracuse, N.Y.: Syracuse University Press, 1953], p. 560). Later the government revised the available positions upward to 130 in the liberal professions (*DV*, no. 281 [December 17, 1941], p. 28), 761 tradesmen, and 34 industrialists (*DV*, no. 93 [May 1, 1942], p. 24).

Many of the prohibitions of the law, for example, against mixed marriages and the holding of positions in Bulgarian societies and certain industries, affected relatively few. The most severe provisions, such as the *numerus clausus*, were mitigated as described above. Bulgarian extremists sarcastically began to call the measure "the law for the defense of the Jews," and anti-Semites like Deni Kostov complained about the number of exemptions granted under article 33, which excluded Jews who had served in the military or had converted to Christianity from most or all of the limitations in the law. Kostov accused judges and officials of selling these exemptions or awarding them too freely.[15]

However, the Bulgarians pursued with ardor one feature of their Jewish policy—confiscation. Article 26 of the ZZN, providing for the registration of Jewish wealth, ominously presaged the enactment of measures to confiscate part or all of that wealth. Despite government claims during the ZZN debate that it would not institute such confiscations of Jewish property, in July 1941 they took the first step toward that goal—one which resembled the German measures of November 1938 after the infamous *Kristallnacht*: a special tax on the Jewish community. Minister of Finance Dobri Bozhilov stated that the chief reason for proposing this tax was the debt the Jews owed Bulgaria for "over sixty years of exploitation."[16] The Subranie enacted a law which required the Jews to submit to the Ministry of Finance a statement of their total wealth within seven days after the law's publication. (They had already registered their property under the ZZN.) All Jews with property valued over 200,000 leva ($2,430) were subject to the tax: 20 percent on property valued above 200,000 leva but under 3 million leva ($36,500), and 25 percent on property valued above 3 million leva. The law applied to all Jewish property in Bulgaria regardless of the citizenship of the owners, and Bulgarian Jews abroad were also liable to the tax.

Half of the tax was due within thirty days, the remainder in six months (except for a special extension for those needing to convert their property to liquid assets to pay the tax). Penalties for nonpayment or attempted fraud on the declaration were severe. Beside triple

---

15. Bulgaria, Narodno Subranie, *Dnevnitsi*, 25th ONS, 2d extraordinary sess. (July 9-16, 1941), pp. 45-46 (Kostov's speech on the bill for a unique tax on the property of people of Jewish origin).
16. Ibid., p. 44. For debate on the law for a unique tax on the property of people of Jewish origin, see pp. 43-65. The text is found in *DV*, no. 151 (July 14, 1941), pp. 1-2.

taxation on the undeclared property, a fine of 3 million leva, and a five-year prison term, the property itself could be confiscated. Jews were forbidden to emigrate until the tax was paid. The law for a unique tax on Jews was the harshest measure against the Jews after the promulgation of the ZZN until the decree-law of August 26, 1942.

In February 1942 the Ministry of Finance also sponsored a bill against real estate speculation.[17] This bill was not directed specifically against the Jews, but was designed to keep the Bulgarian wartime economy under control; and the opponents to the bill in the Subranie, rather than limiting themselves to the sections dealing with Jews, objected to the restrictions imposed on Bulgarians. The law prohibited private persons from owning more than one lot of real estate, with exceptions for government agencies and selected individuals and associations. A special section (chapter II, articles 6-9) concerned foreigners (who could own real estate only under specific conditions, e.g., cabinet approval or international agreement) and Jews. The law forbade Jews, except those in the privileged groups defined by article 33 of the ZZN, to own any real estate except for home or business. The government was to reimburse the Jews over a long period for property liquidated under the law.

The government applied the ZZN and these subsequent laws not only to Bulgaria proper, but after April 1941 to the occupied territories in Greece and Yugoslavia as well. Although Sofia now regarded these provinces as part of the kingdom, Berlin actually recognized only Bulgarian military administration of the occupied territories. The Germans postponed a final settlement, which, to be sure, would have probably awarded the areas permanently to Bulgaria until the cessation of hostilities throughout Europe. Sofia was unhappy with this but could only acquiesce.[18] Almost immediately after occupation began, Hitler pulled most of his forces from the peninsula for use on the projected Russian front, even though the Balkan area was not yet pacified. The Germans relied heavily on their Bulgarian and Italian allies for policing, but Bulgarian occupation included neither Salonika, with its 55,000 Jews,

17. *DV*, no. 32, (February 13, 1942), pp. 1-3. For the Subranie debate see Bulgaria, Narodno Subranie, *Dnevnitsi*, 25th ONS, 3rd reg. sess. (October 28, 1941, to March 28, 1942), II, 803-41.

18. Karl Ritter, deputy political undersecretary of state, to Richthofen, report, April 20, 1941, T120, serial 274, roll 238, frame 177906; Wörmann, report, December 23, 1942, T120, serial 286 (Office of Staatssekretär, Bulgaria, vol. 4, March 1, 1942, to January 31, 1943), roll 244, frame 182201-02; Marin V. Pundeff, "Bulgaria's Place in Axis Policy" (Ph.D. diss., University of Southern California, 1958), p. 410.

governed by the Germans, nor the western parts of Macedonia, where Italian Albania extended. Indeed, until the Italian collapse of 1943 the fixing of the Albanian-Macedonian border was a great problem for the Axis. Italian and Bulgarian forces clashed over the area, which contained rich mineral deposits, and Berlin had to intervene several times with *de facto* settlements.[19]

Sofia regarded the new territory as incorporated into Bulgaria, or rather, as "recently liberated territories" (*novoosvobodeni zemi*), but they treated it as an occupied area. Macedonia, ever since its independence movement had begun in the nineteenth century, had been trying to gain freedom first from the Turks, then from the Serbs, either as an independent nation or as part of Bulgaria. Even though Bulgaria had obtained the territory through Germany's aggression, the Filov government had in 1941 an extraordinary opportunity to prove that the people of Macedonia thought themselves Bulgarian and preferred to be citizens of Bulgaria rather than of Yugoslavia or Greece. At first the Macedonians greeted the Bulgarian conquerors with bread and salt, but the government rapidly dissipated its opportunity. Instead of granting Macedonia autonomy, they introduced hegemony from Sofia. The cabinet appointed mayors and many local officials from Bulgaria for the area without respect to the wishes of the local inhabitants. Even civil servants, for example, officials for banks and public facilities, and clergy came into the new areas from Bulgaria proper. Many Jewish doctors excluded from practicing their profession by the *numerus clausus* were mobilized for the new territories. No new members for the area entered the twenty-fifth Subranie (as none had entered for Dobrudzha). The Subranie gave the cabinet permission to take far-reaching special measures necessary to administer the recently liberated territories.[20] For

19. See files of the Staatssekretär for Bulgaria, vol. 2, found in T120, serial 274, roll 238, especially Clodius and Richthofen (Sofia) to Ribbentrop, April 24, 1941 (frames 177919-20); and Clodius and Otto von Erdsmannsdorf, minister to Budapest, to Ribbentrop, April 28, 1941 (frames 177932-34); vol. 3 (serial 278 [July 1, 1941, to February 28, 1942], roll 237), especially Mohrmann, report, July 8, 1941 (frame 178843); Wörmann, report, July 9, 1941 (frames 178844-46); and Eberhardt von Mackensen, military commander in Rome, report, July 22, 1941 (frames 178867-69); and vol. 4 (serial 286, roll 244), especially Adolf-Heinz Beckerle, ambassador to Sofia after July 1941, reports, August 24 and October 31, 1942 (frames 182069-73; 182144-45).

20. *Zakon za burzo urezhdane neotlazhni vuprosi v osvobodenite zemi* [Law for the rapid settlement of urgent problems in the liberated territories], Bulgaria, Narodno Subranie, *Dnevnitsi*, 25th ONS, 3rd reg. sess., II, 1326. The permission extended to matters concerning emigration which, although at that time directed toward the Greeks, would have great importance for the Jews.

the Jews living in these territories, the change meant their inclusion in the legal structure of Bulgarian anti-Semitism, although the ZZN was not novel legislation in Yugoslavia which had had its own anti-Semitic laws since 1939.[21] Very quickly, the Bulgarians replaced the authoritarian domination of Belgrade with that of Sofia. The initial joy of the inhabitants became despair, and guerrilla resistance against the Bulgarian government was nowhere stronger than in the occupied territories.

After the entry of the United States into the war, Boris was convinced that Germany could not win. (The invasion of the USSR had already shaken his faith in a German victory.) Boris told a confidant that he thought Germany and France would suffer defeat in the war; England would be weakened and impoverished and would not win its war objectives; two nations "would inherit the estate—the Russians and the Americans. The trouble is that they are both too young to know how to manage it."[22] Bulgaria could not escape the inconveniences of warfare. The government applied strong censorship measures and other restrictions such as rationing on the civilian population. The economy was in constant crisis, even though German credits made it appear to be in better shape on paper than it was. These German credits meant only Berlin's increased indebtedness to Sofia. Goods became very scarce causing a black market to flourish. German soldiers and civilians in the country with money and mechandise from home were largely responsible for this, and at one time Bulgaria asked the Reich foreign office to forbid private travel to Bulgaria and eliminate the sending of packages from home to German soldiers.[23]

21. The Jewish Religious Community of Skopje, "Izvestaj o zlocini na okupatora i njihovih pomagaca izvrseni nad Jevrejiste u Skoplju" [Report of the crimes of the occupiers and their collaborators perpetrated on the Jews at Skopje] (undated), p. 1, State Archives of the People's Republic of Macedonia (SAMS), doc. no. 1679 K22-3-1/2; Aleksandar Matkovsky, *Tragedijata na Evreite od Makedonija* [The tragedy of the Jews of Macedonia] (Skopje: "Kultura," 1962), pp. 18-20. For an English edition see Aleksandar Matkovsky, "The Destruction of Macedonian Jewry," *Yad WaShem Studies on the European Jewish Catastrophe and Resistance*, 3 (1959), pp. 206-07. Mr. Matkovsky used unfiled collections of documents from the Military Historical Institute in Belgrade and also documents of the Macedonian Federal Commission for the Investigation of Crimes Perpetuated by the Invaders and their Accessories. Copies of some of these are at Yad WaShem.

22. George Rendel, *The Sword and the Olive: Recollections of Diplomacy and the Foreign Service, 1913-1954* (London: John Murray, 1957), p. 154.

23. Beckerle, report, October 8, 1941, T120, serial 278, roll 237, frames 178950-51. The cost of living on the open market rose almost four times from 1939 to 1944. See David B. Koen, *Ograbvaneto i razoriavaneto na bulgarskoto stopanstvo ot germanskite imperialisti prez vtorata svetovna voina* [The plunder and ruin of

Furthermore, progress of the war heightened the internal political tension in the kingdom. After the Germans invaded the Soviet Union, the Bulgarian government's tolerant attitude toward the BKP ended. The Subranie expelled Communist deputies and the government established political concentration camps. The government also harassed the diplomatic representatives of the Soviet Union. For their part the Communists formed small partisan bands which began guerrilla warfare in Bulgaria. Both the Soviet Union and the Comintern directly and indirectly aided these groups, and the Western allies also sent liaisons and supplies to the partisans. In 1941 and 1942, however, there were not very many Bulgarian guerrillas, and these few worked together with Greek and Yugoslav groups.[24]

In addition to backing the partisan movement, Communist leaders in exile and the Bulgarian Workers' party, their illegal front group at home, agitated for a united front of all anti-fascist elements in the country to oppose the government and Axis alliance. On July 17, 1942, Radio "Hristo Botev" (named after Bulgaria's revolutionary poet killed in 1878), a station transmitting in Bulgarian from the Caucasus, broadcast the program for a Fatherland Front (Otechestven front, OF) drawn up by the foreign bureau of the Bulgarian Workers' party. The twelve-point platform did not contain any strictly socialist provisions but emphasized anti-fascist aims in order to attract participants from all classes in the country. The program included as goals the prevention of further participation by Bulgaria in the war, the removal of Bulgarian soldiers from foreign territory, the withdrawal of Bulgaria from the Axis alliance and in its place adherence to the Atlantic Charter, the cessation of deliveries of Bulgarian produce and minerals to Germany, the return to constitutional rule, the dissolution of fascist organizations in Bulgaria, and the punishment of Bulgarian fascists. Point twelve of the program stated one goal of the OF as "the extirpation of fascist reaction, racial injustice, and national humiliation."[25]

---

the Bulgarian economy by the German imperialists during the Second World War] (Sofia: "Nauka i izkustvo," 1966), p. 240.

24. For the BKP activity during the war see Nissan Oren, "The Bulgarian Communist Party, 1934-1944" (Ph.D. diss., Columbia University, 1960), pp. 201-355; and BAN, *Istoriia*, III, 382-432.

25. *Govori radiostantsiia "Hristo Botev" (23 iuli 1941—22 septemvri 1944)* [Radio station "Hristo Botev" calling (July 23, 1941—September 22, 1944)] (Sofia: BKP, 1950-51), III, 12-14; BAN, *Istoriia*, III, 395. For the foundation of the OF see the BAN history, pp. 394-98; Ruben Avramov et al., eds., *Istoriia na bulgarskata komunisticheska partiia* [History of the Bulgarian Communist party] (Sofia: BKP, 1969), pp. 456-63; Dimo Kazasov, *Burni godini 1918-1944* [Turbulent years 1918-

The BKP's central committee selected a commission led by Kiril Dramaliev and Tsola Dragoicheva to organize the front. Many of the leaders of the other parties, for example, the Democrats and moderate Agrarians, although they opposed the government's policies at home and abroad and were more or less sympathetic to the aims of the front, refused to join the Communists. Nevertheless, the BKP was able to establish a number of OF committees throughout the country, gaining support from other parties. Leaders of the BZNS in exile had formed a Bulgarian National Committee in London which maintained contacts with the OF.

Since the Bulgarian Jews were now by definition enemies of the state, the partisans and OF had a special appeal for them. Many Jewish young men and women, including adolescents, did indeed join the partisan detachments. A memorial volume dedicated to Jews fallen in the fight against fascism lists about 70 Jewish partisans who were killed in the underground.[26] In October 1941 a Jewish Communist, Leon Tadzher, sabotaged a fuel depot in Ruse, one of the very first acts of partisan resistance by anyone in Bulgaria. Adolf-Heinz Beckerle, the new tough German ambassador, wanted fifty prominent Jews from Ruse and fifty from Sofia punished in reprisal for the killing of the German guard. The consistory protested, and the government, which looked unfavorably on the German request, did not comply.[27]

The number of Jewish partisans was about 400 out of a total of 10,000 or about 4 percent,[28] four times their percentage of the population. Besides Tadzher some of the most renowned Jews in the resistance were Violeta Iakova, who, as a member of a *cheta* (guerrilla group) in Sofia, killed General Hristo Lukov in 1943; Menahem Papo, also a member

---

1944] (Sofia: Knigaizdatelstvo "Naroden pechat," 1949), pp. 697-99, 725-28; and Dino Sharlanov, *Suzdavane i deinost na Otechestveniia front: iuli 1942—septemvri 1944 g.* [Creation and activity of the Fatherland Front: July 1942—September 1944] (Sofia: BKP, 1966), pp. 36-65.

26. Central Consistory of Jews in Bulgaria, *Evrei—zaginali v antifashistkata borba* [Jews—killed in the anti-fascist battle] (Sofia: Natsionalen Komitet na Otechestveniia Front, 1958).

27. BAN, Ebroistika, doc. no. 59, "Sabotage in the Benzine Plant of A. D. 'Petrol'—Ruse"; *Evrei-zaginali*, pp. 66-74; Keshales, p. 57; Itso Samuilov, "Zhivot otdaden na Revoliutsiata Leon Tadzher (Ben David)" [A life, devoted to the Revolution—Leon Tadzher (Ben David)], *Godishnik* (of the Bulgarian Jewish Organization), 1 (1966), pp. 127-50; R. F. Kelley, report of U.S. Department of State, "The Situation in Bulgaria up to December 10, 1941," Ankara, Department of State, National Archives record group 59, 874.00/648.

28. For estimates of the total strength of the Bulgarian partisan movement see Oren, pp. 279-81.

of a Sofia group, whose arrest in 1943 was a national press sensation; Emil Shekerdzhiiski, a member of the central committee of the Bulgarian Workers' party and political commissar of the "Dimitur Kaliashki" *cheta* in the Kiustendil district; and Ana Ventura, the daughter of a wealthy industrialist from Ruse, who became a Communist and a leader of the partisan resistance in her native city. Like their non-Jewish counterparts, these partisans were generally young, of both sexes, and involved in the BKP and its various organizations in Bulgaria.[29]

The Decree-Law of August 26, 1942

If left to themselves, the Bulgarians would have continued to implement their Jewish policies along the lines and scope of the ZZN, but the German policy was not so static, and it was this policy which affected all of Europe. The seeds of the second stage of Bulgarian Jewish policy, like those of the first, were planted in Berlin, not Sofia.

The Reich had considered at one time deporting all Jews from Europe to Palestine, perhaps, or Africa. The impossibility of accomplishing this during the war convinced the Nazis to try a different tactic in ridding Europe of the Jews. In the spring of 1941 Hitler and Himmler decided to kill the Jews in territories they planned to conquer in the Russian campaign. Himmler's SS carried out these executions, using special mobile armed detachments, *Einsatzgruppen*. On July 31, 1941, while these killings were going on, Göring as Hitler's deputy gave orders to Reinhardt Heydrich, the chief of the *Reichssicherheitshauptamt* (RSHA), the main administrative body of the SS, to prepare a "complete solution of the Jewish question" throughout Europe. The orders implied that this complete solution meant the annihilation of the European Jews. Göring told Heydrich that all German agencies were obliged to cooperate with him in carrying out his task.

Heydrich soon found out that a general cooperative plan was indeed necessary. The Einsatzgruppen were unable to kill even the Russian Jews fast enough for the German plan; for other areas of occupied Europe and for the allied states, where foreign governments would have to collaborate, their use would be impossible. There were problems concerning foreign Jews, *Mischlinge*, Jews essential to industry, etc. In the fall of 1941 Heydrich called for a general conference with representatives of various ministries and departments interested in the

29. *Everi—zaginali*, pp. 75-95, 108-15. For more on Papo see below, p. 140.

Jewish question. The conference met on January 20, 1942, in Berlin at the RSHA offices. (This became known as the Wannsee conference, after the address of these offices—Am Grossen Wannsee No. 50/58.) Among the fifteen participants were Heydrich; Adolf Eichmann, the chief of the RSHA's section on Jews; and Dr. Martin Luther of the foreign office. The essence of the plan that the conference approved was the deportation of Jews from all over Europe to Poland and their subsequent execution there in vast extermination camps. The plan envisioned sending Jews to these camps even from areas not yet captured, such as England, and from neutral areas, such as Spain and Portugal, with the ultimate goal of no more Jews in Europe. To keep the whole project secret, the Germans and their allies would maintain the fiction that the deportations were for resettlement in a Jewish homeland in Poland.[30]

Heydrich expected difficulties from the Scandinavian countries, but not from Western Europe and the Balkans. In allied states and even in some quisling puppet governments, the RSHA had to rely on the foreign office to clear the way for them. In Southeastern Europe, Rumania, Hungary, and Bulgaria had similar relationships to the Reich, and in these countries the RSHA would have to rely on native cooperation, limiting its role to that of advisor rather than actively carrying out deportations, as, for example, in Greece. The major goal for the Bulgarian government in the framework of the plan for the Final Solution was deportation to Poland of the Bulgarian Jews, including those in the "annexed" territories.

In some respects Bulgaria's Jewish policy was out of step with Germany's, but this problem did not seem insurmountable to Berlin. Bulgaria had thus far proved very willing to comply with German requests and suggestions on Jewish matters. In the summer of 1941 the Germans had easily convinced the Filov government to transfer Jews from labor groups similar to those in which Bulgarians served under the Ministry of War to special forced labor groups under the Ministry of Public Works.[31] In November 1941 on a visit to Berlin, Foreign Minister Popov brought up the difficulties in application of the ZZN, due to intercession by foreign governments, specifically Spain, Rumania, and Hungary, in behalf of their citizens. Popov suggested that the Germans convoke a

30. For the evolution of this Final Solution, see Raul Hilberg, *The Destruction of the European Jews* (Chicago: Quadrangle Books, 1961), pp. 257-66.

31. Beckerle, reports, July 24 and 31, 1941, T120, serial 278, roll 237, frames 178874, 178886. See also CDIA, fund no. 284, op. 1, arh. ed. 7707, pp. 28-29, Bulgarian Jewish Organization Archives, copies of CDIA documents, vol. III.

general European conference to consider the Jewish problems as a whole. Ribbentrop was interested but believed that such a conference would have to wait for war's end when at any rate "all [the] Jews would have to leave Europe." Hitler agreed that the problem was global and that single or partial measures were of little value. (Popov's trip coincided with the preparations for the Wannsee conference.) For the present Ribbentrop advised Popov not to place too much value on foreign protests. The Germans, he explained in example, had ceased to pay attention to American protests on the matter.[32]

Luther of the foreign office thought that bilateral treaties concerning Jews would be preferable to a general treaty.[33] There were several hundred Bulgarian Jews in the Reich and Protektorat (Bohemia and Moravia), and in June 1942 Luther requested the Bulgarian government to repudiate its interests in the rights of these Jews so that they could be deported with others in Germany. Sofia readily agreed and promised to cooperate by supplying detailed lists of Bulgarian Jews residing in the German-controlled areas, but the Bulgarians were anxious that similar treaties be arranged with other states.[34]

Thus, in the spring and summer of 1942, of all of Germany's allies and satellites, the Bulgarians seemed the most ready to cooperate in Jewish matters. Italy, Rumania, Hungary, even Vichy France raised more objections. The foreign office held up Bulgaria as a model for Germany's puppet states, Slovakia and Croatia. The Germans knew that the Bulgarians did not have the same attitude to the Jewish question that they had, but actions and cooperation, not attitudes, were ultimately important.[35]

Both the Germans and the Bulgarians realized that more legislation

32. Report (unsigned) on Popov-Ribbentrop conference at Berlin, November 27, 1941, T120, serial 2330 (Inland II geheim, bundle 54, Settlement of Jewish Question, Bulgaria, 1941 to 1944), roll 1305, frames 486176-85. The Germans might have ignored American protests, but they did not deport to the Polish death camps the handful of American Jews in Germany (Hilberg, p. 289).

33. Martin Luther, Unterstaatssekretär, Abteilung Deutschland, report, December 4, 1941, T120, serial 2330, roll 1305, frames 486187-89.

34. Notice (initialed W), July 2, 1941, ibid., frame 486202; Luther to Beckerle, June 19, 1942, ibid., frames 486203-05; draft of Bulgarian-German treaty arrangement (for Jewish citizens), ibid., frames 486202-07; Beckerle to foreign office, July 6, 1942, ibid., frames 486208-09; Luther to Beckerle, August 5, 1942, ibid., frame 486211; Dr. Stahlberg, legal section, foreign office, report (no date), ibid., frames 486214-15; Beckerle, report, July 9, 1942, ibid., frame 486216; Bulgarian Ministry of Foreign Affairs and Religious Cults, verbal note, July 7, 1942, ibid., frame 486217.

35. Luther to Beckerle, June 19, 1942, T120, serial 2330, roll 1305, frames **486203-05**.

would be needed in the kingdom to implement deportations. The Germans were particularly dissatisfied with the definition of "Jew" and the exemptions in the ZZN. The Bulgarian law relied too heavily on religion, since any Jew baptized before September 1, 1940, was exempt from the law, whether married to a Christian (as in the Nuremberg laws) or not. The Bulgarians also extended complete immunity from the ZZN to Jews who married Bulgarians before January 23, 1941, as well as partial immunity to war heroes, invalids, widows, and orphans. If the Bulgarians extended these definitions and privileges to deportation laws, many Jews would escape the Nazi net, and if the Nazis later decided to proceed against the *Mischlinge* (still being considered in 1942), others in the kingdom would escape as well; for the ZZN did not establish this category.

While the Wannsee conference met and the Final Solution was formulated, Belev was in Berlin under orders from Gabrovski to learn the latest developments on the Jewish question. He reported in June 1942 that the Bulgarian government must prepare the Jews for deportation and take measures for the complete confiscation of Jewish property:

> The radical solution of the Jewish problem in our country would be the deportation of the Jews and simultaneous confiscation of their property. The deportation of the Jews, perhaps, will be possible after the conclusion of the war or the capture from the Allied forces of territory in the east or in Africa. For now, there is no possibility for deportation of the Jews unless Germany is agreed to accept them and settles them in Galicia or elsewhere in Russia. In the meantime until conditions for deportation of the Jews are created it is imperative that the measures concerning the Jews be strengthened while at the same time the supervision of the administration of these measures is strengthened.[36]

Belev had no doubt that the Germans would help deport the Jews from Bulgaria; he had friends among the SS and was certainly privy to the Final Solution. He simply worded his report cautiously, as was customary with all written references to the Jewish policy. Belev also suggested some measures that the government should take. These included limiting the number of privileged Jews as well as the privileges, carrying out new restrictions, transferring Jews from the capital, put-

---

36. Natan Grinberg, *Dokumenti* [Documents] (Sofia: Central Consistory of Jews in Bulgaria, 1945), p. 7.

ting Jewish organizations under government control, and unifying supervision of the Jewish measures under a single agency.[37]

To facilitate the implementation of Belev's report, the government introduced into the Subranie in June 1942 a bill for a "Law to charge the Council of Ministers to take all measures for solving the Jewish question and matters connected with it" (*Zakon za vuzlagane na Ministerskiia suvet du vzeme vsichki merki za urezhdane na evreiskiia vupros i svurzanite s nego vuprosi*). The bill was very simple. It gave the cabinet plenipotentiary authority to pass decrees on Jewish matters, including the alteration of existing Jewish legislation. These would have the force of law until the Subranie later approved or rejected its measures. Theoretically the Subranie still had ultimate control, but it would suit the government better to present the body with *faits accomplis*, than to allow the members to debate the bills. Furthermore, the Subranie would hardly be able to reverse deportations after the fact. The government planned to remove the authority over Jewish matters even further from the Subranie to a body for unified supervision of Jewish legislation and orders, responsible only to the cabinet, as Belev had suggested. Equally important if the cabinet were given law-making powers, the government decrees on Jewish matters would not be subjected to review by the Bulgarian Court of Cassation. While the court had no power to judge the constitutionality or validity of laws, it could review the legality of government decrees and orders. The Bulgarian legal machinery, as already noted, in many cases had liberally interpreted Jewish legislation in favor of the Jews, throwing out government claims of violations against the ZZN.

The opposition in the Subranie was greatly concerned about the legal precedents implied in the bill. (Actually similar legislative powers had been given to the cabinet regarding the new territories.) Members of the right wing in the Subranie also protested, giving similar reasons, apparently fearing loss of their own influence in determining the fate of the Jews and the attendant political advantage they thought they derived from Jew-baiting.[38]

37. Grinberg, *Hitleriskiiat natisk*, pp. 35-38. Grinberg was in the Commissariat for Jewish Questions after the Fatherland Front government came to power in September 1944. At that time the commissariat used its offices to prepare indictments against anti-Semites in the wartime governments, and he had access to commissariat documents, many of which have never been released to the public, with the exception that they have been made available to a few other Bulgarian scholars.

38. For the debate on the bill see Bulgaria, Narodno Subranie, *Dnevnitsi*, 25th ONS, 4th extraordinary sess. (June 22-July 2, 1942), pp. 68-96, 220-22. See also

The major consequence of the June enabling law was the cabinet's decree of August 26, 1942.[39] This was a general anti-Semitic law based on the suggestion of Aleksandur Belev and designed to amplify the ZZN. The decree created a Commissariat for Jewish Questions (*Komisarstvo za evreiskite vuprosi*, KEV) to handle all phases of Jewish matters except those pertaining to the law against speculation and the law for the unique tax on Jews, both of which remained in the province of the Ministry of Finance. Although there was a supervisory council of members from various ministries and institutions, the real power lay with the commissar for Jewish questions appointed upon the recommendation of the minister of internal affairs. In practice, the ultimate fate and even the everyday life of the Jews would be directed almost completely under the authority of this single official. Quite as expected, Gabrovski proposed and the cabinet accepted Aleksandur Belev as the first commissar.

Besides the creation of the commissariat the decree of August 26 introduced a number of other important measures. It changed the definition of "Jew" so that ancestry rather than religion became the most important criterion; reduced privileged categories; and in other ways laid the foundation for fitting the Bulgarian Jews into the framework of the Nazis' plans for Europe. It also prepared the Jewish community for total confiscation of its wealth—an integral part of these plans.

Article 29 stated that "the Jews of Sofia . . . were subject to expulsion into the provinces or outside the kingdom." All unemployed Jews would have to leave by November 1, 1942. From the German point of view, this article and a phrase in article 7, which also referred to deportation, were the core of the matter, for they gave a legal basis for fitting the Bulgarian Jewish community into the Final Solution.

The decree went one step beyond the German laws by excluding a *Mischling* category. A Jew was anyone with two or more Jewish grandparents, even if only one of them had been born a Jew; in other words, even persons whom the Germans would include as *Mischlinge* first degree. *Mischlinge* second degree, that is, persons with one Jewish grandparent, the decree considered non-Jews. After the promulgation of the decree the KEV would handle practically all Jewish matters. According to the decree, the cabinet had to approve commissariat measures, but this was a passive role rather than an active one. The Subranie, which

---

debate on approving the first group of decrees, *Dnevnitsi*, 25th ONS, 4th reg. sess. (October 28, 1942, to March 28, 1943), I, 281, 296-97.

39. For the text of the law see *DV*, no. 192 (August 29, 1942), pp. 1-6.

according to the enabling law of June had ultimate authority for cabinet measures, was now two steps removed from the Jewish question. More efficient than the regular lawmaking machinery of the Bulgarian state, the KEV lessened some of the glaring adverse publicity that the. Jewish policy had brought to the government. It also obviated the need for the king to sign every major decision concerning the Jews, permitting him to avoid some involvement in these matters.

The Subranie, which had been a platform for the opposition to protest anti-Jewish legislation vehemently if ineffectually, was now apparently silenced. There was one more chance when the government in September 1942 brought up for approval a number of decrees based on the enabling legislation, including the decree of August 26. There was a vociferous debate, but the body approved the cabinet's work.[40]

For the next two years the Commissariat for Jewish Questions was to be the major instrument enforcing Bulgaria's (really Germany's) policy in the Jewish community.

The KEV Under Belev

After his appointment Belev rapidly and easily established his department around the group he had assembled in his role as legal counsel for Jewish matters in the Ministry of Internal Affairs. Many of these people were Ratnitsi who had been with Belev and Gabrovski since the two entered the government in the Ministry of Railroads. Anti-Semites naturally gravitated to the KEV; however, most of the commissariat's employees were civil servants who volunteered for the department because its pay rate was higher than that for comparable jobs in other offices.[41] Some saw an opportunity for graft and illegal profits.

The KEV had four sections: administration, public and professional activity, economic activity and agents (enforcing and information authority), and the treasury (called the "Jewish community fund"). The commissar and his personal staff were not included in any particular section. The administrative section handled problems concerning the KEV itself, but also dealt with the organization and leadership of the Jewish communities and the establishment of ghettos and dwelling

40. Bulgaria, Narodno Subranie, Dnevnitsi, 25th ONS, 4th reg. sess., I, 280-301.
41. For the higher pay scale see the letter from the director of the government budget and accounts to the minister of finance, November 19, 1942, section II, "Explanatory Tables," BAN, Ebroistika, doc. no. 41. This letter was a complaint against the regulations proposed by the KEV for operating the Jewish community fund and the size of the budget.

places for the Jews, including the transfer or deportation of the Jewish population. The public and professional activity section took charge of Jewish employment, including that of those Jews who retained certain privileges under the anti-Semitic laws. The economic division handled liquidation and confiscation of Jewish property, the governing of remaining property, and the system of agents and police attached to the KEV. The Jewish community fund both financed the KEV and supported the Jewish communities in Bulgaria.

The KEV's budget allowed it 113 employees. At the beginning of October 1942 Belev had only thirteen in his department. By November 1 this number had increased to fifty-eight, but it was only on November 18 that the KEV moved into its permanent offices on Boulevard Dondukov. At the start of 1943, the commissariat had over 100 permanent employees and almost sixty temporary workers.[42] Besides Belev, the most important officials of the KEV were Iaroslav Kalitsin, chief of the administrative section; Ivan G'oshev, chief of the section for public and professional activity; Dr. Ivan Popov, chief of service for professional activity and a chief inspector; Pencho Lukov, chief of the economic section; Boris Tasev, chief of the KEV's agents; Zahari Velkov Ivanov, chief of the Jewish community fund; and Belev's personal secretaries, Maria Pavlova and Liliana Panitsa.[43]

As provided in the decree-law, Belev drew up the regulations for the KEV's budget and the management of the Jewish community fund. Income for the fund came chiefly from frozen Jewish bank accounts but also from taxes and assessments on Jews and the sale of revenue stamps on KEV documents and forms. Expenditures maintained the commissariat and the Jewish community. The temporary budget from September 1942 to the end of the year provided for an income of 110 million leva ($1,330,000) and expenditures of 30,452,264 leva ($372,000). The director of the state budget complained about certain irregularities in the regulations and about the excessive salaries, but he actually succeeded in forcing only minor technical changes in Belev's handiwork.[44]

42. Commissar for Jewish questions, report to the minister of internal affairs for the period of September 3 to December 31, 1942, pp. 2-3; and report for the period of January 1 to March 31, 1943, p. 2. Both of these reports are from the private collection of Benjamin Arditi of Holon, Israel (hereafter cited as Arditi collection). For the positions filled by the KEV see BAN, Ebroistika, doc. no. 41.

43. In 1945 before the People's Court trial of members of the KEV, Pavlova testified that Kalitsin, G'oshev, and Popov among others were Ratnitsi (Protocols of People's Court No. 7, March-April 1945, II, 375); BAN, Ebroistika, doc. no. 234.

44. "Rules for Governing and Expending the Jewish Community Fund"; "Tem-

The KEV activity against the Jews, aside from arranging with the SS for deportations, fell into three categories—the designation and location of all the Jews in the country, the confiscation of their wealth, and general discriminatory restrictions. The activities overlapped, for some discriminatory and confiscatory measures aided location of the Jews, etc. In general, the confiscation fell to the economic section, while location, designation, and restrictions were the concerns of the sections for administration and public and professional activity. The KEV's very first order concerned liquidators for Jewish enterprises declared illegal by the decree-law of August 26, 1942; but the decrees issued soon after dealt with measures for marking with stars and signs Jewish homes, businesses, and, of course, the Jews themselves.[45] (The ZZN had not required this.)

The task of designating and locating the Jews was logically the first problem to which the KEV had to turn, and a German report from the RSHA indicated that initially Belev encountered some difficulties. The report stated that Filov, without Belev's knowledge, had rescinded the order requiring the wearing of Stars of David for all Jews in mixed marriages, even those not baptized or registered as privileged at the commissariat. At the insistence of Metropolitan Stefan of Sofia, the leader of the Bulgarian Orthodox church, who was blatantly pro-Ally and like other church leaders did not hide his opposition to all anti-Semitic laws, the prime minister cancelled the order also for all Jews who had converted to Christianity, regardless of marital status or registration. The report also accused the minister of justice of interfering with Belev's decrees.

Furthermore, the RSHA statement continued, application of the order regarding stars and house signs was something less than complete for Jews not covered by the new exceptions. There were not enough stars to go around because power rationing at the manufacturing plants delayed their output. Only 20 percent of the quota was fulfilled. Jews who had stars did not bother to wear them or took them off when they saw the laxity of enforcement. Others who did wear them received so much sympathy from their Bulgarian neighbors that they wore them proudly. Some Jews even disregarded the regulation stars of the commissariat and devised their own, which contained pictures of the king and queen.

---

porary Budget for Jewish Community Fund for September 1 to December 31, 1942"; "Explanatory Table for the Temporary Budget"; director of state budget to minister of finance, November 19, 1942, BAN, Ebroistika, doc. no. 41.

45. Bulgaria, *DV*, no. 202 (September 10, 1942), pp. 3-4; no. 214 (September 24, 1942), p. 4; no. 11 (January 16, 1943), p. 24.

The Germans in Sofia took a dim view of this "arrogant behavior" and attributed it to the indifference of the populace. "The broad masses . . . [do not understand at all] that they themselves must participate in the segregation of the Jews." Rumania, Hungary, France, Spain, and Italy protested the application of the decree to their Jewish citizens in Bulgaria. Italy was singularly persistent, presenting more than four hundred urgent notes to the foreign ministry. Moreover, the Italians were allowing Jews to enter Italy fairly easily (the Bulgarians, however, were tightening their exit requirements) and, further, allowing many Jews to become Italian citizens. The Bulgarian foreign ministry made a practice of giving these notes to Belev, the RSHA informants reported, ostensibly to impress him with the need for moderation.[46]

The difficulties of application may have been exaggerated by the RSHA's sources, for in a few months the KEV could see that its orders and decrees respecting markings were observed. Special raids by KEV agents insured such observance.[47] By the end of December almost one hundred and fifty thousand stars and over five thousand circles (for privileged Jews and children) had been distributed or were in stock at the KEV—more than enough to go around. In the three-month period from October 1 to December 31 the KEV prepared thirty-five indictments for violation of its orders, decrees, and regulations. Twenty-nine of these were for failure to wear stars and one for not marking a home.[48]

Along with the marking of Jews, the KEV registered all Jews subject to their authority. Statistics for Jews under Bulgarian administration, although in many cases approximate and not always accurate, revealed the following (see Appendix I):

Area	Number of Jews
Pre-1940 boundaries	51,500
Southern Dobrudzha	500
Western Thrace	4,000
Macedonia	7,200
Pirot (Serbia)	200
Total	63,400

46. Schellenberg to Luther, November 21, 1942, T120, serial 2330, roll 1305, frames 486243-48. See below, pp. 74–75, for Beckerle's modification of this report.

47. Jacob Robinson, *And the Crooked Shall be Made Straight: The Eichmann Trial, the Jewish Catastrophe and Hannah Arendt's Narrative* (New York: Macmillan, 1954), p. 258.

48. Commissar, report for September to December, 1942, pp. 4, 22, Arditi collection.

The total indicates an increase in the Jewish population in the pre-1940 boundaries of 3,000 over the last census, that of 1934.[49] Dobrudzha had been incorporated into Bulgaria, and Dobrudzha Jews were Bulgarian citizens; but Jews from the other occupied areas were not.

The KEV also initiated a regular program of confining Jews to specific residential areas, in other words, establishing ghettos. The ZZN had given the cabinet the privilege of confining Jews to various cities or quarters, but this had never become an established procedure. Now the KEV encouraged its local delegates to restrict Jews to special sections of those cities where consistories were located. In Sofia the Jews were moved to the Iuch Bunar section, the neighborhood of the poorest Jews of the capital, just west of the present center of the city (Sofia district five). However, ghettoization was not completely accomplished either in Sofia or in the provinces.

The KEV also reorganized the Bulgarian Jewish community based on the existing local consistories.[50] Jewish "communities" as legal units (obshtini) were required in and limited to cities with fifty or more Jewish families. Families in towns with fewer than fifty Jewish families were attached to the nearest obshtina. As previously, membership in the obshtina was obligatory for all Jews, but now baptized Jews who met the definition of the decree-law of August 26, 1942, were also included. The obshtini were responsible for keeping complete records of all Jews within their jurisdiction, the local consistory's complete financial activity, and other information concerning the community that might be of use to the KEV.

The legal governing bodies of the obshtini remained the consistories. In Sofia there was, as before, in addition to the local consistory, a central consistory for all Bulgaria consisting of the full complement of seven members. While allowing only one consistory per obshtina, the KEV allowed Sofia, Ruse, and Varna to have Ashkenazi synagogues and religious policies separate from the Sephardic. (The organization established by the Jewish Congress of 1920 had allowed this for Sofia and Ruse, but not for Varna.) As provided in the law, the KEV appointed a non-Jewish delegate to each consistory. The delegate and through him the commissar were the real authorities in each consistory. Members of the consistories, appointed by the commissar, could not refuse to serve without a valid reason, and in many cases the commissar

---

49. Bulgaria, Direction Générale de la Statistique, *Annuaire Statistique du Royaume de Bulgarie*, 29 (1937), p. 25. See above, table 2, p. 29.

50. Bulgaria, *DV*, no. 247 (November 3, 1942), pp. 1-2.

simply kept the body which had been elected. Josef Geron continued as chairman of the central consistory in Sofia.

The KEV's delegates were not necessarily regular employees of that body. In fact, only in Sofia were staff members used: Pencho Lukov for the central consistory—hence the chief of all delegates; and Iaroslav Kalitsin for the local Sofia consistory. Most of the delegates were either district governors, mayors, or police chiefs.[51] The KEV budget, however, allotted a fee for the delegates.

The orders of the KEV's delegates were binding, but local consistories could appeal orders and decisions (of their delegates) to the delegate of the central consistory (Lukov) and ultimately to the commissar (Belev). The delegate designated general duties to the consistory members, including assignments involving the areas of administration, financial and economic activity, religious affairs, education, residence location, employment, and social welfare. Members of the consistories worked without salary unless they had no source of income. Then they could be awarded up to 5,000 leva ($60.80) a month. (A stenographer at the KEV received 4,350 leva a month. Belev received 12,800 leva; Lukov, 8,400 leva.)

The presidents of the local consistories were responsible for seeing that the delegates' and KEV's orders and the consistories' decisions were fulfilled. The KEV delegate decided all disagreements between the president and members of each consistory and confirmed all consistory decisions. The delegate also served as an intermediary between provincial Jews and the KEV, as only Sofia Jews could deal directly with the commissariat. The delegate appointed all synagogue officials on the recommendation of the consistory. The commissar confirmed rabbis and cantors. Schools continued if the obshtina had the means, facilities, and personnel, but the curricula consisted only of professional training. The KEV had the last word on obshtina budgets, but local consistories had a voice.

This KEV plan to work with the existing Jewish consistories disregarded the strong Zionist opinions present in their leadership. Indeed, the ZZN section on international organizations had already proscribed Zionist activity; and the large and varied Zionist press in Bulgaria had ceased. However, while the various groups had stopped operating in the open, they continued to work "underground." An illegal organization operated throughout the war period. They established connections with Zionist leaders and messengers in Istanbul and Switzerland and received funds from these connections abroad. It is outside the scope

51. See Appendix I.

of this study to dwell at length on these Zionist operations beyond the effect that they had on the government's policy toward the Jews. In general, the Zionist groups worked to get people out of the Balkans— the key to which often hinged more on obtaining entrance visas to Palestine from Great Britain than in securing Sofia's permission for the Jews to leave.

Some factionalism existed among the Jews. Native Bulgarian Jews and foreign Jews residing in Bulgaria did not always work together. The latter were most anxious to obtain visas to Palestine, and since Bulgarian Zionist leaders were primarily interested in serving Bulgarians, the foreign Jews had more or less to fend for themselves. Differences apparently existed also among the Bulgarian leadership.[52]

The Jews established an underground consistory of five men, which had connections with the regular central consistory (Leon Farhi, the chairman of the underground group, served on both) and a Zionist, although not exclusively so, orientation. This illegal group could work more effectively than Geron's drafted organization, which was now forced to serve the KEV. Interestingly enough, although the legal consistory was charged with the duty of keeping order among the Jews, after the war the Bulgarian community did not stigmatize the members as collaborators as other European Jews did to such groups in their communities.[53]

In its order on Jewish organization the KEV decreed that living space vacated by limiting rooms in Jewish apartments (under article 25 of the decree law of August 26, 1942) be used primarily to house Jews expelled from Sofia (article 29 of the same decree). However, from 30 to 70 percent of the former Jewish premises, depending on the city, were reserved for needy Bulgarians. (In actual point of fact, KEV and government officials and favorites took over the best quarters.) The KEV began expelling a number of families from the capital, and by the end of March 1943, 680 families (1,904 people) had been forced to leave Sofia.[54]

---

52. Interview with Haim Keshales, former member of illegal consistory, Tel Aviv, Israel, February 1966; interview with Josefico Levi, former member of illegal consistory, Tel Aviv, Israel, February 1966; letters from Bulgaria to officials of Ha-Shomer HaTzier found in the "Moreshet" archives.

53. Interview with Benjamin Arditi, Holon, Israel, January 1966. For a favorable appraisal of the Jewish leaders in Bulgaria, see Benjamin Arditi, *Yehudi Balgariyah bishanah hamishpat hanatzi: 1940-1944* [The Jews of Bulgaria during the years of Nazi occupation: 1940-1944] (Tel Aviv: Israel Press, 1962), p. 282.

54. KEV, reports, December 1942, p. 6; and March 1943, p. 4, Arditi collection.

In addition to designation and location, the KEV confiscated and administered Jewish property. The commissariat planned to deport all the Bulgarian Jews and seize their property. Not all of the documents available on the subject of Jewish confiscations have been opened to the public, but a Bulgarian economist, David Koen, who has had access to them, has made a study of this aspect of the KEV activity and is still able only to estimate the amount of confiscations.[55]

We can approximate the value of Jewish property, but since the commissariat failed in its deportation plans, this does not equal the value of confiscations. Israeli author Benjamin Arditi writes that 29,432 tax declarations were filed with the commissariat,[56] but he does not give the value of the property listed. A member of the Subranie, during debate over the unique tax law, gave as the value of Jewish property 5,612,000,000 leva ($68,200,000), based on 23,000 declarations, almost 40 percent in real estate.[57]

Assuming that the total value of Jewish property was proportional to the total number of declarations filed (using Arditi's figure), the final estimated values would be 7.5 billion leva or about $91 million. Arditi writes that the total assessed unique tax (20-25 percent) on Jewish property was 1,726,871,276 leva ($21 million), which agrees with this estimate. Koen states that the total unique tax assessment was 1,412,283,000 leva ($17 million), about 18 percent lower. Based on these figures, the total value of Jewish property, not including that in the occupied territories which Koen does not write about, would be $75 million.[58] Arditi says that the new territories (not including Dobrudzha) paid 300 million leva ($3,640,000) in taxes.[59] Extrapolating at the same ratio of total value to taxation in Bulgaria (according to Arditi) we find that the Jews in the new territories had property whose value we may estimate at 1.5 billion leva ($18,200,000).

55. David B. Koen, "Ekspropriatsiata na evreiskite imushtestva prez perioda na hitleristkata okupatsiia" [Expropriation of Jewish property during the period of Hitlerist occupation], *Godishnik* (of the Bulgarian Jewish Organization), 2 (1967), pp. 109-10.

56. Arditi, p. 59. Arditi, who has KEV documents in his own possession, does not document this figure.

57. Bulgaria, Narodno Subranie, *Dnevnitsi*, 25th ONS, 2d extraordinary sess. (speech of Nikola Minkov), p. 61.

58. Arditi, p. 59. Once again this is not documented. Koen, "Ekspropriatsiata na evreiskite imushtestva," p. 74. Koen gives as his sources government budget reports. A factor that may have some bearing on the discrepancies is the hope among Jewish survivors in Israel of gaining further restitution from Bulgaria for losses suffered in the war.

59. Arditi, p. 59.

Whatever figure we accept, almost all of this property was under commissariat control. Whether it can be considered confiscated is a matter of semantics. The Jews from the annexed territories were deported, and their property clearly appropriated. Real estate, except that used for the reduced living spaces or permitted businesses, fell under commissariat management or Aryan ownership. The KEV required that the Jews deposit all cash and valuables (stocks, bonds, securities, precious metals, gems, etc.) in frozen accounts which the commissariat controlled. Objects of attributed value—china, works of art, stamp collections, oriental rugs, musical instruments, etc.—were registered and placed at the disposal of the commissariat. Jews could receive from their accounts a maximum of only 6,000 leva ($72.80) per family per month for personal maintenance. They could not sell property valued at more than 10,000 leva ($121) a year without permission.[60] By March 3, 1943, the value of frozen Jewish bank accounts was over 307 million leva ($3,730,000), and the value of property and valuables under KEV control was over 801 million leva ($9,730,000).[61]

Jewish business enterprises and occupational opportunity were severely limited by the ZZN and the decree-law. Belev limited absolutely the number of Jewish business and industrial enterprises to the number permitted by the *numerus clausus,* not allowing privileged Jews (article 33, ZZN) to hold additional spaces, as was the practice previously; but merely giving them first choice of the available openings. Furthermore the number of permissible businesses (excluding artisans and ambulatory merchants) was reduced in February 1943 when the KEV reevaluated the number of available merchant spaces to 412 and permitted no industrial spaces for Jews at all.[62] The maximum Jewish capitalization allowed was 206 million leva ($2,500,000).

The commissariat liquidated all prohibited Jewish enterprises as well as those permitted Sofia businesses whose owners were expelled from the city. Belev's assistants dominated the liquidation supervision committee, and he appointed his cronies liquidators of individual establishments. Graft aside (and Jews who lost their property testified in 1945 that graft was prevalent), the sudden liquidations reduced the value of the property. The KEV deposited the liquidation receipts in

60. Bulgaria, *DV*, no. 202 (September 10, 1942), p. 3; and no. 204 (September 12, 1942), p. 1.
61. Koen, "Ekspropriatsiiata na evreiskite imushtestva," pp. 88-89, 92 (based on KEV account books).
62. *DV*, no. 34 (February 15, 1943), pp. 2-6.

the frozen accounts of the Jewish owners.[63] The total value of these liquidations is unavailable, but Koen, who studied the account books of the KEV, has concluded that the total value of expropriated Jewish property *which can be calculated* was 4.5 billion leva ($54,700,000). (This figure takes into account the inflation of the leva during the war and is reduced to 2.2 billion [$26,700,000] for the 1939 value of the lev.) Koen writes that the calculated expropriations are below the true value, and they include only money collected and property confiscated under the law for the unique tax on Jews, the value of the Jewish community fund, money collected involuntarily for a government loan,[64] the value of buildings taken over by KEV and the rents collected from them, blocked accounts, obligations due Jews which the KEV received from their debtors (less Jewish debts), short-term accounts, movable property, and valuables. They do not include expropriated land, houses, and personal items; confiscated enterprises and the value of capital participation in enterprises from which the Jews were excluded; confiscated property of synagogues, schools, communities, associations, foundations, and nonprofit organizations; the difference between the declared value and market value on property sold; etc.[65]

The KEV as ultimate controller of Jewish property took over the management of Jewish-owned tenements and real estate, and assumed the liabilities as well as the assets of the now defunct or liquidated Jewish enterprises. Belev was insistent that the delegates in the provinces maintain Jewish property in good order, making them liable for any loss in profit due to their negligence. He also established elaborate procedures for proving and collecting claims against Jews, whose liabilities were now the responsibility of the KEV.[66]

The third field of KEV activity encompasses general restrictions placed on the Jews with the intent of excluding them from Bulgarian

63. *DV*, no. 206 (September 15, 1942), p. 18; no. 208 (September 17, 1942), p. 8; no. 241 (October 27, 1942), pp. 1-2; no. 254 (November 11, 1942), p. 12; no. 263 (November 21, 1942), pp. 1-2; no. 285 (December 17, 1942), p. 8; no. 292 (December 25, 1942), pp. 5-7; no. 33 (February 13, 1943), p. 15. For abuses in liquidation procedures see Sofia, Protocols of People's Court No. 7, III, 1071-74 (testimony of Zhak Bohar Menahemov); 1085-90 (testimony of Azaria Aladzhem); and 1099-1101 (testimony of Kemal Tansier Rakov). There are several other examples.

64. Koen, "Ekspropriatsiiata na evreiskite imushtestva," pp. 83-84.

65. Ibid., pp. 109-10.

66. *DV*, no. 206 (September 15, 1942), p. 18; no. 13 (January 18, 1943), p. 26; no. 25 (February 4, 1943), pp. 2-3; no. 115 (May 27, 1943), p. 2.

society. General restrictions against the Jews were similar to laws in other countries under Nazi influence. Article 23 of the decree-law prohibited Jews from owning radios or home telephones. In November and December 1942 Belev issued orders to confiscate all Jewish-owned automobiles, motorcycles, and bicycles.[67] Jews could not frequent certain sections of the city in which they lived. They could visit or patronize only certain public establishments, such as hotels, parks, theaters, and even stores. Finally Jews were forbidden to appear on the streets at all except for four or five hours a day to shop. The ultimate result was that the Jews who were not in labor groups spent nearly all of their time in their cramped quarters. Orders confining the Jews and limiting their movement came from the local governments and delegates rather than from the commissariat in Sofia. Belev encouraged the provincial delegates to issue these orders, but there were no national restrictions. Ironically, in the capital region the Ministry of Internal Affairs issued its restraining orders comparatively late.[68]

Anti-Semitic regulations harassed Jews in a number of other ways. The KEV's order no. 598 of February 1943 closed all non-Jewish schools (with limited enrollment) to Jews. In schools with unlimited enrollment the minister of education determined the number of Jews allowed to enroll.[69] Jews also suffered more than other Bulgarians under the wartime rationing. Many district officials and supply commissars asked to reduce Jewish rations or eliminate entirely their receiving certain items.[70] The KEV outlawed some purely Jewish organizations that had

67. CDIA fund no. 503, ch. p. 247, p. 39. Also fund no. 370, op. 1, arh. ed. 255, p. 4 (order no. 634 [December 9, 1942]), Bulgarian Jewish Organization Archives, copies of CDIA documents, vol. III.

68. For Sofia see Bulgaria, *DV*, no. 29 (February 9, 1943), p. 7. Provincial orders limiting Jewish movement in such cities as Burgas, Vidin, and Karnobat can be found in Bulgarian Jewish Organization Archives, copies of CDIA documents, vol. II. Photostats and actual circulars of these orders can be seen in several other collections. Order no. 709 of Ruse (September 1942) is in "Moreshet" archives, copies of CDIA documents, doc. no. 17. Order no. 10 of Ruse (a reissuance from February 1944) is in the archives of the Centre de Documentation Juive Contemporaine, Paris, doc. no. CCCI-22. Similar orders (e.g., for Shumen, Razgrad, and Silistra) are found in the archives of the Ghetto Fighters' House, Kibbutz Lohamei HaGhetaoth, Haifa, Israel.

69. Bulgaria, *DV*, no. 35 (February 16, 1943), p. 5.

70. CDIA fund no. 190, op. 1, arh. ed. 8569, pp. 2-3 (Razgrad, June 7, 1943); ch. p. 247, p. 88 (Gorna Dzhumaia); ch. p. 247, p. 144 (Stara Zagora, June 18, 1943); and ch. p. 247, p. 97 (Gorna Dzhumaia, November 30, 1943), Bulgarian Jewish Organization Archives, copies of CDIA documents, vol. II.

been permitted under the ZZN. They closed down or restricted libraries and publishing houses.[71] The KEV controlled outright Jewish economic organizations, such as popular banks, credit institutions, and insurance companies.

The compulsory Jewish labor groups were a combination of the defining, liquidating, and restricting activities of the commissariat, but because the Jews were virtually enslaved the groups can be considered principally confiscatory. They began as part of the general compulsory labor service required of all Bulgarian youths. On German insistence, the groups were segregated, placed exclusively under Bulgarian officers, and made a punishment for the Jews rather than an honored duty as for Bulgarians.[72]

Even before the decree of August 26 was issued, the cabinet had on July 19, 1942, ordered Jewish men between the ages of twenty and forty-five to report for labor service.[73] Men were put to work on roads and railway beds in strategic parts of Bulgaria. The Jews' judgment as to whether or not the leaders of these groups were anti-Semites varies. Many of the men called to serve were not used to physical labor, and they could easily have misinterpreted the orders of their superiors as anti-Semitism when in fact the group leader was merely trying to fill his quota. Many Jews who served in these groups did not consider the leadership in general to be anti-Semitic. On the other hand, some who were in labor camps testified to anti-Semitic tirades, petty corruption, and physical cruelty.[74] Jews whom the KEV doctors declared unfit to work were generally excluded from the labor groups, but in some cases such people were sent out.

Having detailed the work of the KEV in carrying out its designatory, confiscatory, and restrictive measures, we should before turning to the chief activity of the KEV, the deportation of Jews to Poland, review the problem of corruption in the commissariat. A distinction, fairly common to all public offices, can be made between outright corruption

71. Deposition of Richard Simontov on file at Yad WaShem, Jerusalem, Israel, doc. no. 03/1710.

72. See above, p. 50.

73. CDIA fund no. 284, op. 1, arh. ed. 7937, Bulgarian Jewish Organization Archives, copies of CDIA documents, vol. III.

74. For labor groups see Arditi, pp. 224-48; and Baruh, pp. 116-24, 137-45, and 178-98. Both of these include reprints and photostats of documents. Sofia, Protocols of People's Court No. 7, II, 1019-26 (testimony of Beniamin Iakov Vaisburg); II, 1044-48 (testimony of Dr. Beniamin Iakov Petrikovski); and II, 1075-78 (testimony of Maks Aron Eshkenazi). These are just three of many testimonies concerning the labor groups.

and "honest graft," or personal advantage gained from information to which a public official is privy because of his position. In the latter case if an official chooses not to take personal advantage, in most cases it will fall to someone else, so that he is not really profiting from a public loss. The official can still faithfully fulfill his duty. "Honest graft" prevalent in the commissariat included the appropriation of Jewish apartments and their distribution to commissariat officials or friends. It also included some benefits derived from the expropriation of Jewish banks and credit institutions. Belev tranferred many funds from these institutions to banks controlled by his friends. Unfavorable testimony at the postwar trials implicated Belev in a grand scheme to benefit from Jewish money placed in the bank Serdika. A KEV inspector, Svetoslav Petrov Nikolaev, asserted in his testimony that Belev and Gabrovski established the Serdika with the specific purpose of holding frozen accounts and confiscated monies. Nikolaev maintained that the bank's officials were members of the Ratnitsi, and that Ratnitsi businessmen received easy credit from the bank. Within one year of its establishment the Serdika vaults held 15 million leva ($182,000) of Jewish money and 90 million leva ($1,090,000) in stocks and bonds. On Nikolaev's advice Bozhilov, the prime minister, after Gabrovski and Belev were dismissed, returned 18 million leva ($219,000) which Belev allegedly had acquired illegally from the Jewish community fund. The inspector further testified that an audit of the bank's books by the Union of Popular Banks showed several million leva unaccounted for.[75] The misappropriation of funds is outright corruption, but the use of frozen Jewish accounts for granting credit to one's friends is an example of "honest graft." Belev, who in a postwar trial was sentenced to death *in absentia* for his activity on the commissariat, was acquitted of the charge of corruption.[76]

Considering the opportunity, outright corruption—the misappropriation of funds, the accepting of bribes, or the general neglect or abuse of duties for personal aggrandizement—was relatively minor in the commissariat. Some corruption, nevertheless, existed. The most important culprit, for reasons that will be obvious in chapter 5, was Dr. Iosif Stefanov Vatev, an optician and investigating doctor for the commissariat. As a matter of circumstance that was typical of the small-town

75. Sofia, Protocols of People's Court No. 7, II, 950-52 (testimony of Svetoslav Petrov Nikolaev).

76. Sofia, Ministry of Justice, Petko Petrinski, President of People's Court No. 7, et al., *Sentence Pronounced by People's Court No. 7*, April 2, 1945, p. 1, BAN, **Ebroistika, doc. no. 42.**

type of entanglements in Sofia society, Dr. Vatev was Gabrovski's brother-in-law.

Vatev investigated medical complaints from Jews wishing to avoid expulsion from Sofia. He would verify medical disability only if given a bribe and presumably was not above fabricating medical excuses. When his assistant, Iordan Lazanov, a KEV agent, told Belev of the doctor's activity, the commissar dismissed both men. Vatev's connections with Gabrovski saved him from further punishment, and Belev threatened Lazanov if he went elsewhere with the story.[77]

The commissariat activity described in this section actually concerned Bulgarian internal regulations. This activity was an intensified continuation of the purposes of the ZZN—putting restrictions on the Jews in Bulgaria. The real nature of changes in anti-Semitic legislation involved the prospective elimination of Jews from Bulgaria (as part of a general European plan) and concerned German-Bulgarian relations. The fulfillment of this new stage of the Jewish question is discussed in the next chapters.

77. Depositions of Maria Borisova Pavlova, Iaroslav Liubenov Kalitsin, Iordan Kirilov Lazanov, Moshe Isak Nisim, Tamara Aaron Beraha, Aaron Rahamin Beraha, Boris David Oliver, and Nisim L. Haim on Dr. Iosif Stefanov Vatev, BAN, Ebroistika, doc. no. 55.

3

Preparation for Deportation

The Dannecker-Belev Agreement

The major work of the Commissariat for Jewish Questions was the arrangement and facilitation of the deportation of Jews from Bulgaria and Bulgarian-occupied territory. This, as we have seen, was part of the general European Final Solution which the Reich drafted at Wannsee. The only references to expulsion in the decree-law of August 26 were the somewhat incidental article 29, which subjected Jews to expulsion from Sofia "into the provinces or *outside the kingdom*" (my italics), and the more direct statement that "the Jewish community is assigned to prepare the deportation of the Jewish population" which was buried in the long article 7.[1] The KEV made its arrangements in secret. Furthermore, although government and court circles privy to the German plans for the Bulgarian Jews had doubts about these plans, the KEV had no misgivings.

The first specific steps in applying the Final Solution to the Bulgarian population involved those Jews resident in Germany and Reich-occupied lands, whom Sofia allowed the Germans to deport in July 1942.[2] At that time the Wilhelmstrasse had also thought it wise to approach the Bulgarians on matters of deportation of the Jews within Bulgaria's jurisdiction, including the some fifty thousand Jews of Bulgarian citizenship. The Germans had little premonition of difficulties. In fact, Luther thought Beckerle might have to delay a request from the Filov government to determine immediately a date when these Jews could be deported. The RSHA was not prepared to deport the Bulgarian Jews until 1943.[3]

1. *DV*, no. 192 (August 29, 1942), pp. 2-3.
2. See above, p. 51.
3. Beckerle, report, July 9, 1942, T120, serial 2330, roll 1305, frames 486208-09.

On the other hand, also in July 1942 the German diplomatic corps in Bulgaria was upset by a mild scandal, an incident which perhaps shook their confidence in Bulgarian cooperation on Jewish matters. Josef Geron, the president of the central consistory of the Jews, sent a congratulatory telegram to the king on the occasion of the fifth birthday of Crown Prince Simeon. Boris replied in a telegram thanking Geron and the Jewish community. Both telegrams were published in the *Bulletin of the Central Consistory of the Jews in Bulgaria*. Beckerle reported that the *Bulletin* ostentatiously publicized this incident and that it caused much comment throughout the nation.[4] There was really nothing unusual about this exchange. The leaders of the Jewish community as officials of the state had social contacts with the court. Geron since his election as president of the consistory had always sent congratulatory letters to the royal family on behalf of the Jewish community on occasions such as royal birthdays, namedays, and national holidays.[5]

It is difficult to believe that no one in the German diplomatic corps, which included a large RSHA contingent working with the Bulgarian police, had been reading the *Bulletin* (written in Bulgarian), but for some reason the exchange of July 1942 was the first to be called to the attention of the Wilhelmstrasse. Perhaps the timing gave Geron's telegram and the king's reply special significance. The exchange occurred a month after the passage of the enabling legislation and a short time before the publication of the decree of August 26, 1942. Beckerle's communication to the foreign office also indicates that the Jews were trying to capitalize on this particular correspondence more than on others and that it was receiving particular notice among members of Bulgarian society. King Boris, to the concern of the Nazis, also took the trouble to explain the August law to Rabbi Asher Hananel, the chief rabbi of Sofia. Beckerle complained to Filov, and Boris replied that if the German minister had any complaints, he should come directly to him.[6]

4. Sofia, *Biuletin na Tsentralnata konsistoriia na evreite v Bulgaria* [Bulletin of the central consistory of the Jews in Bulgaria], 22 (July 7, 1942), p. 37; Beckerle to foreign office, report, July 21, 1942, T120, serial 2330, roll 1305, frame 486218.

5. Sofia, *Biuletin na Tsentralnata konsistoriia*, 22 (October 18, 1941), p. 4; (October 24, 1941), p. 5; (November 14, 1941), p. 7; (January 15, 1942), p. 15; (February 6, 1942), p. 18; (March 13, 1942), p. 23; (May 16, 1942), p. 31; and (May 29, 1942), p. 33.

6. Diary of Adolph-Heinz Beckerle, August 22, 1942, T120, serial 5548H (Foreign Office, Sofia, Group 59/2, Personal Reports, July 20, 1941, to February 16, 1943, Beckerle, I), roll 2651, frames E387609-12.

There is nothing in the German communications with regard to the exchange to indicate that Beckerle was deliberately trying to modify Berlin's high hopes for Bulgarian cooperation on Jewish matters or to forewarn the ministry and RSHA of possible complications in this area; but the fact that Beckerle's report on the exchange of telegrams was included in a report informing the foreign office of the Bulgarians' complete willingness to cooperate on the issue of foreign Jews was an early indication to Berlin that Bulgaria's attitude on the *Judenfrage* was different than had been expected. There were others.

By September the RSHA was ready to give Bulgaria help in establishing Jewish resettlement camps and deportation centers. They inquired about this of the foreign office, but Minister Ribbentrop, aware now that Sofia could not be pushed too hastily on this matter, advised Luther and through him the RSHA to wait patiently and approach Bulgaria with the question of resettlement only at the proper time.[7]

That same month in contrast to their earlier absolute cooperation, the Bulgarian government mildly reproached the Reich about treatment of their Jewish citizens in France. The Bulgarians argued that they had given up their interest in Bulgarian Jews only in lands legally incorporated into Germany, such as Austria and the Protektorat (Bohemia and Moravia), and not in lands merely occupied by the Germans such as Yugoslavia and France.[8] On September 18, Ambassador Smend, of the protocol division of the German foreign office, reported that the Bulgarian commercial attaché, Smedovski, had inquired about the treatment of Jews in the occupied regions. He seemed especially interested in rumors that Bulgarian Jews in France were treated more harshly than Jews of other citizenship. After the decree of August 26, 1942, the foreign office notified Otto Abetz in Paris to apply the restrictions provided, for example, the wearing of stars, to the Bulgarian Jews. Thus, the Bulgarian Jews in France received special attention in September 1942 but whether in general they underwent treatment harsher than the abysmal treatment that all foreign Jews began to receive there is doubtful.[9] The foreign office summarily dismissed these complaints with

7. Luther, memo (*Vortragsnotiz*), September 11, 1942, T120, serial 2330, roll 1305, frames 486224-26. In reference to the RSHA request, Ribbentrop wrote on the memo "*noch warten.*" Franz von Sonnleithner, Büro RAM (Office of the Foreign Minister), to Luther, September 15, 1942, ibid., frame 486223; Luther to Franz Rademacher, foreign office Jewish expert, Abteilung Deutschland, September 15, 1942, ibid., frame 486229.
8. Legationsrat Dr. Stahlberg, report, July 29, 1942, ibid., frames 486214-15.
9. Heinrich Müller, RSHA-Gestapo, to German embassies in Europe, Septem-

the statement that all Jews in the occupied areas were subject to German law.

The inquiries about Bulgarian Jews were minor ones compared to the complaints from other countries, even the complaints that Rumania, Hungary, and Italy sent to Sofia. Ironically, in fact, the same report which dismissed the Bulgarian inquiries suggested that the Bulgarians be told to receive calmly foreign protests to their actions against the Jews. The Germans were not unduly upset over such minor Bulgarian bickering, yet as small as the misgivings were, they were obviously present. Dr. Karl Klingenfuss, an expert on Jewish policies in the foreign office, thought that the Bulgarians were not fully aware of the situation in France because of the machinations of Smedovski. He thought it odd that on the one hand the Bulgarian legation protested the treatment of Bulgarian Jews in France while on the other hand they sought to find a suitable way to implement the Final Solution in Bulgaria and Europe. He "had the impression" that Smedovski was withholding the German explanation from Sofia.[10]

In October, Luther, after talking to Beckerle, decided that the Bulgarians were probably prepared to deport their Jews and offered them the services of the Reich.[11] In a report on the offer sent to the German embassy in Sofia Luther told Beckerle to ask for a lump-sum payment of 250 RM (*Reichsmarks*) per deported person to cover German expenses, but the Germans expected to settle for a lower rate and were prepared to allow the Filov government to bargain over the figure. Besides the cost for German services, Luther was concerned about the legal problems of deporting Jews with Bulgarian citizenship. He advised Beckerle to see to it that deported Jews lost their Bulgarian citizenship by suggesting a law similar to the German decree on Jewish citizenship.[12]

The Bulgarian reaction to the German offer for aid in deportation brought the government's doubts further out into the open. Beckerle reported that the Bulgarians claimed there was a genuine need in Bulgaria for Jewish labor to build roadways and railroad beds. More to

---

ber 4, 1942, ibid., frames 486227-228; Raul Hilberg, *The Destruction of the European Jews* (Chicago: Quadrangle Books, 1961), pp. 407-10.

10.   Smend, report, September 18, 1942, T120, serial 2330, roll 1305, frame 486233; report (initialed J) to Luther, October 9, 1942, ibid., frame 486236; Klingenfuss to Smend, November 19, 1942, ibid., frames 486238-39.

11.   *People of Hesse* v. *Von Hahn*, Ks 2/67 (GStA), 211 (1968).

12.   Report (initialed J) to Luther, October 9, 1942, T120, serial 2330, roll 1305, frame 486236; Luther to Beckerle, October 15, 1942, ibid., frame 486234-35.

the point, he said that Filov would press the issue with the cabinet, which had been in disagreement about Jewish deportations in the past.[13] The Germans proceeded to push for deportations in any case, and late in November, Klingenfuss suggested that an RSHA representative be sent to Sofia to aid in working out details.[14]

On November 21, 1942, Walter Schellenberg, the RSHA espionage chief, sent Luther a secret report containing information on the most serious deviations to date in the Bulgarian establishment's attitudes toward the Jewish question. After the stern measures of August and the establishment of the KEV, Schellenberg wrote, the Bulgarian people believed that the anti-Jewish laws had gone too far. There was a general feeling that things would change for the better for the Jews, and obstacles would be placed in the path of Belev (the most committed source of anti-Semitic policies in Bulgaria). Filov told Beckerle that even the court had strong pockets of Jewish influence. Aleksandur Malinov, the deceased leader of the Democrat party—the political party closest to the crown—who had been the godfather of Princess Maria Luisa, had been married to a Jew. The granddaughter of General Nikolaev, Prince Simeon's godfather, was likewise married to a Jew. Members of the court and the chancellery, and the king himself intervened on countless occasions on behalf of individual Jews. Schellenberg mentioned only one specific case, involving the chief secretary of Boris's chancellery, Stanislav A. Balan, who intervened at the KEV on behalf of a Jew who lived near the summer palace, with the explanation that the king had ordered it.

The report singled out Minister of Internal Affairs Gabrovski for being especially lax on Jewish matters. On September 27 three hundred Jews had marched on the ministry to present Gabrovski with a petition protesting the new anti-Semitic restrictions. In the courtyard before the ministry, Gabrovski addressed the group. In front of the amazed clerks of his ministry, he told the Jews that "they should not be disturbed; the government had noticed everything and the worst had already past." Then Gabrovski personally accepted their petition. Schellenberg said that this gave the Jews new hope and encouraged them to defy and resist the orders of Belev. Schellenberg went on to report that the minister at the end of September refused to allow the press to report measures taken against the Jews for fear of inciting the public. He said that Gabrovski had argued with Belev that the court and

13. Beckerle, report, November 2, 1942, ibid., frame 486237.
14. Klingenfuss, report, November 23, 1942, ibid., frame 486240.

cabinet wanted a milder Jewish policy and that even German econo-
mists argued against strict measures against the Jews because of their
economic importance. Schellenberg was disturbed that Gabrovski had
not yet placed limitations on the Jews in Sofia, for example, restrictions
on entering public places, as had been done in the provinces.[15]

Schellenberg wrote that his report came from "confidential" sources.
Most probably the sources were members of the Bulgarian extreme
right—the Legionaires and Ratnitsi. These groups were trying to convince the Germans to support them in Bulgarian politics—hopefully by
backing a coup. They also had connections with Schellenberg's section
of the RSHA.[16] Many extremists were really not friends of Gabrovski,
whom they regarded as a renegade from their ranks, and were capable
of painting a portrait of him which would make him appear more unsuitable to the Germans than the facts would warrant. Among his colleagues on the cabinet he was the minister closest in sympathy to Nazi
anti-Semitic policies; thus the Germans really had nothing to fear from
him in the way of hindrances to their application of the Final Solution
in Bulgaria.

The espionage chief also relayed some unfavorable observations about
other members of the government. Minister of Justice Konstantin Partov,
he said, suggested not only that the marking of Jews should not be
obligatory, but also that the Jews should not be deported, and especially
that all laws against the Jews should be consolidated into one moderate
law. The Schellenberg report complained about sympathy toward the
Jews within the government faction of the Subranie. It rebuked Metropolitan Stefan as well because of his pressure on Filov regarding the
wearing of stars. Schellenberg also accused the metropolitan of giving
a sermon in September castigating the government for its anti-Semitic
program.[17]

Beckerle, who was in a position to give a more accurate picture than
Schellenberg, commented in December on the espionage chief's report.
He agreed that the populace was disinterested in Jewish measures and
stated further that the government tended to pursue economic measures more strongly than other general anti-Semitic legislation and decrees. He confirmed that the godfathers of Maria Luisa and Simeon
had Jewish connections. The godfathers of the royal children (each

15. Schellenberg to Luther, November 21, 1942, ibid., frames 486242-48.
16. See file on counterespionage and agents in Bulgaria, November 21, 1942,
T120, serial 2320H, roll 1305.
17. Schellenberg to Luther, November 21, 1942, T120, serial 2330, roll 1305,
frames 486242–48.

had more than one) were chosen for political considerations. Malinov was a representative of the people; General Nikolaev was a representative of the army. The general's granddaughter had married and divorced a lawyer, Marko Danailov, the son of the president of the Association for Bulgarian-German Cultural Exchange, and then had married a Jew, whom she had also divorced. This was scandalous to proper Bulgarian society, but Beckerle exonerated General Nikolaev, who had disapproved of the latter match. Without explanation Beckerle wrote that the kings' *chef du cabinet*, Pavel Gruev, was the only member of the court coterie with Jewish contacts. We shall see that this was not entirely accurate.

Beckerle also supported Gabrovski, writing that he did not know anything about the incident in front of the Ministry of Internal Affairs and suggesting that the description may have been exaggerated. The minister may have accepted the petition. Beckerle did not know.

Only Italian Jews, who were few in number, were excused from wearing stars. The report's claim that Filov had rescinded the order for baptized Jews and Jews in mixed marriages was not correct and the government was paying no heed to Stefan's petitions.[18]

A shrewd diplomat, Beckerle pleaded Sofia's case to the Wilhelmstrasse and that of the German foreign office to the Bulgarian government. His dispatches to Berlin make him appear moderate. Yet Filov in his diary complained that he was too friendly with right-wing extremists in Bulgaria and was an extremely limited person.[19]

Schellenberg's November report had accused Bulgaria, both government and populace, of a lack of understanding of the Jewish question. Beckerle moderated this view, and the Bulgarians bore him out. In a verbal note of November 2, the Bulgarian Ministry of Foreign Affairs informed Berlin that Bulgaria was willing to deport its Jews but needed them for public labor. Beckerle suggested that the Bulgarians proceed to arrange the deportations and hold out just those who were needed for labor gangs. They could deport the latter at a later time. The government asked the Reich to send a German advisor to help with deportation arrangements. The government also requested that the Germans handle Bulgarian deportations in connection with those from Rumania because Bulgaria was unable alone to deport even part of its Jews. The connection is somewhat cryptic and part of the reason for asking that the Jewish question be handled in Rumania and Bul-

18.   Beckerle, report, December 14, 1942, ibid., frames 486274-77.
19.   Filov, "Diary," entry for February 27, 1942, *Naroden Sud*, no. 2, p. 2.

garia at the same time was probably concern over world opinion and possible Allied bombings as punishment for Bulgaria's deportation of the Jews. Beckerle had probably first suggested the possibility of the two countries deporting their Jews together to encourage Sofia. The Bulgarian verbal note said that 250 RM was too high a price; some of the Jews' wealth was needed to aid Bulgaria's own economy.[20]

The foreign office and RSHA agreed to send to Sofia Theodor Dannecker, who had been in charge of Jewish policies in Paris. He had left his post in France because of a throat ailment but was now ready to return to work. The Wilhelmstrasse expected the SS man to complete his work in Bulgaria within nine months. In Sofia, Dannecker joined Karl Hoffmann, police (gestapo) attaché there. Franz Rademacher, in charge of Jewish policies in Luther's department, stated that he did not want the matter of price to impede the Bulgarian negotiations and insisted that Beckerle have a free hand in determining the cost of deportation. Klingenfuss, who paid particular attention to this matter, conceded the argument but maintained that 100 RM per person was an absolute minimum.[21]

In Sofia Dannecker worked closely with Belev from December to February to draw up a plan for deportation. Yet even while they discussed the details of deportations, Berlin and Sofia could not resolve other differences regarding the Jews. Beckerle suggested that Gabrovski arrange an anti-Semitic exhibit in Sofia, but the minister hesitated because he did not want adverse publicity at the time of the arrangement for deportation. Gabrovski, like other government leaders, thought that the less said about the Jews, the better. Beckerle convinced Gabrovski to hold some sort of anti-Jewish exhibit, but Filov when approached on the matter also refused. The prime minister's will prevailed, and an anti-Communist exhibition was held instead (Gabrovski was even reluctant to handle this). Beckerle informed Berlin and explained that some of the difficulties in Bulgaria's attitudes toward the Jews arose because the Jews in Bulgaria were workers and because the presence

20. Beckerle, report, November 16, 1942, T120, serial 2330, roll 1305, frame 486261; Bulgarian Ministry of Foreign Affairs to German embassy, verbal note, November 2, 1942, ibid., frames 486262-63.

21. Rademacher to Müller, March 19, 1943, ibid., frame 486264. This communication discusses events which occurred in November 1942. Otto von Hahn, foreign office, Abteilung Deutschland, to Legationsrat von Willenberg, foreign office, Abteilung Personal, January 2, 1943, ibid., frame 486268; RSHA (signature illegible) to Luther, December 10, 1942, ibid., frames 486270-71; Klingenfuss to Sofia, December 4, 1942, ibid., frame 486272.

of other minorities in the country prevented a full understanding of the nature of the Jewish question.[22]

Nevertheless, despite some government waverings, the KEV cooperated fully with the Germans, and for Berlin the practical talks between the commissar and the RSHA representative were much more important than the quibbling at higher levels. Belev and Dannecker finished their plans in February 1943. On February 4, Belev sent to his superior Gabrovski a report notifying the minister that the Reich was prepared to help the Bulgarians deport their Jews. The report outlined some of the general problems to be considered in the first deportation as well as some of the more prominent specific problems. About ten to twenty thousand Jews would be transferred from Thrace (Belomorie) and Macedonia along with "undesirable" (*nezhelatelni*) Jews from within the prewar boundaries of the state. These latter Jews would lose their Bulgarian citizenship on leaving the kingdom. The KEV's delegates would prepare lists of Jews who were to be deported. These Jews would be gathered at suitable concentration centers, transferred to camps at rail stations, and taken by special trains to areas under German authority. Jews were not to pass through Turkish or Greek territory on their way from Thrace to German-administered territory. (This would involve routing along track not normally used.) The deportations would start at the beginning of March and end in about a month. The Jews would remain in the camps near the rail stations at least ten to fifteen days and possibly a month. Belev insisted that all Jews to be deported be rounded up at once to prevent flight. They would be allowed a small amount of baggage, but no money or valuables. The KEV would collect and administer all remaining Jewish property. The operation would require the service of the labor armies, the chief commissariat of supply, the director of police, the chief director of public health, the chief of the welfare service (Service for the General Poor), the director of railroads (who would work with his counterpart from Germany), the director of the post office, and the general staff. The commissar for Jewish questions was to be the key operative for the Bulgarians. Since the whole operation was to be carried out in secret, the KEV would tell the Jews not that they were being deported, but merely that they were to be relocated in another part of Bulgaria.

22. Beckerle, reports, January 22 and February 10, 1943, ibid., frames 486278-80, 486290; Filov, "Diary," entries for September 26 and 27, 1942, *Naroden Sud*, no. 2, p. 8.

In point two of his report, Belev stated that if the government deported the Jews of Thrace and Macedonia, it would be well to deport the Jews from the old territories. Otherwise those remaining would live in constant fear of deportation and cause much anxiety and concern throughout the country. In point three he said that if this were not done and only Jews of Macedonia and Thrace were to go, then at least measures must be taken to prevent panic among the Jews in the old boundaries of Bulgaria. It would be necessary to draft all Jewish males from the age of eighteen to forty-eight into forced labor camps and to take strict measures to secure against flight.[23]

Belev learned from Dannecker that Gabrovski and Beckerle had agreed on the principle of deportations already. Belev's differentiation between Jews from the old territories and those from the new indicates that the government had not yet decided to deport the Jews from old Bulgaria. For reasons which we shall discuss later, Bulgaria could more easily undertake the deportation of Jews from the newly acquired lands. However, because Belev, and presumably Dannecker, wanted to deport Jews from the old territorial limits as well, they made provisions for including "undesirables" in the agreement.

Dannecker informed his superior, Adolf Eichmann, of the projected arrangements on February 5, and Beckerle reported to the foreign office a few days later.[24] Both, however, mentioned deportation only of Jews from the new territories. They said that the Bulgarian Jews could be deported later, but for now they would go to work camps.

Dannecker also sent Eichmann a report on February 8 which discussed some serious objections being raised in Bulgaria that Belev had related to him. The Italian ambassador had objected that Jews who were married to Italians were forced to wear stars. Then the ambassadors of Spain, Portugal, and Switzerland also protested on behalf of their citizens. The result was that all Jews in mixed marriages were exempted from wearing stars, even if they were married to Bulgarians or to stateless persons, and all Jews married to Jews, no matter what their citizenship, were required to wear them. Dannecker also reported that the weakening of the resolve of some of the government officials alarmed Belev. These officials had often done business with the Jews in the past. Also many foreign Jews—formerly German, Polish, Czecho-

23. Belev to Gabrovski, February 4, 1943, in Natan Grinberg, *Dokumenti* [Documents] (Sofia: Central Consistory of Jews in Bulgaria, 1945), pp. 8-11.
24. Beckerle, report, February 8, 1943, T120, serial 2330, roll 1305, frame 486284; Dannecker and Beckerle, report, February 8, 1943, ibid., frames 486285-87.

slovakian, and Austrian citizens—were becoming Italian, Spanish, and Portuguese citizens. Many Sephardic Jews were becoming Spanish citizens, and many Jews in Macedonia and Thrace were obtaining Italian citizenship.[25]

In any case Belev hastily implemented the projected plan of deportation while the issue was still a matter of unresolved debate in the cabinet.[26] On February 3, the day before his report to Gabrovski, Belev had issued orders to the delegates of the commissariat to make lists of Jews living in their jurisdiction according to family, stating sex, age, profession, and address; and to send copies to the KEV by February 9.[27] With this information the KEV's statistical director prepared lists of Jews to be deported from the new territories.[28]

In February, Iaroslav Kalitsin, as chief of the commissariat's administrative section, and the *ad hoc* director of the Thracian deportations, reported to Belev on his preparations for the latter. There were two problems: the location of the concentration points and the means of transporting the Jews there. Logistical factors, particularly the burden of transferring vast amounts of construction material to one place, led to Kalitsin's suggestion that three concentration points be built in Bulgaria along the route from Thrace to the Danube. The first of these was Radomir—a city some thirty miles southwest of Sofia, famous for the republican uprising in the army stationed there at the end of World War I. The second concentration area, Kalitsin decided, should be Dupnitsa (today Stanke Dimitrov), a town some sixty miles south of Sofia. The third area should be Gorna Dzhumaia (today Blagoevgrad), the largest of the three, some thirty miles south of Dupnitsa in the Struma Valley—the chief city of Bulgarian Macedonia.

The second problem involved the transportation of Jews from Thrace to the concentration points in Bulgaria. Kalitsin proposed the use of trains and trucks, the latter especially for use in the port city of Kavala, where 2,000 Jews lived and where there was no train. (The track runs from Ksanti to Drama, some thirty-five miles north of the port.)[29]

25. Dannecker and Beckerle to Eichmann, February 8, 1943, T120, serial 2330, roll 1305, frames 486288-89. Mussolini's Italy, the primordial fascist state, did not really see the Jewish question in any respect as the Reich did. See Hilberg, pp. 421-32.

26. Dannecker to Eichmann, February 16, 1943, T120, serial 2330, roll 1305, frames 486293-94.

27. The order is reprinted in Grinberg, *Dokumenti*, pp. 11-12.

28. Ibid., p. 12.

29. Kalitsin to Belev, February 16, 1943, in ibid., pp. 12-14.

On February 22 Belev and Dannecker signed an official agreement for the deportation of the first 20,000 Jews (without regard to sex or age) into German hands.[30] The agreement called for a total of six deportation centers in Bulgaria and the occupied territories (Skopje, Bitola, Pirot, Gorna Dzhumaia, Dupnitsa, and Radomir). Bulgaria would be responsible for costs. Jews in mixed marriages would not be deported, while Jews with Bulgarian citizenship would lose it on leaving the country. Point eight of the agreement stated "in no case will the Bulgarian government ask for the return of the deported Jews."

Dannecker informed Eichmann of the agreement on February 22 over the telephone.[31] Several days before, Berlin had completed details on the use of German railroads for deportations.[32]

After the agreement, Belev proposed the following problem for implementation by the KEV: "To be deported outside the kingdom all Jews of Thrace and Macedonia and a definite number of Jews from the old boundaries, in all 20,000 people, by the end of the month of May 1943 at the latest, according to the agreement with Germany."[33] The KEV's general plan devised in response to this problem called for the deportation of 8,000 Jews from Macedonia and Pirot, 6,000 from Thrace, and 6,000 from the old territorial boundaries. The KEV planned first to concentrate Jews in those cities in Thrace and Macedonia having local consistories (with the exception of Shtip whose Jews would go to Skopje), and then to send the Thracian Jews to the Bulgarian departure centers. The KEV would also send Bulgarian Jews to these camps (and Pirot) as well. The gathering process would begin with the Thracians in early March and subsequently the KEV would round up Bulgarian and Macedonian Jews. Deportations from all six departure centers were to begin at the end of March.

To supervise operations in the Sofia region, where the Bulgarian camps were located, and Pirot, Thrace, and Macedonia respectively, Belev assigned KEV section chiefs G'oshev, Kalitsin, and Velkov, with other KEV officials to work under them. Velkov and Kalitsin were in charge of the other regions of Bulgaria as well. G'oshev was responsible for the economic aspects of deportation; Pencho Lukov, for legal matters;

30. See Appendix II.
31. Dannecker to Eichmann, February 23, 1943, T120, serial 2330, roll 1305, frames 486296-99. One copy of the agreement which Dannecker was to send did not arrive. None is present in the German records. Memo (signed "St"), March 2, 1943, ibid., frame 486300.
32. Eichmann to Hahn, February 18, 1943, ibid., frame 486301.
33. Grinberg, Dokumenti, p. 16.

and Hristo D. Bakurdzhiev, an assistant chief of section at the KEV, for the tranfer of Jews to the Germans.[34]

At its meeting of March 2, 1943, the cabinet, using its authority under the enabling legislation, issued a series of warrants (*postanovleniia*) approving the deportations. Gabrovski proposed these warrants on the basis of reports made by Commissar Belev on February 16, six days before the agreement with Dannecker was concluded.[35]

The first warrant (no. 113) concerned the mobilization of commissariat personnel to prevent resignation or loss through military draft. The cabinet, following the regulations of civilian mobilization, mobilized all personnel, temporary and permanent, male and female, of the Commissariat for Jewish Questions until May 31, 1943. This meant that the members of the commissariat could not resign their positions or refuse to perform their assigned tasks under penalty of law. They could not be preempted by the military draft. All of the ministers except Partov, who was not present, signed this warrant; however, to preserve secrecy, the cabinet decided not to publish it in the *Durzhaven Vestnik*.[36]

The cabinet issued warrants ordering the minister of railroads to transport without charge Jews from Thrace, Macedonia, and old Bulgaria to places indicated by the commissariat[37] and gave the KEV the right to requisition private and public buildings and premises for use as temporary camps for the Jews.[38] The cabinet also arranged to take away the citizenship of all Jews deported across the borders, in accordance with article 15 of the Law for Bulgarian Citizenship, which provided that Bulgarian citizens who were not of Bulgarian nationality lost their citizenship if they emigrated, even as a result of international treaty.[39] On Belev's and Gabrovski's requests, the cabinet also permitted mobilization of local civilian officials to maintain and guard

34. KEV, plan for deportations, in ibid., pp. 16-23.
35. Ibid., p. 23.
36. Belev to Gabrovski, February 16, 1943; Gabrovski to Filov (no date); Bulgaria, Council of Ministers, 113th warrant, 32nd protocol, March 2, 1943; ibid., pp. 23-26.
37. Belev to Gabrovski (no date); Bulgaria, Council of Ministers, 114th warrant, 32nd protocol, March 2, 1943; ibid., pp. 26-28.
38. Belev to Gabrovski (no date); Gabrovski to Filov (no date); Bulgaria, Council of Ministers, 115th warrant, 32nd protocol, March 2, 1943; ibid., pp. 28-30.
39. Belev to Gabrovski (no date); Gabrovski to Filov (no date); Bulgaria, Council of Ministers, 116th warrant, 32nd protocol, March 2, 1943; ibid., pp. 30-32. For the relevant section of the citizenship law, see *DV*, no. 288 (December 20, 1940), p. 21. Bulgaria had had experiences with the exchange of population after World War I.

Jewish property and real estate left behind until this property was liquidated. The KEV reserved the right to designate these officials later.[40] Moreover, on the matter of liquidation and control of Jewish property, Belev and Gabrovski asked the cabinet to issue a warrant declaring that all real estate of the deported Jews would be confiscated for the advantage of the state. The KEV would sell movable property belonging to the deported Jews for the advantage of the local community in which the Jews had lived.[41]

All of these warrants were really implementing actions for warrant no. 127, which charged the commissariat "to deport from the borders of the country in agreement with the German authorities up to 20,000 Jews, *inhabiting the recently liberated territories*" (my italics).[42] As with most of the other warrants, the cabinet based its authority for this on the enabling legislation of June 1942. As in the cases of the other deportation decrees, all cabinet members present signed warrant no. 127, and it was not to be published in the *Durzhaven Vestnik*. These details are significant, for in the essential warrant no. 127 the limiting reference to the *recently liberated territories* had important consequences.

It is obvious from the nature of the implementing warrants (arranging for transportation from all over Bulgaria, forfeiture of citizenship, etc.) that the cabinet was making provisions for the deportation of Jews from the old territorial boundaries as well as "the recently liberated territories." Indeed, in Gabrovski's report for warrant no. 113 he mentioned the plan to deport undesirable Bulgarian Jews along with those of Thrace and Macedonia. The question then remains: Why did the cabinet in its most important decree authorize only the deportation of Jews from the new territories? Unfortunately, available documents do not reveal the answer, and speculation must supply it.

The Dannecker-Belev agreement called specifically for the deportation of Jews from the new territories, probably because the Nazis thought that it would be less controversial to begin deporting Jews from the occupied lands than from Bulgaria proper. Nevertheless, even

---

40. Belev to Gabrovski (no date); Gabrovski to Filov (no date); Bulgaria, Council of Ministers, 117th warrant, 32nd protocol, March 2, 1943; Grinberg, *Dokumenti*, pp. 32-35.

41. Belev to Gabrovski (no date); Gabrovski to Filov (no date); Bulgaria, Council of Ministers, 126th warrant, 32nd protocol, March 2, 1943; Grinberg, *Dokumenti*, pp. 35-38.

42. Gabrovski to Filov (no date); Bulgaria, Council of Ministers, 127th warrant, 32nd protocol, March 2, 1943; Grinberg, *Dokumenti*, pp. 41-43, reproduced in Appendix III.

before the final draft of the agreement was completed, Belev began plans to deport some Jews who came from within the old boundaries.[43] It seems rather unlikely that the original wording of the final agreement was unintentional on the part of Belev, but he thought it necessary to change the document afterwards by crossing out the qualifying words "from the new Bulgarian lands Thrace and Macedonia" in its opening statement.[44] This change in the wording was an obvious move to include Jews from old Bulgaria in the agreement. In warrant no. 127 the cabinet repeated the wording of the agreement as originally stated, even though the clear intention was to deport Jews from old Bulgaria anyway.

Any explanation for the warrant's wording seems inadequate. The government felt it had a freer hand acting in Thrace and Macedonia because of the power which blanket legislation had given them in 1942, enabling legislation similar to that concerning the Jews; but the legal basis for the deportations was the enabling Jewish legislation, which could have been applied and, in fact, in implementing proposed Bulgarian deportations, was applied to the Jews from old Bulgaria as well. The government might have expected more objections concerning the Bulgarian Jews than the Thracian and Macedonian, but the whole operation was to be strictly secret in any case. There is no doubt that the Bulgarian government regarded the new territories with special concern. There was a general move on the part of Bulgaria to rid these areas of non-Slavic elements, especially Greeks, whom Sofia attempted to deport into German-occupied Greece;[45] but this only indirectly affected the decision to deport the Jews from this area. The cabinet issued the warrant on the basis of the original Dannecker-Belev agreement. More specifically, as in the case of the other warrants, they approved with no change the phrasing in Gabrovski's reports. (The only major change in any of Gabrovski's proposals was the decision not to publicize the warrants as the minister had intended.)

Thus, it was Gabrovski who was really responsible for the wording of warrant no. 127, although the cabinet could have changed it had they thought something odd. The minister of internal affairs evidently phrased the proposed decree in his report with exact reference to the

43. See Belev's report of February 4, 1943, Grinberg, *Dokumenti*, pp. 8–11; see also above, pp. 77–78.

44. Grinberg, *Dokumenti*, p. 16.

45. Wörmann, reports, February 18 and March 29, 1943, T120, serial 267, roll 225, frames 173822, 173871-78. The Germans did not allow Bulgaria to expel the Greeks.

original Dannecker-Belev agreement. Could the wording of the warrant have been an oversight? If so, it was an oversight of which (as we shall see below) members of the cabinet were aware. This discrepancy between authorization and plan is most essential to subsequent actions.

Later on in March, Gabrovski sent an amended report proposing the deportations established by the Dannecker-Belev agreement. This report asked for a new warrant similar to warrant no. 127 but with the words "and lodged in camps in the cities Skopje, Pirot, Gorna Dzhumaia, Dupnitsa, and Radomir" inserted following "inhabiting the recently liberated territories." The cabinet passed Gabrovski's new proposal, which meant that both Jews from the new lands and Bulgarian Jews encamped in the departure centers could be deported.[46] The available copy of this new warrant reproduced in Natan Grinberg's *Dokumenti* does not indicate the exact day in March on which it was issued. It would seem likely, however, that the cabinet issued the new warrant and that Belev also modified the February 22 agreement only after the events of March 9 revealed the shortcomings of warrant no. 127. (Grinberg, who had an opportunity to examine the original Bulgarian version of the Dannecker-Belev agreement, believes that Belev used the same pen and ink to cross out the qualifying passages that he used to sign the document. This does not necessarily preclude, however, his changing the agreement some time after the signing.)[47]

Arrangements for Deportations

The KEV deportation plan divided the kingdom into five separate areas: Macedonia, Thrace, Pirot, the Sofia region, and the remainder of the country. The commissariat had to resolve two basic administrative problems dependent on the particular areas. First, the Jews in the new territories (Macedonia, Thrace, and Pirot) did not hold Bulgarian citizenship (excluding mobilized persons from the interior), while persons from the rest of Bulgaria did. Secondly, Belev planned to deport all the Jews of the first four areas with the exception of the city of Sofia; therefore, only in the other regions would the KEV need to select Jews for the first deportations.

Belev scheduled the deportation of Thracian Jews first and then in order those from the old territorial boundaries, Pirot, and Macedonia.

46. Gabrovski to Filov (no date); Bulgaria, Council of Ministers, warrant (no number); Grinberg, *Dokumenti*, pp. 43-44. Reproduced in Appendix III.
47. Grinberg, pp. 16, 43-44.

The plan everywhere provided for three stages: the congregation of Jews at a central point in their own town (or the closest consistory town); the transfer to one of the six departure centers, a process which in Thrace required several days; and the deportation from the centers to Poland. The first step in the procedure—congregation—was scheduled for Thrace on March 4, for Bulgaria on March 9, for Macedonia on March 11, and for Pirot, in the smallest of the operations, at an unspecified time after the Bulgarian collection.

The commissar ordered the officials charged with carrying out the deportations in the new territories to their posts at the end of February to survey the regions and make the proper arrangements for arresting the Jews, detaining them in their home cities until transfer, transporting them, establishing departure centers, etc.[48] In all areas the KEV officials employed local police, military, and civilian authorities to help in the deportation process. Everyone from the governor of Thrace to the district agronomist of Pirot was obliged to serve the KEV in its operation.[49]

Through a series of carefully delineated plans and instructions, Belev insured that the procedures for deportation would be efficient and homogeneous everywhere in the kingdom and occupied lands. The commissar's own set of instructions established the overall plan, but regional instructions implemented it in the different areas, and local plans drawn up by the district police chiefs provided for proper application of rules in each of the cities.[50] All of the commissariat and government officials stressed attention to the most minute detail, including, for example, elaborate plans for sealing Jewish homes to protect them against looting[51] and instructions to the guards to prohibit the Jews from "singing, shouting, whistling, scratching the walls of the vehicles, smoking, and lighting fires" during transport.[52]

Because of the ultimate outcome of this first attempt at deportation,

48. Ibid., pp. 44-45, 151; Hristo Bakurdzhiev to Belev, Pirot (no date), pp. 138-42.

49. For a detailed description of the deportations, see ibid., pp. 44-184.

50. See especially *Obshti uputvaniia* [General instructions] distributed to delegates of the Commissariat for Jewish Questions, ibid., pp. 47-49; Ts. Gruev, police commandant, report (no date), pp. 65-69; T. V. Kolibarov, police commandant in Seres, report, March 3, 1943, pp. 71-73; Al. pop Stefanov, district police chief in Dede Agach, report (no date), pp. 81-83; I. Dzhamdzhiev, police commandant in Ksanti, report (no date), pp. 84-86; A. Trifonov, police commandant in Kavala, and Sl. Ionchev, KEV inspector, report (no date), pp. 90-91; Hristo Bakurdzhiev to Belev, Pirot (no date), pp. 139-42.

51. *Obshti uputvaniia*, ibid., pp. 148-49.

52. Kalitsin, "Instruktsii" [Instructions], ibid., p. 62.

two aspects of the KEV's preparations are of special interest—the selection of Jews from among the communities within the old territorial
boundaries and the actions which the commissariat took prior to the
deportations in the cities of southwestern Bulgaria where they planned
to deport the total Jewish populations. On February 22, the day the
Dannecker-Belev agreement was signed, Pencho Lukov sent a letter
(numbered 5712) to most of the KEV delegates in old Bulgaria requesting information on the Jews. Lukov wanted, within twenty-four
hours, lists of all Jews who were "rich, prominent, and generally well
known [bogati, po-vidni i obshtestveno proiaveni]." The list should
include, Lukov wrote, all those whom the delegates considered, or who
demonstrated themselves to be, leaders among the Jews, defenders of
the Jewish spirit (evreiskiia duh) in the local community, or supporters
of antigovernment ideas or feelings. Belev wanted not only to eliminate
agitators and decimate the Jewish leadership and morale, but also to
realize the greatest initial profit from the deportations. Lukov required
the delegates to include on their lists the names of members in each
Jew's family, together with the sex and age of each one. The lists were
not to include Jews privileged under article 33, paragraph 1, of the ZZN
(converted Jews, Jews married to Bulgarians), Jews with foreign citizenship, or Jews in mixed marriages (with people "of Aryan origin").[53]
On the other hand, Jews with rights under article 33, paragraph 2 (war
heroes, war orphans, etc.) were liable for inclusion on the lists.[54] On
the twenty-third Belev himself sent letters to the KEV delegates and
district governors in the Sofia and Vratsa regions asking for information
within five days on all Jews in their districts, listed according to families.[55] The commissar selected from all the submitted lists those whom
he wished to deport.

The method of preparing the lists varied from city to city, as the
attitudes of the commissariat delegates to the operation varied. Some
prepared the lists with enthusiasm; some with misgivings. Belev's stipu-

53. This is one of the few times the word "Aryan" appears in the Bulgarian
treatment of the Jewish question.
54. Pencho Lukov to the delegates of the KEV in Vidin, Lom, Berkovitsa,
Ferdinand, Vratsa, Pleven, Ruse, Razgrad, Shumen, Dobrich, Provadiia, Varna,
Burgas, Iambol, Kurdzhali, Haskovo, Plovdiv, Pazardzhik, Stara Zagora, and Nova
Zagora, February 22, 1943, Grinberg, Dokumenti, p. 170. Lukov did not send letters
to Chirpan, Dupnitsa, Gorna Dzhumaia, Karnobat, Kiustendil, Samokov, Sliven, and
Sofia, all of which would also take part in the operation. The consistories of Nevro-
kop and Silistra had by this time been disbanded.
55. Belev to delegates of the Jewish communities and district governors in the
Sofia and Vratsa regions, February 23, 1943, ibid., pp. 170-71.

lations for Jews to be included left most of the burden of judgment on the local delegates. In a few cases, Belev and his delegates could not agree on the lists, and the commissar ordered revisions or additions or made them himself.[56] The Subranie representative Ivan Nedelkov, who was also the KEV's delegate in Vidin, wrote Belev that it was possible to include all Jews under the instructions of letter no. 5712, because all of them openly expressed joy over Axis reverses demonstrating "manifest antigovernment ideas and feeling."[57]

Many of the delegates concentrated on people whom they considered defenders of the Jewish spirit or suspected of antigovernment behavior because wealthy Jews, especially after the confiscatory measures of the preceding months, were hard to find. The authorities selected Jews because they were "often seen [gathered] in the . . . synagogue" (Ferdinand), they supported the Jewish "spirit" (Vratsa), they performed "questionable acts" (also Vratsa), and for similar reasons. One Jew from Pleven was included on the list because he had supported the republican side at the time of the Spanish Civil War. The delegate from Kazanluk characterized the persons on his list with such notations by their names as "a known anarcho-Communist," "a perpetrator of propaganda in favor of the USSR," "one who had maligned German leaders," "insolent," "unruly," etc.

An interesting incident demonstrating the arbitrary nature of the lists occurred in Plovdiv, Bulgaria's second largest city. From a combined total of over 200 families selected by the delegate, Belev determined to deport 148. He designated the first 148 families on the list; however, while typing the final papers, the typist inadvertently omitted families number 95 and 97 from the delegate's group; thus, families number 149 and 150 were added at the end to make up the difference. On such capricious grounds as this rested the Jews' fate.[58] The KEV offices received the names of about 9,000 Jews (3,000 families) which the local delegates considered subject to deportation. From these Belev selected over 8,400.[59]

56. Grinberg deals with the preparation for deportations in the individual cities within the old boundaries of Bulgaria on pages 172-81 of his *Dokumenti*. With a few exceptions he does not include any of the commissariat's documents.

57. Ibid., p. 174.

58. Ibid., pp. 177-78.

59. Ibid., pp. 172-81. Grinberg gives most of the statistics for individual towns in his text. Only the following documents are included: Nikola Anastasov Ikonomov, KEV clerk, report, Sliven, March 18, 1943, p. 173; Hristo P. Dimitrov, KEV delegate at Stara Zagora, report, February 25, 1943, p. 178; Ivan Popov, report, Sofia (no date), p. 180; Boris Tasev to Mayor Georgi Efimov of Kiustendil, Kius-

On March 5 the commissar met with most of the delegates from old Bulgaria or their representatives and talked with each one individually about the impending action.[60] The KEV arranged with the Bulgarian State Railway (*Bulgarski durzhavni zheleznitsi*, BDZh) to prepare the transfer of about 5,800 persons from various stations in the kingdom to Pirot and Radomir on March 10 and 11. In the southwest no transportation was needed. Belev selected for deportation native Bulgarian Jews ranging from groups of less than fifty to some of over a thousand, and from almost every community in the country. The authorities planned to keep most Bulgarian Jews separate from those of Thrace, whom they concentrated at Gorna Dzhumaia and Dupnitsa.[61] On March 8 Belev sent the names of the selected Jews to the regional (*oblastni*) police chiefs with letters of instructions on the procedures for arrest.[62]

The cities of southwest Bulgaria commanded special attention both because the departure centers were there and because in consequence the KEV included all Jews in the area in the planned operation. In Dupnitsa, Asen V. Paitashev, a commissariat chief of service, administered the camp and also had charge of deportations of the local community of 1,050 Jews. Paitashev, when he arrived in the city, placed all Jews under house arrest from February 25 until March 2 and stationed guards at the intersections of the Jewish quarter. Only children of ten years of age or under were allowed on the streets in order to shop for their families.[63]

Belev sent Ivan Tepavski, a clerk from the Ministry of Internal Affairs, to Gorna Dzhumaia. Like his colleague in Dupnitsa, he was in charge of both the camp and the deportation of the local community, and on March 7, he reported to Belev that he had made all preparations for the arrest of the 184 local Jews.[64]

In Kiustendil, Boris Tasev, the chief of the commissariat's agents, arranged for the deportation of that city's 980 Jews. Tasev arrived in the city on February 26 with his immediate superior for the Sofia region, Dr. Ivan Popov, chief of the KEV's administrative section. In the afternoon, Popov met with the district governor, who had promised full

tendil, March 5, 1943, pp. 180-81; Tasev, report, Kiustendil, March 6, 1943, p. 181; and Maria Pavlova to Radomir departure center, Sofia, March 5, 1943, p. 181.

60. Belev to KEV delegates, March 2, 1943, ibid., p. 171.

61. Commissariat for Jewish Questions, Plan for the Transfer of Jews by Railroad (no date), ibid., p. 172.

62. Belev to regional police chiefs, March 8, 1943, ibid., p. 171.

63. Dupnitsa, Jewish Committee of the Fatherland Front, report, October 13, 1944, ibid., pp. 107–08.

64. Ibid., pp. 179-80.

cooperation. From the police registry Tasev prepared a list of the Jews living in the city and designated the warehouse of the former Jewish firm Fernandes as a temporary concentration center.[65] Tasev requested that Mayor Georgi Efimov, the KEV delegate, allow him to collect necessary furnishings for the camp from Jewish households.[66]

Ivan Popov also supervised the administration of the departure centers in southwest Bulgaria. On March 10, he wired the KEV that everything in Radomir, Dupnitsa, and Gorna Dzhumaia was ready for receiving the Bulgarian Jews. (The Thracian Jews had been arriving at the latter two camps all week.) At the same time, Hristo D. Bakurdzhiev in Pirot reported that all was ready there for the influx of about 2,000 Sofia Jews.[67]

In its final preparations, the KEV, although it maintained secrecy on the one hand, also tried to arrange for the illusion of popular support. On March 8 Popov sent telegrams to the special representatives in Kiustendil, Dupnitsa, and Gorna Dzhumaia ordering them to send expressions of thanks from the citizens, mayors, benevolent associations, and others to the cabinet and the KEV after the Jews left their cities.[68]

Belev's final list of Jews from the pre-1941 boundaries came to almost 2,500 more than his proposed 6,000. However, there were fewer than 11,500 Jews in Macedonia and Thrace, so that Belev's figure for deportations from old Bulgaria brought the number up to 20,000. Except in the southwest where all the Jews were marked for deportation, Belev tried to follow his criteria for selection. Nevertheless, these criteria—wealth, prominence, or subversive behavior—were highly subjective, and in any case many arbitrary decisions were made in selection—decisions such as those made in areas where there were few or no Jews fitting the criteria or those decisions made by Belev himself as to whom he would or would not choose from the submitted lists. Since the KEV wished to deport whole families rather than individuals, there was the additional factor that kinship determined the fate of some Jews, particularly children and wives. Ivan Nedelkov's remark that all Jews were antigovernment reveals a basic flaw in Belev's argument that some Jews were more likely candidates for deportation to Poland than others. If the Nazi New Order was by definition an enemy of the Jew and vice

65. Tasev to Popov (no date), ibid., p. 180.
66. Tasev to Georgi Efimov, mayor of Kiustendil, March 5, 1943, ibid.
67. Bakurdzhiev, report (no date), ibid., pp. 181-82.
68. Popov to district governors in Kiustendil, Dupnitsa, and Gorna Dzhumaia, March 8, 1943, ibid., 96-VI (Grinberg has inserted six pages numbered 96-I to 96-VI between pages 96 and 97).

versa, all Jews were indeed fit for deportation. Everyone in the KEV hierarchy, probably in the government hierarchy, realized this and knew that, once the deportations began, it might be difficult not to conclude with the whole Jewish population. This indeed was Belev and Dannecker's plan.

The Peshev Protest

Despite the KEV's elaborate precautions and intense concern to conceal the plans, preparations, and procedures for the deportations, they were not completely successful. It is hard to imagine how they could keep such a massive plan totally undisclosed in any case. Various concerned Jews and Bulgarians became privy through one means or another to the KEV scheme and attempted to exert their influence to halt it.

When the police began gathering the Jews in Plovdiv (March 10), Dimitur Stankov, a prominent citizen, left for Sofia to persuade Filov to change the impending orders. Kiril, the bishop of Plovdiv (who later became the patriarch of Bulgaria), sent a telegram to the king threatening a campaign of civil disobedience, including personally lying down on the railroad tracks before the deportation trains, if the planned operation was carried out. The Holy Synod sent a letter of protest on behalf of the Jews. The president of the writers' union, Stiliian Chilingirov, and another noted writer Trifon Kunov went to see the king and the prime minister on behalf of the Jews.[69]

However most effective protest in March really originated with the Jews themselves. Eminent Jews in Sofia learned of the proposed deportations through several sources. Liliana Panitsa, Belev's secretary, had ties of friendship with several Jews in the capital, including Mr. and Mrs. Nisim (Buko) Levi. (He was the vice-president of Geron's central consistory.) These ties, of course, were not known to Belev. At the end of February, Miss Panitsa told Levi that the Jews of Macedonia

---

69. Haim Keshales, "Tova se sluchi v onezi dni: Belezhki za zhivota na evreite v Bulgariia prez 1939-1950 godini" [It happened in those days: notes on the life of the Jews in Bulgaria during the period 1939-1950] (unpublished manuscript deposited in Yad WaShem, Jerusalem), pp. 92-93; Benjamin Arditi, *Yehudi Bulgariyah bishanah hamishpat hanatzi: 1940-1944* [The Jews of Bulgaria during the years of Nazi occupation: 1940-1944] (Tel Aviv: Israel Press, 1962), pp. 287-90; Misho Leviev, ed., *Nashata blagodarnost* [Our thanks] (Sofia: Sbornik "Kadima" [1946], pp. 81-89; interview with B. Piti, January 1966, Jaffa, Israel (this information has subsequently been published under the title *Te, spasitelite* [They, the rescuers] [Tel Aviv: n.p., 1969]); Sofia, Protocols of People's Court No. 7, III, 1007-12 (testimony of Kosta Nikolov Rusinov).

and Thrace were to be deported to Poland, and at the end of the first week in March she told him and others that some Jews from old Bulgaria, including Levi himself, would also be deported.[70]

Moreover, on February 25, Haim Rahamin Behar of Kiustendil while in Sofia visiting relatives met Vatev, the commissariat doctor, near the consistory office. Vatev told him that he knew a great secret and asked Behar what it was worth to him. Behar bribed Vatev to talk and hence learned of the impending deportations. Behar told David Oliver, a friend of Liubomir Lulchev, the king's confidant. Lulchev, after asking at the court about this, told Oliver that the rumor was false. However, Behar heard the same story from others—his friends, Vladimir Kurtev, a prominent member of IMRO, and Avraham Alfasa, the former president of the local Sofia consistory, who had also learned the secret from Miss Panitsa. Behar received a telephone call from the Kiustendil district governor, Liuben Mitenov, to come back to Kiustendil the next day, the 27th. On his return, Mitenov also told him the plan for deportation. Mitenov asked Behar to raise 300,000 leva ($3,700) to help him try to find some way to save the Jews. After he spoke with Mitenov, Behar informed leaders of the Kiustendil Jewish community, and the story became widespread.

On the one hand, many Kiustendil Jews were seized with panic and depression. Resignedly, they began to prepare for the deportation, choosing the things they would need to take with them, giving other items to Bulgarian friends. However, some Jews sought a way out. A group of men led by Behar began to raise money for Mitenov. Until March 6, Behar reports, the Jews were at a loss as to what to do to save themselves. Then on that day they decided to ask Bulgarian friends to go to the capital to intervene for them.[71]

By March 6 Behar and his associates collected 900,000 leva. They gave Mitenov his requested 300,000 leva and gave another 300,000 leva to Vladimir Kurtev, the Macedonian leader, and others to use to bribe people in the KEV. The Jews also tried to bribe members on the staff of Boris Tasev, the KEV's representative in Kiustendil.

Mitenov had helped Behar learn the final orders for Kiustendil, given

70.   Sofia, Protocols of People's Court No. 7, V, 1498 (testimony of Buko Levi); and interview with Buko Levi, Tel Aviv, Israel, December 1966.

71.   Deposition of Haim Rahamin Behar, Archives of the Union of Bulgarian Immigrants (*Ichud Olei Bulgariyah*), Tel Aviv, Israel, reprinted in Keshales, pp. 84-86. Iako Baruh in his account of the events claims that the Bulgarians on their own initiative decided to form a committee to travel to Sofia on behalf of the Jews (Yad WaShem, doc. no. 03/1705, pp. 3-4). These accounts and, others cited in **note 73** are also the sources for the events described on the following pages.

by Belev personally on a visit during the first week in March. On March 4 at 9:00 P.M. a curfew had gone into effect for the Jews of the city. On the tenth of March the Jews would be taken to the Fernandes tobacco warehouse to prepare for their transfer to Radomir.

In accordance with the plan to seek help from Bulgarians, the Jews sought out their friends. Several Bulgarians including Petur Mihalev, Subranie representative for the third Kiustendil district, agreed to help the Jews, but some who were asked did not. At any rate, a delegation of five Bulgarian residents of Kiustendil arranged to go to the capital on behalf of the Jews. Behar emphasizes that the activity originated among the Kiustendil Jews without direction from the central consistory, although communication between the two cities was maintained when possible. Other accounts indicate that it was in Sofia, not Kiustendil, that the main defense of the Jews took place, although all agree that the germ of the action came from the provincial city.

Iako Baruh was an official of the illegal Zionist center in Bulgaria who distributed visas to Palestine for the Jewish agency. In this capacity he had occasion to deal *sub rosa* with men prominent in the Bulgarian government, including cabinet ministers who were interested in obtaining such visas for their friends. Nowhere, do the bizarre paradoxes of Bulgarian "anti-Semitism" stand out so clearly as in these connections of Baruh with the government officials who were trying to save Jewish friends at the same time that they were passing legislation to destroy the Bulgarian Jewish community.

Samuel Baruh, Iako's brother, was in Kiustendil as a mobilized pharmacist working in a Bulgarian apothecary shop. Governor Mitenov told him of the deportation plans. Because Jews were not allowed to use telephones or telegraphs without permission, Baruh asked a friend of his brother's to contact Iako in Sofia and ask him to use his influence to save the Jews. The same night "an influential Macedonian" (presumably Kurtev) also informed Iako of the situation.

As the Jews of Sofia had become privy to the KEV's secret, they had sought support primarily among members of the political opposition, both in and out of the Subranie, who had demonstrated their distaste for the anti-Semitic policies—men like Mushanov, Stainov, Metropolitan Stefan, Dimo Kazasov, Damian Velchev, etc. Baruh, however, could appeal directly to the government. Working feverishly from hour to hour, Baruh called on his contacts for aid. He first went to see the secretary of the cabinet's chancellery, Georgi K. Serafimov. This man told Baruh that the Germans had forced the deportation operation on the government and that there was no hope for the Jews. Baruh did not give up. He went to see Gabrovski's chief secretary with whom he had attended Sofia University. He gave Baruh the same unpromising report. The cabinet had already made the decision; it could not be changed. (Baruh also went to see the Swiss ambassador, Charles Redard, an official of the International Red Cross.) Beginning to despair, Baruh next turned to the minister of trade, Nikola Zahariev, whom he had helped to obtain entrance visas to Palestine. Zahariev told him once again that nothing could be done. No one dared to help the Jews for fear of being accused of taking Jewish bribes; in addition, "the Germans would take cruel revenge." However, Zahariev revealed to Baruh the cabinet's Achilles' heel. *The cabinet's decree authorized only the deportation of Jews from "the recently liberated territories" and not those from the pre-1941 boundaries.* Zahariev felt himself powerless to press this issue because he believed that if he did so, the government would not only dismiss him, but punish him as well.

Baruh took the agricultural minister's hint that he should somehow use this vital information. He called on another classmate, the Subranie representative from the first Kiustendil district—Dimitur Peshev, a vice-president of that body.

Early in the morning of March 7, Baruh and Peshev had a two-hour conversation. Baruh told the deputy everything he knew of the events in Kiustendil, including the preparations being made to carry out the deportations. He also informed him of the discrepancy between the cabinet's decree and its planned operation. Baruh writes that all this was up to then unknown to Peshev. The representative could not believe that these things were going on without his knowledge. However, he promised that he would verify the account and uncover the whole story. If what Zahariev said was true, Peshev was confident that they could stop the deportations. The men arranged to meet the next day.

Peshev called Mitenov and the police chief in Kiustendil, both of whom confirmed Baruh's account. At their meeting the next day Peshev told Baruh that he would confer with several other representatives, his friends, as he felt that only collective action could be effective. Baruh told him of the commission that was coming from Kiustendil and was expected in Sofia at eight o'clock that evening. Peshev decided that protest would be most effective if they waited for the commission's arrival.

Meanwhile, in Kiustendil the KEV continued with its plans. On March 6, Boris Tasev reported by phone from the governor's office to G'oshev in Sofia, and Tasev and Governor Mitenov learned the final date and hour of the departure of the Kiustendil Jews for Radomir at the same time. That same day Tasev visited the secretary of the municipality to obtain lists of mobilized Jews. In the presence of other city officials, the secretary began asking the special representative about the details of the concentration. Tasev told the secretary that he did not need to know these things, that rumors would spread throughout the city. The assistant mayor told Tasev that it was no longer a secret since the governor had officially announced the deportations and the date of the roundup. He also told Tasev that Mitenov had informed Samuel Baruh. Until then Tasev had not known the secret was out.

On March 8 Tasev conferred with Mitenov and Mayor Efimov. He suggested that the Jews be gathered a day earlier, that is, on March 9, rather than on March 10. In the afternoon, when Tasev again had occasion to visit the governor, he found there Petur Mihalev, who began questioning him about the action. The KEV official was disturbed that the deputy knew about the proposed action. That same evening, Tasev learned of the special delegation of five planning to visit the capital on behalf of the Jews, and he sent an agent to the station to investigate. Actually only two of the five were able to board the train to Sofia. Local Ratnitsi detained the others. One man's home was surrounded, and the mob pelted him with stones when he tried to leave. Kiustendil in the crisis did not really demonstrate solid support for or against the Jews, but was rather a microcosm of the forces and doubts at work in the entire country.

On the evening of the eighth, Mayor Efimov announced at a public meeting, in response to a question from the floor, that the Jews would be gathered in camps on the tenth. Because of the actions and anxiety of the Jewish community, the Bulgarians in Kiustendil were by this time aware of the tension in their city. Tasev told Mitenov that he was afraid that because the secret was out he would be blamed. Sarcastically, Mitenov responded that he should not worry because the Jews were only going to the interior of Bulgaria.

On the morning of March 9, in Sofia there gathered in Peshev's office a number of Jews and Bulgarians including the deputies Mihalev, Tasko Stoilkov (from Sveti Vrach), and Dimitur Ikonomov (from Dupnitsa); Kurtev; Col. Avram Tadzher, the most prominent Jewish army officer; Iako Baruh; and other Jewish leaders. Fortuitously the fourth regular session of the Subranie was reconvening that afternoon after several days' recess. The men at the meeting decided that the best time to confront the government with their knowledge of deportations was just before the Subranie convened. The Jews retired to their favorite coffeehouse to await the outcome, and the Bulgarians proceeded to insure more support from the Subranie.[72]

Between five and six, while the members of the Subranie were gathering in the chamber, Peshev invited Gabrovski into his office, where a group of representatives awaited him. Gabrovski at first denied that there was a plan for Jewish deportation, but the protesters gave him irrefutable proof—accounts of the preparations in Kiustendil—and also told him that they knew that the deportation of Jews from the old boundaries of Bulgaria contradicted the wording of the cabinet's decrees. The men said that they were quite prepared to raise this matter in the Subranie, causing at least a public scandal and perhaps even a government crisis. The minister went to confer with Filov. After a brief conference Gabrovski returned to Peshev's office and informed the assembled representatives that the order could not be reversed; however, the prime minister had agreed to postpone for another time the deportation of the Jews from old Bulgaria. The available documentation of these events neither indicates nor entirely precludes that Filov contacted the king on this matter before giving his decision to Gabrovski. Nevertheless, the timing and nature of the decision leads this author to believe that the prime minister did not contact Boris at this time.

It was 7:00 P.M.; the concentration of the Jews was scheduled to begin at midnight. Peshev asked Gabrovski to countermand the orders by telephoning the various cities where the Jews would be collected. The minister replied that he would have his secretary telegraph the orders. Peshev wanted immediate action, and he himself then called Mitenov in Kiustendil and informed him on behalf of Gabrovski that the action was to be stopped. Dimitur Ikonomov likewise called Dupnitsa, passing on the same information. Realizing that the representatives were going to call their districts one by one, Gabrovski took the phone and called his secretary, issuing orders to telegraph all the cities within the old boundaries cancelling the orders for rounding up the Jews. The telegraphed message did not reach its destinations until the next day, March 10. In Plovdiv, Pazardzhik, Samokov, Haskovo, Shumen, and some other cities the police rounded up the Jews on schedule and assembled them in schools, synagogues, or warehouses to await deportation to Poland; but when the orders came through, these Jews were released.

The Jews of Sofia and Kiustendil learned of the postponement im-

72. Arditi, p. 287. Arditi was present at this meeting.

mediately from the representatives. Tasev was informed of the change by Buko Konforti, a leader of the Kiustendil Jewish community, when he called Konforti concerning the gathering of supplies for the collection point. Tasev then went to the offices of Mitenov where he verified the account. When he called the KEV, Lukov told him to return to Sofia. Tasev attributed the failure of the action to four causes: the publication by the district governor of Dupnitsa of orders regarding the roundup of the Jews; the proximity of Kiustendil to Skopje and Thrace where deportation activity had already begun; the gathering of supplies from the Jews for the camp at Radomir (as Tasev himself proposed); and the notification of the mayor and district governor of Kiustendil of the action. In other words, Tasev thought that a successful operation would have to have been carried out in almost complete secrecy. The KEV could not trust even government officials to carry through the plan.[73]

The postponement relieved the situation, but Peshev was not satisfied. During the next weeks the KEV carried out its operations in Thrace and Macedonia, and there remained the possibility of reinstituting the operation in Bulgaria proper, which was after all in Filov's words merely postponed. There was a feeling of despondency among the Jews in the country. Those Bulgarians in favor of and others against Jewish policy hardened their lines. Both Boris and Filov at this time expressed sentiments of theoretical anti-Semitism, a different tack from the essentially practical motivation which had characterized the previous period.

On March 17 Peshev and forty-two other members of the Subranie, mostly from the government faction, sent a letter of protest to Filov condemning the government's Jewish policy.[74] The signers of the protest, although they stressed their loyalty to the government, accused it of acting against the prestige and interest of the nation. They deplored the measures which would expel the Jews from the country

73. The above account (from p. 91) of these events in March is taken from the following documents: Sofia, Protocols of People's Court No. 7, V, 912-19 (testimony of Iako Baruh); Yad WaShem doc. no. 03/1705; and Bulgarian Academy of Sciences, Institute for Balkan Studies, Section for Hebrew Studies archives, doc. no. 62 (hereafter cited as BAN, Ebroistika). Both of the latter are depositions of Iako Baruh; all three of these accounts by Baruh are essentially the same but are not identical. Boris Tasev, report (no date), BAN, Ebroistika, doc. no. 366 (also reprinted in Grinberg, *Dokumenti*, pp. 182-84); Haim Behar, deposition, Archives of the Union of Bulgarian Immigrants (*Ichud Olei Bulgariyah*), reprinted in Keshales, pp. 84-86. The three accounts corroborate each other although minor differences on specific points are apparent. For additional accounts see Arditi, pp. 286-90, and Keshales, pp. 81-103.

74. See Appendix IV for a list of the signers.

ultimately leading to their deaths, a harsh accusation since the Final Solution was not public knowledge.[75] The names of the signatories were impressive. They included Andro Lulchev, the brother of the king's advisor; Dr. Petur K'oseivanov, the nephew of the former prime minister; and Dr. Ivan Vazov, nephew of the famous author. Several representatives from southwest Bulgaria who helped originate the action in March signed the protest—Peshev and Mihalev of Kiustendil, Ikonomov and Sotir Ianev of Dupnitsa, and Tasko Stoilkov of Sveti Vrach; but others from the region significantly did not. Representatives from Gorna Dzhumaia, Radomir, Ihtiman, Petrich, and Samokov did not sign, nor did Kovachevski, the third representative from Kiustendil. Mushanov signed although he was a member of the opposition. On the other hand, Petko Stainov, because he was an opposition representative, did not wish to sign the protest proper, but attached a statement giving it his full support. The greatest surprise on the list of signatories was that of the right-wing opposition leader Aleksandur Tsankov. He may have been trying to embarrass the government rather than befriend the Jews, but the German favorite also had been conspicuous by his lack of anti-Semitic statements during the debates on Jewish policy in the Subranie hall.

Peshev presented the protest to Filov on the morning of March 19. Filov was greatly disturbed by this demonstration, and in his diary he attributed it to the great harmful influence of the Jews in Bulgaria. Before accepting the protest he had requested a meeting with Peshev to see if they could come to terms, but the deputy insisted on a public statement. That afternoon Slaveiko Vasilev, a deputy from Pazardzhik, led a group of government supporters in objecting to the protest. Filov told them that the situation was most grave and that he would call a meeting of the Subranie majority.

The next day Filov spoke of the protest to Iordan Sevov, Boris's most influential advisor, and convoked a cabinet meeting to discuss the letter. He persuaded the cabinet to use the protest as a test case for the government's majority in the Subranie. He would ask for a vote of confidence and the removal of Peshev as vice-president. Those members of the government faction who refused to withdraw their names from the protest would lose their standing with the Subranie majority. The time was suitable, wrote Filov, feeling confident of victory, for bringing this matter out in the open. The legislative session was near

75. A copy of the March 17 protest is in the archives of the Kibbutz Lohamei HaGhetaoth.

its end, and the Jewish question would make a good subject for a campaign platform if new elections were held. Filov preferred a small sure majority to a larger group of uncertain supporters. Petur K'oseivanov sent a letter to the prime minister withdrawing his name from the protest. Spas Marinov of Belogradchik spoke to Filov about withdrawing, but the prime minister insisted on a letter.

The next week, on March 24, the majority—114 strong—caucused to discuss the protest. The debate was long and intensive. All members of the majority faction voted their support of all government policies including those involving the Jews. They also withdrew the protest. On the question of censuring Peshev, sixty-six voted yes and thirty-three no. There were eleven abstentions; four members had left the hall before the ballot. Petur K'oseivanov was among those who did not attend. Filov asked Peshev to resign quietly, but the vice-president refused. He claimed that the letter of protest was his own idea and accepted sole responsibility. He started to argue with Filov, warning him that he (Filov) would be sorry for this deed, and the prime minister admitted that all men must bear the responsibility of their actions. Filov wrote in his diary that he had actually called the meeting to expose Peshev's attempts to topple the government or at least embarrass it. He believed that the meeting was a success, but that there was a contradiction to be found in the behavior of those representatives who voted their complete confidence in the government, yet refused to censure Peshev, since the government was making this an issue of confidence; but he did not press this matter.[76]

On Friday, March 26, the first order of business at the Subranie session was a brief proposal by Dr. Atanas Popov on the removal of Peshev from his post. As soon as President Hristo Kalfov opened the meeting and called Dr. Popov to the tribune, a number of representatives began calling for the right to speak first. Peshev, who wanted to resign publicly in protest, called to the president to allow him to make a statement. A number of other deputies, including Stainov, Mushanov, Tsankov, and Angel Durzhanski, an opposition Agrarian and future minister in the Fatherland Front government, demanded the floor. Popov very quickly read his motion, demanding that Peshev lose his position because he no longer had the confidence of the majority. The opposition benches greeted Popov's statement with stamping of feet and shouting. Peshev demanded to be allowed to place his resignation before the

76.   Filov, "Diary," entries for March 19, 20, and 24, 1943, *Naroden Sud*, no. 3, p. 3.

Subranie. Stainov complained that Popov's resolution had not been distributed to the deputies. Kalfov, ignoring the uproar, read a motion bringing Popov's proposal before the body and announced that since the reasons for the motion were well known, they should vote at once. Shouting, Peshev questioned the propriety of voting him "no confidence" without allowing him to defend himself. Mushanov, Tsankov, Stainov, Ivan V. Petrov, and Durzhanski shouted for the floor, and there were cries of "scandal," "shame," "unprecedented," "unconstitutional," etc. Kalfov took the vote, which, of course, passed the measure, and the majority applauded.[77]

The opposition was not denied its day in court, however. The third item of business (after the approval of a trade treaty with Croatia) concerned the approval of a number of cabinet decrees passed since October 1942 and applied in the new territories on the basis of the law giving the cabinet emergency legislative powers there.

The fourteen decrees under discussion did not pertain to the Jewish question. They dealt chiefly with matters such as finance, public relief, building, etc. One of them concerned an amendment to the decree on citizenship for the new territories passed in 1941. This was part of a government effort to expel Greeks from Macedonia and Thrace. Petko Stainov chose to use this decree as a means of bringing up the matter of Jewish deportations. His argument was that according to prevalent international law citizens of lands occupied by another state automatically became citizens of that state from the date of annexation. Therefore not only the Greeks, but also the Jews, of Macedonia and Thrace were *in fact*, if not under Bulgarian law, Bulgarian citizens and could not be forcibly expelled from Bulgaria. Besides appeal to legalistic reason, Stainov called out to emotion by declaring that they were sending women and children to their deaths and that Bulgaria was exchanging a government based on law for one resembling a dictatorship. Kalfov urged him to regard his conscience in respect to decency while he spoke. Several government delegates subjected Stainov to a verbal bombardment during his speech, particularly Bozhil Prashtilov of Ruse, who harassed Stainov for his Anglophile opinions and accused the professor of treason.

Stainov's speech reopened the Peshev issue. Mushanov followed Stainov to the tribune and repeated his views. Then Todor Kozhuharov (from Sofia), a signer of the protest and a former cabinet minister,

77. Bulgaria, Narodno Subranie, *Dnevnitsi*, 25th ONS, 4th reg. sess., II, 1157-58.

spoke exclusively on the protest without even referring to the scheduled items of business. Government deputies called to him to speak to the subject on the agenda, that the Peshev item had been disposed of; but Kozhuharov insisted on giving his reasons for signing the protest—purely moral grounds, a small nation's only weapon in an international state system based on power politics. Because the debate was open, a number of government delegates took the podium to defend the demotion of Peshev and the government's Jewish policy. The last speaker, Hristo Statev, from a Plovdiv rural district, made a speech which was progovernment rather than anti-Semitic, and the debate ended quietly. Finally, somewhat anticlimactically, the Subranie approved the government decrees for the new lands.[78]

Beckerle reported the events to Berlin, emphasizing that Tsankov's participation in the protest was antigovernment rather than pro-Jewish. In general, he tried to play down the protest. He saw as the important point the fact that Peshev was removed and that even the members of the government faction who had signed the protest voted for measures concerning government security.[79]

Thus, it seemed then that the protest was a failure. The government had a sufficient majority not only to keep the parliament's confidence, but also to punish those who maintained their protest. They even succeeded, albeit not completely, in keeping any debate on Jews out of the Subranie chamber. At the same time deportations were in progress. Jews from the occupied territories were on their way to Poland, and to all who were aware of this it seemed obvious that the remaining Jews in Bulgaria would go next.

78. Bulgaria, Narodno Subranie, *Dnevnitsi*, 25th ONS, 4th reg. sess., II, 1163-71. (Pages 1167-70 are missing from all copies.) See also Filov, "Diary," entry for March 26, 1943, *Naroden Sud*, no. 3, p. 3.

79. Beckerle, report, March 26, 1943, T120, serial 267, roll 225, frames 173863-64.

4

Deportation from the New Territories

Thrace

The deportation of the Thracian Jews began on March 4, 1943, even before Peshev conceived his protest. In all the cities of eastern Thrace with major Jewish populations—Giumiurdzhina, Dede Agach, Kavala, Drama, Ksanti, and Seres—the special commissariat representatives proceeded in a similar manner, according to the instructions worked out by Belev and Iaroslav Kalitsin, who directed deportations in the region. For the duration of the action, the police placed the cities under blockade and curfew, beginning sometime after midnight until seven or eight in the morning. Shortly before the action began at 4:00 A.M., policemen in groups of three received their instructions, including the lists of Jewish families to be assembled and the necessary equipment for sealing the Jewish homes. The Thracian Jews may have been aware that something grave was about to occur, but they did not know the exact time of the operation. The abrupt awakenings in the middle of the night surprised them. Following Kalitsin's plan, the police informed the Jews that the government was sending them into the interior of Bulgaria and that they would return to their homes shortly.

Jews were marched through the main streets of the cities, their numbers swelling at each intersection until they reached their destinations —the tobacco warehouses which served as temporary camps. The Jews remained in the camps for one or two days, and the KEV then sent them to the major departure centers at Dupnitsa and Gorna Dzhumaia. The police reported very few untoward events in the roundup of the Jews in Thrace. Most importantly, disturbances in the streets, they observed, were avoided. Actually many citizens became aware of the events and maintained both discreet and open contacts with the Jews—hiding their valuables, passing food, openly sympathizing, etc. The German and

Bulgarian authorities attributed these breaches of popular discipline to Greeks, but they would naturally be reluctant to admit that Thracian Slavs, whom they regarded as Bulgarians, expressed sympathy toward the Jews. There is also Jewish testimony singling out Greeks for showing friendship to the Jews. Yet there is no evidence to support the belief that the Slavs at large were more anti-Semitic than the Greeks.[1]

Expulsions of Jews in the individual Thracian cities are summarized in table 4. The approximate census taken by the KEV in 1942 shows

TABLE 4

DEPORTATIONS FROM THRACE

City	Most Significant Leaders of Operations	Number of Expulsions	
		Persons	Families
Dede Agach	Aleksandur pop Stefanov (district police chief); district governor (unidentified)	42	12
Samothrace		3[a]	—
Drama	Victor Altunov (inspector at Ministry of Internal Affairs and KEV special representative); Tsv. Gruev (police commandant); G. Kortenski (leader of motorized platoon in Drama and head of temporary camp)	589[b]	153
Giumiurdzhina	Illia Dobrevski (inspector at KEV and special representative); Aleksandur		

1. Fr. Dräger, consul, Kavala, report, March 9, 1943, T120, serial 2330, roll 1305, frame 486308. Sofia, Protocols of People's Court No. 7, III, 933 (testimony of Dr. Maer Aron Moshona) (witnesses with "Dr." before their names are mobilized Jewish physicians unless otherwise noted); III, 843 (testimony of Natan Grinberg—Grinberg testified that both Greeks and Slavs helped the Jews); also III, 1405 (testimony of Todor Mihailov, a Bulgarian sailor who befriended Jews at Kavala).

Accounts of the roundup procedure in the various Thracian cities are recounted in Natan Grinberg, Dokumenti [Documents] (Sofia: Central Consistory of Jews in Bulgaria, 1945). He reprints documents and supplies additional text. The most important of these, listed by city, are as follows: Drama, including two undated reports by Gruev before and after the action, pp. 65-69; Seres and Ziliahovo, including Vasilev to Kalitsin, March 2, 1943; Kolibarov, reports, March 3 and 9, 1943; and Vasilev, report, March 24, 1943, pp. 69-74; Giumiurdzhina, including Dobrevski to Kalitsin, March 1, 1943; and Dobrevski to Belev, March 22, 1943, pp. 74-81; Dede Agach, including pop Stefanov, report (no date) sent before the action; and an unsigned report sent to Drama on March 7, 1943, pp. 81-83; Ksanti and Sarzh-Shaban, including Dzhamdzhiev, report (no date) sent before the action, and report, March 8, 1943; Petev to Kalitsin (no date); and Petev to Kalitsin, March 8, 1943, pp. 83-89; Kavala, including Trifonov and Ionchev, report (no date) sent before the action, and report (sent to Belev), March 25, 1943, pp. 89–96-II.

TABLE 4 (Continued)
DEPORTATIONS FROM THRACE

| City | Most Significant Leaders of Operations | Number of Expulsions | |
		Persons	Families
	Hristo Peichev (retired master sergeant and head of temporary camp); Vasil Liubenov (colonel of Giumiurdzhina garrison); Boris Georgiev (commandant of district police headquarters)	878	264c
Kavala	Slavcho Ionchev (inspector at KEV and special representative); A. Trifonov (police commandant); Simeon Nikolov (chief of 1st police district and head of temporary camp)	1,484	393d
Pravishte		19	5e
Tasos		16	5f
Ksanti	Ia. Kalitsin (KEV chief of section and representative); I. Dzhamdzhiev (police commandant); Dobri Petev (asst. mayor and commissariat's delegate); Tr. Petkov (district police chief at Sarzh-Shaban); V. Kaipakov (chief of 1st police district and head of temporary camp)	526g	144
Sarzh-Shaban		12	5
Seres	M. Vasilev (inspector in Ministry of Internal Affairs and KEV special representative); T. V. Kolibarov (police commandant); Geno Kunev (chief of 1st police district and head of temporary camp)	471	111
Ziliahovo		18	5
Total		4,058h	1,097

SOURCE: KEV, report, March 1943, pp. 6-8, from the private collection of Benjamin Arditi, Holon, Israel (hereafter cited as Arditi collection). See also reports from the KEV's representatives in Thrace listed in note 1. For German figures on deported Jews from Thrace, see Wagner, report, April 3, 1943, T120, serial 2330, roll 1305, frames 486326-30; Hoffmann, report, April 5, 1943, ibid., frames 486316-21. Wagner stated that 4,219 Jews were deported. This is also the number of Jews who left from Lom (see below, p. 121). Hoffmann's figure, 4,221, apparently represents an adjustment. Although the latter is now the accepted number, it is short of the true figure of Jews deported from Thrace and Pirot, including those who died before reaching Lom. Discrepancies in the two sets of Bulgarian figures (the KEV's report and local reports) are unexplained, but statistics compiled by the Bulgarian bureaucracy are habitually inconsistent. We cannot assume that the KEV's report

3,975 for the five commissariat centers[2]—obviously an underestimated figure. According to a Greek commentator, in 1940 there were 5,490 Jews in that part of Thrace which Bulgaria occupied; and according to the KEV, there were 4,273 in 1943.[3] We see that even before the Dannecker-Belev agreement there was about a 20 percent drop in the Jewish population, most of which represents Jews sent south into Greece.

From table 5 we see that about 200 Jews escaped deportation from Thrace. Most of these Jews were foreign citizens. The Bulgarians sent citizens of nations occupied by Germany to Poland, but those of neutrals and independent Axis allies, such as Italy, Spain, and Turkey, generally escaped although some Jews of such foreign citizenship may have been deported.[4] A number of these Jews were Greek citizens and escaped deportation because of illness, work on labor gangs, or some other circumstance.[5]

2. See Appendix I.

3. For 1940, see Rabbi Michael Molho, ed., *In Memoriam: Hommage aux victimes juives des Nazis en Grèce* (Salonika: Salonika Jewish Community, 1948), p. 164. The author of this section, Joseph Nehama, does not include Jews from the small villages listed in the commissariat reports. Nehama in his figures for Thrace in 1940 mentions 1,000 Jews from Dimotika, 197 from Nea Orestia, and 40 from Soufla. These towns are all close to the Turkish border and hence were occupied by German forces. Their Jewish populations are not included among the 5,490 (see Froh, OKW staff Berlin, report, April 21, 1943, T120, serial 274, roll 238, frame 177908). For the 1943 population see KEV report, March 1943, Arditi collection. This does not include the three Jews from Samothrace mentioned in the Dede Agach reports.

4. See, for example, Sofia, Protocols of People's Court No. 7, III, 969 (testimony of Dr. Nisim Davidov).

5. The KEV claimed that all Jews not deported were foreign citizens. Benjamin

---

Table 4 notes (continued)
represents a later calculation, as figures for Kavala are lower than those in the local report. I used the KEV's report for convenience and consistency, but there is really little other reason for preference. The entire population of Samothrace was omitted from the KEV's report; thus in that case, I added the local figures.

a. The KEV report of March 1943 does not list these Jews.

b. Ivan Tepavski, the KEV special representative at Gorna Dzhumaia, reported receiving 592 Jews from Drama, including 2 late arrivals.

c. Local reports list 863 Jews from 264 families deported from Giumiurdzhina.

d. For Kavala, Ionchev lists 1,477 Jews from 381 families, to which should be added 24 Jews (not grouped according to family) deported after March 24, for a total of 1,501 Jews.

e. For Pravishte, Ionchev's report lists 5 Jews from 1 family.

f. For Tasos, Ionchev lists 16 Jews from 3 families.

g. According to the local report, this includes a woman from Kavala who was visiting Ksanti.

h. This total of 4,058 is less than the actual number because of persons not recorded in the commissariat records (see below, p. 127). Local reports total 4,049 Jews from at least 1,079 families. The various German totals of 4,219 or 4,221 include Pirot.

TABLE 5

STATISTICS CONCERNING DEPORTATIONS FROM THRACE

City	Jews Living in Eastern Thrace		Jews Deported		Jews Not Deported	
	Persons	Families	Persons	Families	Persons	Families
Dede Agach	44	12a	42	12	2	—
Drama	592	154	589b	153	3	1
Giumiurdzhina	904	271	878	264c	26	7
Kavala	1,657	485	1,484	393c	173	92
Ksanti	537	144d	526	144	11	—
Pravishte	19	5a	19	5c	0	—
Samothrace	3e	—	3e	—	0	—
Sarzh-Shaban	11	4	12	5f	0h	—
Seres	471	111g	471	111	0	—
Tasos	16	5a	16	5c	0	—
Ziliahovo	19	5	18	5	1	—
Total	4,273	1,196	4,058	1,097	216	100i

SOURCE: These figures come from table 4, above, and from KEV report, March 1943, pp. 6-8, Arditi collection.

a. Local reports indicate that only 42 Jews (12 families) lived in Dede Agach, 5 (1 family) in Pravishte, and 16 (3 families) in Tasos.

b. Ivan Tepavski at G. Dzhumaia reported receiving 592 Jews from Drama.

c. The local reports listed 863 Jews (262 families) deported from Giumiurdzhina, 1,501 (381) from Kavala, including 24 not listed by family, 5 (1) or all from Pravishte, and 16 (3) or all from Tasos.

d. Grinberg's recopying of Dzhamidzhiev's report lists 536 people living in Ksanti before the action. However, this is apparently a misprint or a mistake in the original, as the report also specifically lists 525 Jews deported and 12 not deported.

e. The KEV report does not list these Jews, and the local report does not give a figure for the number of families.

f. In the KEV report, from which the population and deportation figures are taken, there is no explanation for the discrepancy. Both the report and reports from Sarzh-Shaban agree, however, that 12 Jews (5 families) were deported.

g. This is the figure in the KEV report and Kolibarov's reports on the action. Vasilev in his letter to Kalitsin, March 2, however, recorded 476 inhabitants.

h. This figure is presumed.

i. These figures are not the actual difference between the total number of Jews in Thrace and the number of those deported because of the discrepancy in the figures from Sarzh-Shaban. Furthermore, about 60 deportees, not recorded in the KEV records, must be deducted.

The Jews in Thrace were not permitted to be Bulgarian citizens by the regulations of the 1940 Law of Citizenship, the ZZN, and the cabinet decrees regarding the recently liberated territories. Most of them

Arditi, *Yehudi Bulgariyah bishanah hamishpat hanatzi: 1940-1944* [The Jews of Bulgaria during the years of Nazi occupation: 1940-1944] (Tel Aviv: Israel Press, 1962), p. 141, quoting KEV report, March 1943, p. 11. This section of the report was not available to me (see bibliographical note on sources).

held Greek citizenship. As the threat of war and nazism reached into the Balkans, many families gained or reclaimed Spanish citizenship, basing their claims on Sephardic ancestry. The Italians even more freely granted citizenship to Jews in this area. Indeed, some Thracian and Macedonian Jews left for Italian territory and escaped the German-Bulgarian action. The Italian motives seem to stem more from humane origin than from any possible political motivation caused by the conflict with Bulgaria in this region. Roman Catholic clerics in the Balkans apparently played a major role in obtaining citizenship papers for Jews. Also many priests and diplomats protested the fate of the Jews in Bulgarian-occupied territory. The Roman Catholic Bishop at Skopje, Stiliian Tschekoda, protested the deportation of thirty-one Jews converted between 1941 and 1943. The police chief, Bogdanov, refused to intervene, and the bishop then insisted on visiting the camp. The Italian consul at Skopje; the Spanish ambassador at Sofia, Sr. Julio Palencia; and other ministers protested on behalf of their citizenry.[6]

According to local reports, one Jew from Seres who survived missed deportation because of illness. In Ksanti seven Jews were in labor camps, three had gone to Giumiurdzhina before the action, and two were under arrest. (Thus twelve Ksanti Jews were not deported in the action; however, since one Kavala woman accompanied the Ksanti Jews, the commissariat's total deportees from the city is five hundred twenty-six—a difference of eleven from the total Jewish population.) In Giumiurdzhina the commissariat reported that twenty-one Jews (six families) were foreigners. In addition, the local account listed one Jew in prison whom the authorities did not send, a family of four who had asked for asylum in the Turkish consulate, and two individuals who worked in labor groups. At the time of the account, the KEV had ordered one of the Jews in the latter category to a departure center, and presumably the other followed, for the Jews not deported from Giumiurdzhina amounted to twenty-six. As for the Jews in the consulate, Ivan Dobrevski wrote that diplomatic measures must be taken to release them. Their fate is not recorded. The local report, however, notes only eight hundred sixty-three Jews deported while the commissariat's report had eight hundred seventy-eight—perhaps including Jews deported after the local report was filed. For Drama the local report indicates

6. Hoffmann, report, April 15, 1943, T120, serial 2330, roll 1305, frames 486316-21; also Artur Witte, general consul, Skopje, draft of report, May 18, 1943, ibid., frames 486309-13; Pedro Ortiz-Armengol, counselor at the Spanish embassy, to author, Washington, D.C., April 18, 1968.

that one Jew remained because he had been mobilized as a druggist; the account does not indicate whether or not he was a Bulgarian citizen. No reason is given to explain why the remaining Jews were not included in the action from Dede Agach (the local report indicates that only forty-two Jews—the number deported—lived there before the action, not forty-four, as in the commissariat's figure) and from Kavala, where the bulk of Jews not deported resided.[7]

Many foreign citizens were rounded up in the Bulgarian action in Thrace and later released. Jews of Bulgarian citizenship, mobilized in Thrace, were also arrested, but the authorities released them after the events of March 9. Some Jewish men from Thrace were conscripted to work in the labor gangs preparing roads and railroads in southwest Bulgaria. Belev sent letters to Lt. Col. Iliev Rogozarov, head of the labor service, inquiring about these Jews. On February 27 Ionchev sent a letter to Kalitsin informing him of Kavala Jews working on a railroad bed in Bulgaria. The only available list of Jews in the work gangs is in a KEV letter sent to the minister of public works asking that six Ksanti Jews be turned over to the district governor at Sveti Vrach for transfer to Gorna Dzhumaia.[8] Belev sent these laborers and some other Jews (including laborers from elsewhere) who arrived late at Gorna Dzhumaia to Skopje to be deported with the Macedonians. Grinberg writes that they numbered forty-two. There were other Thracian Jews working in Bulgarian labor camps whom the KEV arrested too late to include in any action and who hence survived.[9]

Belev ordered his men in Thrace as elsewhere to ask the civic leaders in the various cities to send messages of gratitude to the KEV and the government for deporting the Jews. Although written under this pressure, the messages were not necessarily insincere. On the other hand, even though the content and tone indicate hearty approval, the senders would not necessarily have been anti-Semites in normal times. Chau-

7. Belev to Rogozarov, March 13, 1943, Grinberg, *Dokumenti*, p. 122; Ionchev to Kalitsin, February 27, 1943, p. 123; Ts. Donchev, KEV clerk, to Ministry of Buildings, Roads, and Public Works, Division of Temporary Labor Service, March 22, 1943, pp. 123-24.

8. Ibid., p. 124. There is no indication whether all or only some of these Jews were included in the final report drawn up by the KEV.

9. Kolibarov, Ziliahovo, to Kalitsin, March 9, 1943, ibid., p. 73; Dzhamdzhiev, Ksanti, report, March 8, 1943, pp. 85-87; Donchev to Ministry of Public Works, March 22, 1943, pp. 123-24; Dobrevski, Giumiurdzhina, to Belev, March 22, 1943, pp. 76-80; Gruev, Drama, report (no date), p. 69; report (unsigned), Dede Agach, March 7, 1943, p. 83; Ionchev to Belev, March 26, 1943, pp. 92–96-II (see also Grinberg's text, p. 124; KEV, report, March 1943, p. 8, Arditi collection.

vinists and civil servants, especially in a contested area like Thrace, are ready to support their government even in the most unwise or immoral ventures. Many of these civic leaders were anti-Semites because the government's policy was anti-Semitic.[10]

According to the reports of the KEV's agents, they accomplished the Thracian operation very efficiently. It did, in fact, proceed as planned without any significant deviations. However, the agents' reports do not show the tragedies and hardships that occurred along the way. The Jews were evicted from their homes without adequate warning; placed in camps without sufficient food, water, toilet facilities, and medical service; and subjected to delousing operations and humiliating searches, which caused loss and damage to the little property the police allowed them to bring with them. The long journey in open cars through Thrace was difficult. Many fell ill, and a few died. Some women gave birth. Observers who were not part of the commissariat's network reported unbelievable misery: cries of fear and despair among the expellees, including the lame and sick, children, the aged, and pregnant women; as well as harsh and sometimes brutal treatment, both physical and psychological, by the guards and officials. On the other hand, occasionally an official pressed into service against his will, perhaps feeling the KEV's unfairness himself, treated the Jews decently.[11]

10. Popov to Kiustendil, Dupnitsa, and Gorna Dzhumaia district governors, March 8, 1943, Grinberg, *Dokumenti*, p. 96-VI. This is one of the extant KEV instructions on the subject of appreciative letters. Grinberg also relates a statement by Dobrevski in which the agent said that Kalitsin and Belev ordered him by telephone to arrange these messages, p. 96-IV. There are several examples of these messages on pp. 96-III–96-IV, including these among others: Liuben St. Tsekov, president of the Drama trade association, and Kiril Todorov, secretary, to Filov, March 8, 1943, pp. 96-III–96-IV; Babalekov, president of the Drama workingman's association, and Secretary Benev to Filov, March 8, 1943, p. 96-IV; Zapro Rupelski, president of the Macedonian Adrianople volunteers in Seres, to Gabrovski, March 8, 1943, p. 96-IV; Antonov, president of soldiers' association in Giumiurdzhina, to Belev, March 8, 1943, p. 96-IV; Necho Deianov, president of the Organization of Cavaliers of the Order of Bravery, to Belev (no date), p. 96-V; Shtipliev, mayor of Ksanti, to Gabrovski, March 6, 1943, p. 96-V; Georgi Uzanov, president of the accounting college in Kavala, to Filov (no date), pp. 96-V–96-VI.

11. For unfriendly accounts of the deportations by observers not attached to the KEV see Dr. Bentsion Solomon Kadmon, former manager of the community apothecary in Giumiurdzhina, statement (no date), ibid., pp. 80-81; Dr. Marko Avram Perets (from Sofia, but mobilized in Sarzh-Shaban), statement (no date), pp. 88-89; Boris Georgiev Bozukov, criminal investigator in Kavala, statement (no date), pp. 96-II–96-III (as a local official Bozukov with others was pressed into service by the KEV); also the following testimonies from Sofia, Protocols of People's Court No. 7: III, 872-73 (testimony of Todor Benov, official of Bulgarian National Bank in Ksanti); III, 883-85 (testimony of Petur Nedelchev Radev, mobilized civil-

At Demir-Hisar and Simitli, where the track gauge changed, the Jews had to transfer trains. KEV officials tried to accomplish the transfer as swiftly as possible to keep both trains and rails free. Since this was also a "rest" station for the thousands of Jews coming through and because the standing time at the station was very long, disorders arose frequently among the travelers, and the officials mistreated them. Jews arrived at Demir-Hisar four or more hours before departure. Invalids on stretchers and women ready for childbirth passed through the terminal, but Atanas I. Ovcharov, the KEV supervisor, held no one back. When the Thracian operations were concluded, Ovcharov, Ivan Popov at Simitli, and Kalitsin, oblivious to the suffering, expressed satisfaction with them.[12]

The Bulgarian Red Cross assigned about thirty Jewish nurses from Sofia to various parts of the country where the KEV planned deportations. Three came to Demir-Hisar and one to Simitli. When they arrived at the stations, the KEV officials humiliated and verbally abused them. Ovcharov ordered their baggage searched for letters, parcels, and money they might be carrying for the deportees. At Simitli Ivan Popov asked Nora Levi, the nurse there, why she did not wear a Jewish star. (The Red Cross chief in Sofia had forbidden the nurses to wear any emblems on their uniforms besides that of the organization.) In contrast, Ovcharov explicitly prohibited his nurses from wearing stars when the Jews arrived in order to avoid trouble among the deportees. With the arrival of the Jews, Ovacharov tried to limit contact between the nurses and the expellees as much as possible, allowing the former to perform only the routine duty of distributing hot water.

---

ian, Dede Agach); III, 885-86 (testimony of Harizan Iordan Harizanov, official of BNB in Drama; Harizanov did not participate in the action but witnessed the trains carrying the Jews while returning to Thrace from Sofia); III, 886-92 (testimony of Dr. Nisim K'oso, member of the Drama health service, a Bulgarian Jew who traveled with the Drama Jews to Gorna Dzhumaia); III, 1030-32 (testimony of Zlato Hristo Atanasov, cashier of the BNB in Seres); III, 1099-1101 (testimony of Kemal Tansier Rakov, from Sofia mobilized in Sarzh-Shaban); IV, 1378-82 (testimony of Petko Lalovski, district attorney in Giumiurdzhina); IV, 1395-1402 (testimony of Iordan Rainov, mayor of Giumiurdzhina and a secret member of the BKP). There are many other similar testimonies in the protocols. Karl David Gaten'o, a KEV official assigned to action in Kavala and Drama, also gave an unfavorable account of the operation at the 1945 trial (IV, 1314-18). For official commissariat versions of the action, see reports listed in note 1 above.

12. Ovcharov, report, March 12, 1943, Grinberg, *Dokumenti*, pp. 96-VI–98 (Ovcharov also wrote daily reports which are not reprinted in Grinberg except for a few minor excerpts [p. 96-VI], revealing the brutality of the guards toward the Jews); Popov, report (review of Thrace, March 25 to April 6, 1943) (no date), pp. 103-04; Kalitsin, report (no date), p. 104.

He refused all special requests (for aspirins, etc.). H. Atanasov, the Red Cross chief at Demir-Hisar, testified later that Ovcharov forbade him to give out aspirin or quinine except in extreme cases.[13]

The first stations on the Thracian Jews' journey to Poland were the departure centers in southwest Bulgaria—Gorna Dzhumaia and Dupnitsa. In all, over 2,500 Jews actually went to the former camp and fewer than 1,500 to the latter. Apparently only the Giumiurdzhina and Ksanti Jews went to Dupnitsa, and the KEV ordered the entire remainder to Gorna Dzhumaia.[14]

In Gorna Dzhumaia the commissariat confined the deportees in three different places. Most Jews were held in the Rainov tobacco warehouse and the School of Economics; but some stayed in the progymnasium. The Jews had to walk over a mile from the station to the camps. These camps received five tons of flour from the local Commissariat of Supply and rented three ovens for the baking of bread. The Jews at Gorna Dzhumaia received about five ounces of bread a day. Ivan Tepavski, a KEV deputy chief of service and the camp's commandant, also bought onions, beans, rice, etc., in smaller quantities to prepare hot food (bean soup) for the Jews. The camp commander purchased dried goat's meat and mutton for use on the trip north. Observers unfriendly to the commissariat described the fare as meager and of poor quality. Dr. Iosif Konfino, who worked in the camp, in his statement for the Peoples' Court suggested that the camp administrators stretched soup for one meal for use at two and stole what they saved from the food budget.

Medical services in the camp were performed by six Jewish doctors. Most of the Jews had some sort of illness, if only a cold, so that as elsewhere medical supplies and services were insufficient. Although

13. For events at Demir-Hisar and Simitli see text and documents in Grinberg, *Dokumenti*, pp. 96-VI–103, including Ovcharov, March 12, 1943, report, pp. 96-VI–98; Rosa Mois Iakova (nurse at Demir-Hisar), statement (no date), pp. 98-99; Dr. Marko Avram Perets, statement (no date), 100-02; Dr. Iosif Konfino, statement (no date), pp. 102-03. These statements of survivors are presumably from depositions filed for the People's Court. See also Sofia, Protocols of People's Court No. 7, III, 788-93 (testimony of Dr. Iosif Konfino); III, 886-92 (testimony of Dr. Nisim K'oso); III, 892-94 (testimony of Hristo Mihailov Atanasov, official of the Bulgarian Red Cross at Demir-Hisar); IV, 1288-92 (testimony of Dr. Buko Isakov, who traveled with the Jews). A copy of Miss Levi's statement is in Bulgarian Academy of Sciences, Institute for Balkan Studies, Section for Hebrew Studies archives, doc. no. 367 (hereafter cited as BAN, Ebroistika).

14. Ivan Tepavski, camp commandant, report, March 7, 1943, Grinberg, *Dokumenti*, pp. 108-09; unsigned report "Vlakovete" [Trains] (no date), pp. 111-12.

Tepavski reported no serious illness, Dr. Iosif Konfino, one of the camp physicians, said that the officials did not isolate some of the children suffering from whooping cough and other contagious diseases. At the School of Economics there was only one water faucet for use by 1,500 people and at the warehouse only one for the 1,000 there. The Jews had no soap, since the search committees had confiscated this upon their entrance into the camps. The camps had one toilet per 300 to 500 people, and the areas around some of these facilities were impossible to clean because of poor drainage. Kalitsin, inspecting the departure center, ordered the Jews to rearrange their cramped quarters so as to allocate space more efficiently. Konfino stated that during the trip from Simitli to Gorna Dzhumaia someone died from hunger or exposure in almost every train. In the camp there were from one to three deaths daily.

At the departure centers the authorities revised the story of resettlement in the interior of Bulgaria. Now they said rather that the government had made arrangements with the British to send the Jews to Palestine and that they were to leave the camps for ports on the Adriatic and Black Seas. Dr. Nisim K'oso testified that the Jews did not believe it.[15]

At Dupnitsa, Asen V. Paitashev represented Belev, but the camp commandant was the local police chief. On Belev's order Paitashev prepared the camp in one of the tobacco warehouses in the city, adapting parts of the warehouse for use as kitchen, infirmary, washrooms, and toilets. The Dupnitsa garrison provided a five-man sentry for the camp, but local police handled the major portion of camp security. The city's chief of public health with the aid of Jewish doctors in the camp provided medical service.

The first Jews (those from Giumiurdzhina) straggled into the camp on the evening of the seventh. Paitashev later wrote Belev that it was obvious that these Jews, poorly dressed, some in tatters, were extremely poor. He reported no incidents on the march from the station to the camp, but residents of the town were very curious to know who these people were and where they were going. According to observers and witnesses not connected with the KEV, living conditions and provisions were as poor in this camp as they were at Gorna Dzhumaia.

Some Bulgarians and civil servants in Dupnitsa asked Paitashev to imprison the Jews from the town in the camp as well. The representative wrote the commissar that these people felt that the Jews were causing the scarcity of goods and inflated prices. Paitashev ordered the Jews of the city to collect provisions for the camp. The leaders of the community later reported that they gathered ten wagonloads of supplies, but that the authorities did not allow them to enter the camp to see to their final distribution. According to a survivor of the camp, Dr. Marko A. Perets, very little reached the Jews; instead, the guards and administrators used the provisions themselves.

The Jews within the camp submitted to two separate searches. Perets recalled that at the first search the authorities collected about 50,000 leva ($607) from the little remaining to the Jews, but he had no knowledge of the results of the second. A Dupnitsa doctor who was called into the camp, gave up 20,000 leva ($243) which he never regained. (Paitashev told him that he had spent the money for provisions for the camp.)

In fifteen days at the camp five died. Paitashev allowed the dead to be buried in the Jewish cemetery in the town. This was the only contact (aside from that of the doctors) permitted between the Jews in the camp and those of the town.[16]

After the deportations from Thrace the KEV liquidated the movable property of the deportees. As in all of Bulgaria, the commissariat already controlled Jewish-owned real estate. The liquidators deposited money realized from the sale of Jewish property in the frozen accounts of the owners, if known; otherwise, they transferred the money into the Jewish community fund. Since the government confiscated the accounts of Jews "leaving" Bulgaria in any case, this distinction was a matter of little consequence to the deportees. Nevertheless, the KEV preferred to have the money in the fund, which they could use more freely, rather than in frozen accounts. Thus Belev asked commissariat delegates in Thrace to store items in such a fashion as to prevent their identification as belongings of specific individuals. The delegates did this, under the pretext of accomplishing the liquidation as quickly as possible, by eliminating the time needed for careful registration by

16. For information on the Dupnitsa camp see Grinberg, *Dokumenti*, pp. 105-08, including Paitashev to Belev, March 20, 1943, pp. 105-06; Dr. Marko Avram Perets, statement (no date), pp. 106-07; and Jewish Committee of the Fatherland Front (Dupnitsa), October 13, 1944, statement, pp. 107-08. Dr. Nisim Chelebi Bentsion, February 15, 1945, statement; and Sotir Dimitrov Katsarov, statement (no date), in BAN, Ebroistika, doc. no. 367.

owner and the recording of items by type. In this manner, most of the money realized from the liquidations went to the Jewish community fund. In some cities virtually all of it did so. Only in Kavala did the liquidators make any systematic attempt to designate owners. Here the committee placed items in boxes with an identifying inventory. In other cities the authorities piled the Jewish property in warehouses without regard to order. Officials also haphazardly stored valuables confiscated at the temporary camps in Thrace, again with the exception of Kavala, where the police commandant took care to arrange things properly. Nonetheless, the Kavala liquidation committee still committed some of the worst looting.

Reports of the commissariat mentioned some cases of looting, especially in Giumiurdzhina and Kavala, but these the commissariat claimed were minor, and most of the items were recovered. The KEV ignored the wholesale looting and dubious sales and distribution of goods by government and commissariat officials themselves. The liquidations took place in two stages. First, the government agencies and designated bureaus had the right to buy things at minimum prices or to procure such items as footstuffs gratis. Then the KEV sold the remainder at public auction to Bulgarian citizens. Dr. Popov reported that the German-Bulgarian trade society, a private organization claiming to be a public institution, had obtained some furniture at the first sale, but that he had made them return these items. However, despite occasional maintenance of strict order, direct and indirect forms of graft marked the whole Thracian liquidation activity. Officials of such government agencies as the military and police took items or bought them at a minimum, to be given or sold to friends and relatives, or to be sold to merchants and secondhand dealers for a personal profit. Even items destined to be sold at public auctions—furniture, bedding, clothes, crystal, silverware, etc.—the liquidators sold to friends, often at prices only fractions of the minimum value. By complicated procedures involving middlemen, some of these things found their way back to the commissariat officials charged with selling them. The most common practice in these cases was to move the goods out of Thrace to the officials' homes in the interior. Officials sold many items to local merchants at a low price in return for a rebate. Others took goods from the warehouses against falsified receipts without sale. Persons from all groups connected with the sales took part in this looting: policemen, judges, KEV officials, laborers, government employees on the liquidation committees, etc. The conspiracy was so thick that when Mayor

Rainov of Giumiurdzhina, the delegate of the KEV, tried to expose the looting carried on by the KEV's special representative Ivan Dobrevski, the chief of police, and the assistant mayor among others, he was unable to bring prosecution proceedings because the president of the district court was also involved. The police chief replaced Rainov as delegate. Later when the evidence became too great to hide, Belev arranged the transfer of some of those involved elsewhere. It is possible that the regional governor for Thrace also participated in the lootings.[17]

In all, the Jewish community fund realized 6,163,978 leva from Giumiurdzhina, 4,162,272 from Drama, 5,803,380 from Kavala, 2,528,175 from Seres, and 1,978,079 from Ksanti, for the total of 20,635,884 leva ($257,000).[18]

Pirot

Nowhere did the KEV so harshly carry out deportations as in the area of Pirot—the small section of eastern Serbia, about 40 miles northwest of Sofia, transferred to Bulgaria in 1941. The technique of the operation was similar to that in Thrace. On March 11 Miss Panitsa telephoned Hristo Bakurdzhiev, who directed the local operation, and told him to begin. On the next day, police patrols, using prepared lists, roused the Jews from their homes; ordered them to gather up their valuables; gave them less than half an hour to pack their baggage; and

17. Dr. Ivan Popov, reports, "Po otnoshenie subirane divizhimostite na evreite i tehnoto suhranenie" and "Po otnoshenie podgotovkata i prodazhbata na veshtite" [In regard to the treatment of gathering the movable property of the Jews and their maintenance] and [In regard to the treatment of the preparation and the sale of personal effects] (no date), Grinberg, *Dokumenti*, pp. 125-29; Klechkov, governor of Thrace, to mayors and KEV delegates in Thrace, April 7, 1943, p. 125; Boris Iv. Indzhiev, inspector at KEV, report (no date), pp. 129-30; Kadmon, excerpt of report (no date), pp. 130-34; unsigned letter sent to the regional prosecutor in Drama, October 7, 1943, pp. 134-37 (this concerns looting by officials in Kavala). Grinberg writes (p. 125) that the KEV archives contained many receipts and transaction papers dealing with the confiscated items—too numerous to reprint in his book. For other documents dealing with confiscations, see Sofia, Bulgarian Jewish Organization Archives, copies of CDIA documents, vol. IV. See also Sofia, Protocols of People's Court No. 7, IV, 1378-82 (testimony of Petko Lalovski).

18. KEV order no. 865, March 13, 1943, cited in Grinberg, *Dokumenti*, p. 124; Svetoslav Petrov Nikolaev, inspector at KEV, excerpt from report (no date), p. 124; Popov, reports, "Po otnoshenie subirane" and "Po otnoshenie podgotovkata," pp. 125-29. See also Grinberg's text, p. 125. He gives no figures for percentage or amount deposited in frozen accounts. There is also no account of the fate of the property of Dede Agach Jews and those of the minor communities, as to whether they are included with the larger communities near them or are simply not considered in the total given.

sealed their houses. Following the sealing, the patrols marched the Jews to the Pirot gymnasium and interned them there until time for the actual deportation.

A group of three policemen and two officials of the district government acting under a search committee led by Bakurdzhiev himself thoroughly searched men, women, and children, forcing them to strip completely. Even those few decencies observed in the operation in Thrace were absent in Pirot. Not only did the searchers take valuables, but they systematically looted the luggage of the Jews.

The operation included all Jews in the city, even those with Bulgarian citizenship whom the government had mobilized and sent there from Bulgaria. Bakurdzhiev reported that they rounded up 188 persons, including a woman from Bitola, Macedonia. Several families escaped for the time being. One student hid in a small village near Pirot for several days, but in the end he returned to the city and joined his family in the gymnasium. The Jews interned included 27 with Bulgarian citizenship whom the KEV did not deport. Commissariat records indicate that 186 non-Bulgarian Jews (52 families) lived in Pirot and that 185 (52 families) were eventually deported. There is no documentary explanation as to what happened to the other person. At the time of deportation on March 19, 158 Jews left Pirot for Sofia to join the trains from the deportation centers in southwest Bulgaria (see below, p. 118). Again the documents do not explain the discrepancy between the number of Jews deported on March 19 and the number that one would expect, 161 (188 interned less 27 with Bulgarian citizenship). Bakurdzhiev reported that after the deportation, police discovered 5 Jews hiding on the road to Skopje and these left with the Macedonian Jews, but it seems unlikely that they were from the group interned. The authorities did not consider any Jews too ill to travel, and they did not report any deaths either at the gymnasium or the local hospital, where 4 old Jews were sent to await deportation; but death is the most likely explanation.

At the gymnasium the Jews voluntarily surrendered about 390,000 leva ($4,500). After this the search committee uncovered an additional 20,000 leva and some gold (coins, plate, etc.) which they deposited in the Bulgarian National Bank in Belev's name rather than in the accounts of the owners.

The Jews remained in the gymnasium for a week until the departure date. Conditions were inadequate: food was meager and toilet facilities exceptionally bad. One inmate reported that the salon of the gymnasium had only one small container for all inmates. There was "almost a deluge of urine in the hall."[19] The police isolated the Jews from the citizens of Pirot, but some of the latter managed to smuggle in packages of food to their friends and neighbors. The Pirot police served as the guard in the gymnasium as well as for the transport to Sofia, which took place on March 19.

The officials of the operation treated the inmates with great cruelty. Witnesses at the trial of KEV officials in 1945 accused Georgi Popov, the district governor and regular commissariat delegate, and Push-karov, the police chief, of rape. Pushkarov threatened to kill one wo-man's children and give her to the guard barracks unless she submitted to him. The guards frequently beat the prisoners severely. The officials attempted to force bribes from the Jews. Witnesses claimed that the money registered at the search was much less than that actually taken. Popov permitted one wealthy man to leave the gymnasium in order to raise money to bribe his way to freedom and permission to travel to Istanbul. The documents do not indicate if he gained his freedom. Per-haps he accounts for the discrepancy of one in the commissariat's rec-ords of the deportations. Bulgarian citizens, who remained incarcerated for several days after the deportations, had to sign false statements say-ing that the authorities took nothing from them.

The leading officials of the Pirot region also participated in the sys-tematic looting of Jewish homes. Not only did Pushkarov deliberately sabotage the public auctions by hiring a crowd to disrupt orderly auc-tion proceedings, but the authorities also engaged in outright theft. Bakurdzhiev tried to account for some of the loss by declaring that the military in the Pirot garrison had misunderstood the commissariat's de-cision allowing them to buy Jewish items at cost and had demanded the goods gratis. Many Jewish survivors testified that they saw Pirot officials carrying off their possessions. The members of the government occu-pied the finer Jewish homes, and the town's officials accused each other of wholesale looting. Belev sent two high KEV officials, G'oshev and Lukov, into Pirot to investigate the irregularities, and later the govern-ment conducted an inquiry; but apparently they thought the evidence insufficient to warrant bringing proceedings against the Pirot officials. During the investigation the police threatened and bullied the Jews to keep them quiet. Money realized from the sale of Jewish property amounted to 3,571,645 leva ($43,300), of which the liquidators gave 1,127,025 leva ($13,700) to the Jewish community fund and deposited the remainder in the frozen accounts.

19. Leon Nisim Shalom, statement (no date), Grinberg, *Dokumenti*, p. 150.

In September of 1943 the government sent the remaining Jews in Pirot (Bulgarian citizens) into the interior of the country. The property which they had been able to retain in March they lost at that time.[20]

From the Departure Centers to Poland

Responsibility for the transfer of the Jews from the departure centers to areas under German authority belonged primarily to the Bulgarian State Railway and the KEV. On February 22, the day that the Dannecker-Belev agreement was signed, the KEV informed the railroad of the impending action. The commissariat and the railroad worked out the details together.[21]

The transport of the Thracian Jews to Lom required two trains. The BDZh scheduled the first to leave on the morning of March 18 with about 2,000 from Gorna Dzhumaia, stopping at Sofia for an hour and a half and reaching Lom at 3:38 a.m. on the nineteenth. The second train with 600 Jews would leave Gorna Dzhumaia on the nineteenth following a similar schedule, but gathering Jews at Dupnitsa (1,500) and others from Pirot (200) at Sofia, and arriving at Lom on March 20.

Ticketing and scheduling arrangements were drafted by Dr. Iosif Petkov, economic director of the railroad; Nikov of the economic office of the railroad; and "the girl who worked in Nikov's office"—not further identified. All three could answer inquiries about the arrangements. The passengers from Gorna Dzhumaia, Dupnitsa, and Pirot traveled to Sofia without tickets. At Sofia the railway representative ascertained how many persons on each train were in groups under four years of age (having the right to travel free), between four and ten (being able to travel at half fare), and over ten (requiring adult fare), but billed all for laborers' tickets—one-half regular fare. The Jews traveled from Sofia to Lom with one group ticket issued in the names of the leaders of the group who were assigned by the director of police or the chief

20. Ibid., pp. 138-51, including Bakurdzhiev, report (no date), pp. 139-42; Stefan Nikolov Stamenov, chief of taxing authority in Pirot, statement (no date), pp. 142-47; Aleksandur N. Sokolov, director of the Bulgarian National Bank in Pirot, statement (no date), p. 147; Iosif Levi, Bulgarian citizen, statement (no date), pp. 147-50; and Leon Nisim Shalom, student and Bulgarian citizen, statement (no date), p. 150; KEV, report, March 1943, pp. 6-7, Arditi collection; Sofia, Protocols of People's Court No. 7 (testimonies of Bulgarian citizens Mois Haim Eshua, III, 896-99; Isak Levi, III, 899-901; and Sami Meranda, III, 901-08).

21. Commissariat for Jewish Questions to Bulgarian State Railway, February 22, 1943, Grinberg, Dokumenti, pp. 110-11.

of uniformed police. From Lom the Jews traveled through Vienna to Katowicz in Poland under the responsibility of Dannecker, and later the Germans notified the commissariat of the cost of this part of the journey. (The Bulgarians were responsible for fares.) Before boarding the Danube barges which took them to Vienna, the Jews waited in the trains. The KEV also reimbursed the BDZh for this cost. Officials of the railway arranged with the KEV for locations where the trains could wait at the Sofia and Lom stations. At the second stop, Lom, the Jews had to wait several days.

The Bulgarian police served as guards on the trains not only through Bulgaria in conjunction with the Germans, but also up to Katowicz. Guard groups on the trains consisted of a police chief, two senior officers, and forty ordinary officers. Other guards served as security officers for the Thracian and Pirot Jews. (The local Pirot police guarded trains bringing Jews from that city to Sofia.) The KEV scheduled the departure from Lom on four barges March 20 to 22, and arranged for guard groups of fourteen to thirty-two to accompany them—altogether two full groups, or eighty-six men.[22]

On the March 18 train from Gorna Dzhumaia there were actually 1,985 Jews (121 under the age of four and 216 more between four and ten). The trains on March 19 carried 692 Jews from Gorna Dzhumaia (47 under four and 59 additional between four and ten); 1,380 from Dupnitsa (75 under four, 175 more between four and ten); and 158 from Pirot (4 under four, 12 between four and ten). The Thracian group leaving the departure centers, not considering those on the Pirot train, had 4,057 Jews (681 of these were children ten or under). During their fortnight's journey from Thrace some late arrivals and a few newborn children had been added to the original group (which numbered 4,058 according to KEV reports) but a number of Jews had died.

Kalitsin reported that the trip to Lom proceeded in proper order. Red Cross officials met the trains at Sofia and Lom, and at Sofia distributed 300 quarts of tea, 40 quarts of milk to children and the ill, and water for use on the trains. Kalitsin wrote that the Red Cross personnel gave their services conscientiously, providing sufficient medication, e.g., aspirin, to Jews as needed. The Jews had food for fifteen days— bread, marmalade, sugar, pressed meat, and cheese.[23]

There exists another account of this fateful trip which contradicts Kalitsin's favorable version of the Jews' journey to "resettlement in the

22. KEV-BDZh agreement (no date) ibid., pp. 112-16.
23. Kalitsin, report (no date), ibid., p. 116.

East." Mrs. Nadeia Vasileva was a nurse who had grown up near the Jewish quarter of Lom. The trains arrived in Lom on March 19 and 20; the barges left on March 20 and 21. Mrs. Vasileva learned of the Jews' presence at the station while at a friend's near the depot where she could hear the Jews in the cars screaming for water in Bulgarian, Greek, and Ladino. She filled a bucket with water and went to the trains, but the armed guard (local Lom police) ordered her to halt. Lom is a small city of a few thousand and Mrs. Vasileva knew the guards. With both threats and pleading they ordered her to stay back, but her determination weakened their resolve and she began to distribute water to the Jews. A large crowd of Jews, Bulgarians, Gypsies, and Turks gathered; and shortly a detachment of German and Bulgarian guards arrived, led by Slavi Puntev, Belev's cousin who was the KEV. delegate at Lom and also served as chief of the Red Cross in the city.

He yelled at Mrs. Vasileva, "Who asked you to do these crazy things? Go back! I am going to have you arrested!"

Her account follows:

Then he said to the policeman, "Disperse the crowd; arrest all Jews; arrest this woman also!" He turned toward me and asked, "Don't you know who I am?"

"I know that you are Slavi Puntev and you are the President of the Merchants' Association and of the Red Cross. Don't you know me? I am a nurse and I am doing my duty."

"Who asked you? Who gave you permission?"

"I didn't ask permission from anybody—nobody asked me to do anything. On the contrary, the policemen were going to shoot me, but their hearts are not of stone and they let me give water to these poor wretches."

"You go back home before it is too late." All were looking. Suddenly he told them, "She is crazy."

The police dispersed the crowd and sent Mrs. Vasileva away. A bit later, however, she returned. This time the guard let her through to help distribute items apparently collected by the Red Cross from the Jewish community of Lom—matches, candles, cigarettes, lemons, apples, yogurt, etc. A doctor from the government hospital confided to Mrs. Vasileva that, although the local Jews had prepared all these items, she had better say that they came from the Red Cross. Puntev examined the items for concealed messages and gave his official approval for the distribution to begin. Mrs. Vasileva continues: "I started the distribution with the help of two or three Gypsies, and filled the utensils that were handed through holes or through a narrow window. But the smell was nauseating and the dirt awful. I did not have enough water to wash the utensils."

The guard did not permit Bulgarians, except for a designated few, near the trains, but they allowed local Gypsies to help. Mrs. Vasileva reports that some of the helpers were selling the items, including water, to the Jews. A railroad worker tried to hose down the cars and the personal pans which the deportees had used for defecation and now had to use for drinking, but his task was hopeless. The dried salted goat's meat, which was a staple of their diet, had, along with the extremely crowded conditions, increased the Jews' thirst. A man had died three days before and his body remained in the car. A woman had just given birth and she had no clothes for the infant. Many people had contracted dysentery.[24]

Svetoslav Nikolaev, the chief auditor of the commissariat, also had occasion to find fault with Puntev. The delegate received from the passport bureau over 100,000 leva ($1,210) confiscated from the Jews and another 40,000 leva ($486) confiscated by customs, along with some miscellaneous valuables. On Nikolaev's inquiry later in the year concerning what had happened to the money, Puntev replied that he had deposited it in the BNB. Nikolaev checked the account number which Puntev gave but found no reference to it. Trying to reach the delegate again, the auditor discovered that Puntev had dropped out of sight. Nikolaev learned from an official of the bank that Puntev had tried to make a belated deposit the day before, but the bank had already closed. A customs official reported that Puntev wanted him to falsify the receipts by recording only 40,000 instead of 100,000 leva confiscated. Nikolaev ordered Puntev's arrest. The delegate had destroyed the docu-

---

24. Nadeja [*sic*] Slavi Vasileva, "On the Catastrophe of the Thracian Jews: Recollection," *Yad WaShem Studies on the European Catastrophe and Resistance,* 3 (1959), pp. 295-302. A copy of the Bulgarian original is in Paris, Centre de documentation Juive Contemporaine, doc. no. CCCI-23. As he did for the Sofia stopover, Kalitsin described a much happier picture of Lom than did Mrs. Vasileva. See Kalitsin, report, March 24, 1943, Grinberg, *Dokumenti,* pp. 116-17.

Incidentally, although Hitler planned to include Europe's Gypsies in the Final Solution, the Bulgarians made no plans to deport the Bulgarian Gypsies (in number about 80,000 or 1.3 percent of the population according to the 1934 census), nor did the Germans ask Sofia to do this. There were only a few laws and decrees limiting their freedom, for example article 24 of the decree-law of August 26, 1942, prohibiting marriages between Gypsies and Bulgarians and local orders restricting rations for Gypsies more than Bulgarians.

ments with the true figures of the confiscations. However, the inspector knew Puntev's accounts were about 60,000 leva short.

Nikolaev also accused Puntev and his wife of stealing clothes which the Sofia rabbinate had collected for the deported Jews. The Red Cross distributed most of these to the Jews but assigned some left over to the poor and orphans in Lom. The customs officials gave the clothes to Puntev, but the latter told the representative of the Lom welfare association that there was no excess. Mrs. Puntev did give some of the clothes to her favorite charity and also some to her cleaning woman. Puntev himself sold the remainder to peasants and Gypsies.[25]

The first ship, *Kara G'orgi*, left Lom at 2:00 p.m., March 20. The second, *Voivoda Mashil*, left that evening. Two, *Saturnus* and *Tsar Dushan*, left the next evening. Each ship had 875 to 1,100 passengers, and in all 4,219 Jews left. As arranged, a Bulgarian guard went along; and Bulgarian doctors, whom the commissariat had requested from the director of public health, traveled with the Jews as well. Jewish doctors of Bulgarian citizenship did not accompany the ships, for the Germans would not have allowed them to return. Kalitsin reported once again that the departure took place without incident.[26]

According to reports that Grinberg found in the commissariat archives, the four doctors apparently traveled on only the last two ships, *Tsar Dushan* and *Saturnus*. The *Tsar Dushan* was accompanied by a smaller barge on which some deportees traveled in order to ease the burden on the vessel. Although most of the security force was Bulgarian, German guards supervised the operation. The most prevalent illness among the Jews was malaria; but there were cases of bronchial diseases including pneumonia, gastric illness, nervous and arthritic disorders, influenza, and others. Seven died on the *Tsar Dushan* and one on the *Saturnus*. The Germans removed the dead from the ships at ports along the Danube. The journey to Vienna on the *Tsar Dushan* lasted about ten days, and food ran out; but the Germans gave the Jews more at Budapest. (The *Saturnus* reached Vienna after only five days.) The Bulgarian doctors left the convoy at Vienna, from which the Jews traveled on to Katowicz and then Treblinka. The authorities placed Dr. Hristo Mendizov, who traveled with the *Tsar Dushan*, in custody for a

25. Nikolaev, report, November 29, 1943, Grinberg, *Dokumenti*, pp. 117-19; Kalitsin, report, March 24, 1943, pp. 116-17.

26. Kalitsin, report, March 24, 1943, ibid., pp. 116-17. Four thousand two hundred nineteen is four greater than the recorded number of people on the trains (not taking into account births and deaths)—4,057 from Gorna Dzhumaia and Dupnitsa and 158 from Pirot. There is no explanation for the discrepancy.

few hours in Vienna for replying to anti-Semitic remarks which officials made there, but the Germans released him when a physical examination assured them that he was not Jewish.[27]

Macedonia

The last Jews the KEV deported in the Bulgarian operation were those from Macedonia. The action began there a week after that in Thrace and also after the curtailed preparations in the interior. Many Macedonian Jews, therefore, were aware of their impending fate. Before the actual concentration procedure began, over a hundred Jews escaped across the border into Italian-held Albania.[28] In order to prevent further escapes of this nature Sofia reinforced its Albanian border patrol.

As mentioned above, the KEV had originally planned to have two camps in Macedonia, in the largest cities, Skopje and Bitola. Each city had over three thousand Jews, and each, like Ksanti, was the regional center of a Bulgarian administrative *oblast*. However, Bitola had no convenient point in which to establish a departure camp, so the commissariat chose to use only the buildings of the state tobacco monopoly in Skopje. Belev assigned Peiu Draganov Peev, assistant chief of service at the KEV, to the operation in Skopje, working under Zahari Velkov, chief of the entire Macedonian deportation. The commissar himself made several trips into Macedonia, where in fact the largest single Jewish deportation action occurred.

The commissariat population statistics for Jews in Macedonia before the action were as follows:[29]

City	Persons	Families
Bitola oblast		
Bitola community	3,342	813
Skopje oblast		
Shtip community	546	141
Skopje community	3,493	1,079
Total	7,381	2,033

27. Drs. Nikolov and Mihailov, report (no date), ibid., pp. 119-21; Drs. Mendizov and Tsenov (no date), pp. 121-22; Dr. Mendizov, excerpt from report (no date), p. 122; Sofia, Protocols of People's Court No. 7, III, 817-21 (testimony of Dr. Mendizov); *People of Hesse* v. *Von Hahn*, Ks 2/67 (GStA), 236 (1968).

28. Grinberg, *Dokumenti*, p. 81; Aleksandar Matkovsky, "The Destruction of Macedonian Jewry," *Yad WaShem Studies on the European Jewish Catastrophe and Resistance*, 3 (1959), p. 252.

29. KEV, report, March 1943, p. 6, Arditi collection.

Prewar statistics for the Jewish population of Yugoslavia are:[30]

City	Persons	Families
Bitola	3,351	810
Shtip	551	140
Skopje	3,795	1,181
Gevgelija	11	3
Kriva Palanka	5	1
Kumanovo	13	7
Veles	8	2
Elsewhere in Macedonia	28	6
Total	7,762	2,150

Immediately after the invasion of 1941 this figure increased slightly because of emigration from Serbia, but apparently over five hundred Jews left Macedonia between April 1941 and September 1942.

Procedures for rounding up the Jews followed the same general rules established for Thrace and Pirot. The process began March 11. In Bitola and Shtip local police arrested the Jews and then sent them by rail to Skopje.

The harsh life at the tobacco warehouses of Skopje repeated the conditions of the warehouses and schools of Thrace, Pirot, and southwest Bulgaria. Field posts and a cordon of police armed with submachine guns guarded the camp. Inadequate space, food, and toilet facilities, together with the strictness of the regime and brutality on the part of some of the guards, made the few days' wait for ultimate deportation an ordeal for the Macedonian Jews. As in the other areas, the authorities told the Jews that the government was relocating them in the interior of Bulgaria. The Macedonians hardly credited the lie, for the rumors of the fate of Jews across the border were widespread. According to Draganov's figures, 7,215 Jews entered the camp on March 11: 3,351 from Skopje, 3,313 from Bitola, 551 from Shtip [sic]. Twenty-five followed shortly thereafter. The number of inmates included 2,300 under sixteen; 1,100 of these under ten.[31] Aleksandar Matkovsky, who

30. "Elaborat za zlodelata na okupatorite i nivnite pomagateli nad jevrejskoto naselenie vo Makedonija" [Exposition of the crimes of the occupiers and their agents against the Jewish population in Macedonia], April 2, 1946, p. 1, MHI-Yad WaShem, invoice no. 16.378; Matkovsky, "Destruction," pp. 207-08. In the KEV's figures Jews in the villages were included with their consistories—only three in Macedonia.

31. "Elaborat za zlodelata," p. 3, MHI-Yad WaShem; "Nemacki zlocini prema Jevrejima" [German crimes against the Jews], p. 6, ibid., invoice no. 16.490; un-

has written a monograph on the Macedonian deportations, calculates that over 7,300 Jews passed through the Skopje camp altogether, including some whom the authorities later released or who managed to escape.

The Bulgarians released sixty-seven Macedonian physicians and pharmacists with their families because of their great need for men in these professions. They released foreign citizens in the Skopje camp as well—seventy-four Spaniards, nineteen Albanians, and five Italians, twelve of whom the Germans later rearrested.[32] In addition two escaped, so in all one hundred fifty-five Jews who passed through the camp at Skopje escaped the Final Solution. Four Jews died in the camp before deportation. We have seen that some of the Jews in the camp came from Thrace and Pirot (Grinberg gives the number of these as forty-seven). A number of the 7,381 Jewish inhabitants of Macedonia (according to the commissariat's census) did not go through the camp. Most of them had fled to Albania before the operation.

The KEV representative in Skopje, Draganov, had grave difficulties with Bulgarian officials in the area because of maladministration, probably corruption. On March 25 in the midst of the deportations the district governor, Dimitur Raev, fired Draganov and asked Belev to send a replacement. Belev felt that Raev had usurped his authority and sent Paitashev, who was finished in Dupnitsa, as an aide but did not confirm Draganov's dismissal. The latter, however, resigned. Later, at the postwar trials, Draganov blamed his trouble in Macedonia on insufficient and incompetent officials.[33]

The inmates of the Skopje camp left Macedonia for Poland on three transports: March 22, March 25, and March 29. From Skopje the route passed through Nish, Gurlitsa (in Italian-held territory), and Lapovo (occupied by the Reich), crossing Albanian, Serbian, Croatian, Hun-

titled statistical table of March 11 roundup, February 23, 1946, ibid., invoice no. 16.378.

32. "Izveshtaj na Anketnata komisija," p. 7, MHI-Yad WaShem; Aleksandar Matkovsky, *Tragedijata na Evreite od Makedonija* [The tragedy of the Jews of Macedonia] (Skopje: "Kultura," 1962), p. 85; idem., "Destruction," pp. 242-43.

33. Grinberg, *Dokumenti*, pp. 165-66; Sofia, Protocols of People's Court No. 7, III, 1037 (testimony of Todor Lulchev, inspector at commissariat). The latter refers to a statement by Draganov during the testimony in which he said that he was no longer in authority after March 16, but Grinberg (in his text without documents) writes that Draganov did not leave until after the second transport (March 25). Matkovsky, in his article ("Destruction," p. 250), lists Draganov as commandant at the time of the third departure (March 29), but in the Macedonian version he writes (*Tragedijata*, pp. 91-92) that Paitashev replaced Draganov during the third transport.

garian, and German territory into Treblinka in the Generalgouvernement (Poland). The Bulgarian State Railway arranged for transport
along routes which differed slightly station to station, but followed the
same general path. G'oshev of the economic section and Draganov paid
the BDZh for the KEV, and bought the tickets for the Jews from Balkan,
a Bulgarian travel agency. At Lapovo the German guard took over the
train from the Bulgarians. As in the other deportations, the Bulgarian
guard groups—one for each train—consisted of forty-three men; the
German groups had thirty-five.

According to Matkovsky, the first transport carried 2,338 Jews; the
second 2,402; and the third 2,404—total 7,144. Twelve persons died en
route. These figures are from German documents not specified by the
author but in all probability are the most accurate. KEV records conflict. Grinberg lists 2,409 persons (659 families); 2,399 (611); and 2,315
(527), with 42 additional from Thrace on the last transport—7,165
(1,797), including the Thracians not listed by family. Draganov's records, reproduced by Matkovsky, have a third total figure—7,069, which,
however, seems too low. One hundred ninety-six Macedonian Jews
returned to Yugoslavia after the war—116 from Albania, 15 from German POW camps, and 65 survivors from various concentration camps.
Presumably only the last group was among those deported.[34]

After the deportations the KEV liquidated Jewish personal property
in Macedonia through committees in the three cities: Skopje, Bitola,
and Shtip. Government bureaus and organizations and certain private
institutions received permission to buy Jewish property at a minimum
price, and the commissions offered the remainder at public auction.
German authorities and institutions at Skopje took their pick of Jewish
property.

Dr. Ivan Popov, who visited Macedonia in May 1943, was not pleased
with the progress of the liquidations. In Skopje the commissions had

34. Matkovsky, *Tragedijata*, pp. 86-93; "Destruction," pp. 243-52; Grinberg,
Dokumenti, p. 184. German reports in Berlin give 7,240, which is undoubtedly inaccurate. Perhaps it is the number initially interned in the Skopje camp. Police attaché Hoffmann reported that 7,122 Macedonian Jews left Skopje, a figure closer to
the consensus; and this is now the legally accepted figure. Wagner, report, April 3,
1943, T120, serial 2330, roll 1305, frames 486326-30; compare Witte, report, March
18, 1943, ibid., frames 486309-15; and Hoffmann, report, April 5, 1943, ibid., frames
486316-21.
    For Jewish and Bulgarian accounts of life in the camp at Skopje see Matkovsky,
Tragedijata, pp. 72-85, and "Destruction," pp. 231-43; Albert Safarti, survivor,
statement (no date), Grinberg, *Dokumenti*, pp. 160-62; Sofia, Protocols of People's
Court No. 7, III, 1032-42 (testimony of Todor Lulchev).

liquidated property from only 63 of about 600 Jewish homes and in Bitola from 198 of about 400. Besides liquidating too slowly, the commissions, Popov complained, were not realizing sufficient profit from the sale of the property. Popov accused the government offices, entitled to buy supplies before the public auctions, of abusing this privilege. He said that the officials bought not only office needs, but such domestic items as chinaware, kitchen utensils, wardrobes, sewing machines, pianos, general household furniture, and fine cloth. The inventory of items at the storage warehouse was unsystematic and inaccurate. He reported many thefts, and charged the liquidation officials with neglect of duty. He ended his report with a request for a KEV inspector to come to Macedonia to examine further liquidations. The delegate at Bitola, who found the liquidations nerve-racking, requested two.

Popov expected liquidation sales to amount to over 50 million leva ($607,000) in Skopje and 33 million leva ($402,000) in Bitola. In fact, liquidations in Skopje realized only 12,070,960 leva ($146,000) and in Bitola 19,564,486 leva ($238,000). In addition, the liquidators realized 1,477,268 leva ($17,900) for Shtip. In all, liquidations amounted to 33,112,714 leva (over $402,000). This statistic does not include money, jewelry, and other valuables confiscated at the Skopje departure center, for which there are no figures available.

The profits for liquidation were deposited in the frozen accounts of the Jewish owners when known. In one of the most gruesome aspects of the entire operation in Macedonia, the Bulgarian National Bank sent deposit statements addressed to the Jewish owners, in care of the KEV, after the owners had already been killed in Treblinka.[35]

35. For liquidations see Matkovsky, *Tragedijata*, pp. 96-101, and "Destruction," pp. 253-55; Grinberg, *Dokumenti*, especially Popov, report, May, 1943, pp. 166-68, and Dzhambizov to KEV, May 21, 1943, p. 168. Many examples of BNB deposit statements sent to deported Jews in care of the KEV are in SAMS, Yugoslavia, collection of Jewish Religious Community of Skopje, e.g., box no. 466. Also in the archives are examples of German requests for Jewish property (Protocols no. 17796, 17883, and 17887). One such is reprinted in Matkovsky, "Destruction," plates 14–15. For material related to the entire deportation operation in Macedonia, see Matkovsky, *Tragedijata* and "Destruction," and documents from the MHI-Yad WaShem collection. See also Grinberg, *Dokumenti*, pp. 151-68, which contains besides those documents mentioned above, Berta and Mino Noah, survivors, statement (no date), pp. 152-53; Dzhambizov, report (no date), pp. 153-54; Albert Safarti, excerpts of statement (no date), pp. 154-55, 160-62, and 164-65; Bahchevandzhiev, report, March 7, 1943, pp. 155-57; "Plan na deistvie v vruzka s izselvaneto litsata ot evreiski proizhod" [Plan for activity in connection with the deportation of persons of Jewish origin], in Shtip (unsigned, no date), pp. 157-58; Liubomir Vasilev Panev (director of BNB in Shtip), statement (no date), pp. 158-60; and KEV, notes for transport of Macedonian Jews (no date), pp. 162-63. The archives of the Organiza-

According to estimates from the most reliable statistics, the Bulgarians deported approximately 4,075 Jews from Thrace; 158 Jews from Pirot; and 7,160 Jews from Macedonia—in all, 11,393. This total is based on German and Bulgarian transport figures adjusted for recorded deaths in the camps (the deaths among Thracian Jews are not precisely recorded). The figures for each area include those Jews who may have lived in another area; for example, the forty-odd Thracian Jews deported from Macedonia are included in the Macedonian total rather than with the Thracian Jews. Commissariat figures for Jews before the deportation indicated that 4,273 Jews lived in Thrace, 186 in Pirot, and 7,381 in Macedonia, for a total of 11,840 in the entire occupied area. According to these figures, some 447 Jews escaped the deportation. Most of these were foreign citizens. Some fled before the operation or hid while it was in progress.[36]

The Bulgarians realized for the Jewish community fund over 20 million leva ($243,000) from liquidations in Thrace. This did not include money deposited in the Jewish frozen accounts, money and valuables confiscated at the camps for the advantage of the commissariat, or any real property which the government had systematically confiscated earlier. Furthermore, the money realized at the liquidation sales was well below the actual market value. In Pirot the Jewish community fund

---

tion of Jewish Religious Communities of Yugoslavia at Belgrade contain an unpublished manuscript by Jakov Aroesti, "Izjaiva o deportaciji Bitoljskih Jevreja" [Report of the deportation of the Bitola Jews] (no date), doc. no. 2191 H22-3-1/31. This besides a short text on the fate of the Bitola Jews has biographical notes on all the Jews who lived in that city before the deportation. Testimony in Sofia before People's Court No. 7 includes that of Hristo Slovev Hristev (a Bulgarian official at Skopje), III, 1006-07; Todor Lulchev, III, 1032-42; and Hristo S. Drenski, III, 1044.

Matkovsky relies heavily on documents and testimony presented to the Macedonian Federal Commission for the Investigation of Crimes Perpetrated by the Invaders and Their Accessories. These documents were, at the time of his article in the Yad WaShem studies, not cataloged; but two large boxes, inventory numbers 16378 and 16490, containing the documents pertaining to Macedonia, are in the Military Historical Institute at Belgrade. Some of the documents are in the MHI-Yad WaShem collection.

36. German records in Berlin without stating the source give the totals as 4,219 from Thrace, including Pirot, and 7,240 from Macedonia, or 11,459, Wagner, report, April 3, 1943, T120, serial 2330, roll 1305, frame 486329 (Nuremberg doc. no. NG-4180). Other German figures give 4,221 coming from Lom and 7,122 from Skopje (11,343 total), Hoffmann, report, April 5, 1943, ibid., frame 486316 (NG-4144). Hoffmann's is the figure accepted in postwar trials in the West (see *Time*, July 12, 1968, p. 24). This article concerns the trial of Adolph-Heinz Beckerle in Frankfurt. Another report containing a general list of deportations for all Europe gives the total as 11,364. Korherr, inspector of statistics, SP and SD, to Himmler, April 19, 1943 (NG-5193).

realized over 3.5 million leva ($42,000) from liquidations, in Macedonia over 33 million leva ($402,000). The liquidations in all three areas brought in a total of over 56.5 million leva (approximately $700,000). Jewish wealth in the new territories was valued on the order of $18 million (see above, p. 62).

Expenses for the deportations in the new territories are itemized as follows:[37]

Expense	Cost
Train fare for Thracian and Pirot Jews	721,114 leva
Steamship fare for Thracian and Pirot Jews	4,093,417
Transport fees for Thracian and Pirot Jews from Vienna to Poland	2,301,007
Train fares for Macedonian Jews	7,144,317
Damages to state tobacco monopoly warehouse at Skopje	1,264,608
Camp expenses (mainly wages and fees) for Bulgarian employees	5,748,463
Total	21,272,926 leva ($257,000)

Even the reduced amounts realized in the liquidations covered the total expense adequately. Besides the payment for fares in German-held lands, the 250 RM per person which the Germans requested came to, for 11,343 deportees (using Hoffmann's figures), 2,825,750 Reichsmarks (94.8 million leva or $1,150,000). The Bulgarians thought this price was too high, and in fact no price was either agreed upon or paid.[38]

37. Grinberg, Dokumenti, pp. 169-70.
38. Report (signature illegible), March 3, 1943, T120, serial 2330, roll 1305, frames 486304-07; Raul Hilberg The Destruction of the European Jews (Chicago: Quadrangle Books, 1961), p. 482.

5

The Failure of
the Deportations
from Bulgaria

World Opinion and the Bulgarian Jews

The tragedy of the Macedonian and Thracian Jews and the impending threat to the Jews inside the old territorial boundaries aroused concern and agitation on their behalf, not only inside Bulgaria, but also abroad.

Iako Baruh, when he was seeking support against deportations in March 1943, told Swiss ambassador Redard, an official of the International Red Cross, of the imminent tragedy. On March 11 the ambassador had a meeting with Filov regarding the Bulgarian Jews. Although the danger for the Jews in the interior was over for the time being, the ordeal of the Thracians was in full progress. The ambassador offered to telegraph the British authorities to urge the admission of the Jews into Palestine. Filov replied that it was already too late, for in a few days they would be deported to Poland. "That means that they go to their death," the ambassador rejoined. Filov protested that the Jews were only going to Poland to work, as Bulgarians were working in Germany. The ambassador answered that the situation was not the same and that the Jews in Poland would meet with grave inhumanity. The prime minister angrily replied that it was not time to speak of inhumanity when the Allies were destroying the great cities of Europe. Four days later Filov had an audience with the king, mainly concerning the Jews. Boris told him cryptically to remain "firm." The king, without very specific instructions, was leaving matters in this serious crisis to his subordinates.[1]

1. Filov, "Diary," entries for March 11 and 15, 1943, *Naroden Sud*, no. 3, p. 2. The portion of Filov's diary published in *Naroden Sud* and some other newspapers, which is the only portion available for public research, identifies Filov's visitor of March 11 only as "he." However, German sources confirm that this was the Swiss ambassador Redard. It certainly was not the king as Arditi suggests in his *Roliata na Tsar Boris III pri izselvaneto na evreite ot Bulgariia* [The role of King Boris III in

Somewhat later two officials of the International Red Cross, Dr. Edouard Chapuissa and David de Trotz, came to Bulgaria from Switzerland on behalf of the Jews. They spoke with the king, Metropolitan Stefan, and others. At their audience with the king late in May, Boris assured the Red Cross emissaries that the Bulgarians would not send the native Jews out of the country, although they would deport foreign Jews, especially Poles. Boris said, however, that it was necessary to expel the Jews from Sofia. This meeting occurred at a time when the king and the government's attitude changed radically in respect to the Jews, as we shall see below.[2]

In the spring of 1943 the Allies were awakening to the tragic fate of the Jews in Europe. They now gave particular concern to the Jews of the Balkans as the West learned that the Nazis were directing their immediate plans against them.[3] Some limited foreign concern about Jews in Bulgaria had existed even before the ZZN,[4] and Bulgarian Jews had attempted to arouse sympathy abroad among Jews in Western countries.[5] However, any concentrated effort did not begin until the end of 1942.

By the summer of 1942 rumors of the tragedy inside Nazi-occupied Europe had leaked to the West. Dr. Gerhardt Riegner, chief of the Geneva office of the World Jewish Congress, learned of the Final Solution from a German in Geneva in August 1942. Well over a million Jews were already dead. Riegner notified Stephen Wise, the foremost rabbi in the United States, and Sidney Silverman, M.P., in Britain. Wise brought the matter to the attention of Sumner Welles, undersecretary of state. The story remained secret until November 1942,

the deportation of the Jews from Bulgaria] (Tel Aviv: n.p., 1952), p. 30; Beckerle, report, March 12, 1943, T120, serial K782 (Inland II geheim, Jewish Travel to Palestine), roll 4201, frame K207336.

2. Dr. Edouard Chapuissa (Geneva) to Eli Eshkenazi, president of the Jewish Scientific Institute in Sofia (no date but probably 1948), in Bulgarian Academy of Sciences, Institute for Balkan Studies, Section for Hebrew Studies archives, doc. no. 56 (hereafter cited as BAN, Ebroistika); Hoffmann, report, June 24, 1943, T120, serial 267 (Office of Staatssekretär, Bulgaria, vol. 5, February 1, 1943, to September 10, 1943), roll 225, frames 173953-56 (Nuremberg doc. no. NG-096).

3. Burton Y. Berry, United States consul at Istanbul, reports, March 13 and 23, 1943, Department of State, National Archives record group 59, doc. nos. 874.4016/65 and 874.4016/66.

4. Emanuel Celler, representative of the 10th district of New York in the House of Representatives, to Cordell Hull (no date); Shipley to Celler, October 21, 1940, ibid., doc. no. 874.4016/48.

5. Vitali Haimov and Abraham Achiferlich to Henry Monsky, president of the B'nai B'rith in Omaha, Nebraska, through Ambassador George Earle, January 29, 1941, ibid., doc. no. 874.4016/54.

while the State Department verified rumors. In the meantime another million Jews died at the hands of the Nazis. On December 17, 1942, the Allies officially acknowledged and condemned the Nazi policy of extermination.[6]

In the fall of 1942 Jews from Bulgaria in New York and Palestine founded a committee to rescue the Jews still in the kingdom. Jaques Asseov, a very wealthy tobacco merchant, was named president and Sigmund Ritel vice-president. This group worked closely with international Zionist organizations. Their first goal was somewhat modest— the admission of 500 Bulgarian children into Palestine.[7]

In general, the Jews in the United States, not exclusively the Jews from Bulgaria, but the entire community, despaired of ameliorating the European situation. Hilberg indicates that the B'nai B'rith had already given up the Jews in Nazi hands for lost, and that its major concern was postwar problems. However, interest in the Jews expressed by the State Department at the end of 1942 and the beginning of 1943 gave the Jews new hope, and new rescue efforts began.[8] Important American government officials were indeed now concerned about the fate of the European Jews, but some career officials in the State Department and those British leaders who knew that the Jewish rescue, if successful, would run counter to their Palestine program tried to moderate this concern.[9]

The English did agree to allow 5,000 Jewish children into Palestine. The Swiss embassy in Sofia relayed this to the government at the beginning of February 1943 (a month before the meeting between Ambassador Redard and Filov over the fate of the Macedonian and Thracian Jews). These Jews were not necessarily to come exclusively from Bulgaria; but all would probably have to pass through Bulgarian territory, no matter what their point of origin. Beckerle disapproved of

6. Raul Hilberg, *The Destruction of the European Jews* (Chicago: Quadrangle Books, 1961), pp. 718-19. Hilberg details rescue operations throughout the period, pp. 715-38. For concern over the Bulgarian Jews in the House of Commons, see Great Britain, *Parliamentary Debates* (Commons), 5th ser., 388 (1943), p. 1683; and 390 (1943), p. 699.

7. Benjamin Arditi, *Yehudi Bulgariyah bishanah hamishpat hanatzi: 1940-1944* [The Jews of Bulgaria during the years of Nazi occupation: 1940-1944] (Tel Aviv: Israel Press, 1962), pp. 311-14, including a printed copy of a telegram sent by Vitali Nachmias, secretary of rescue committee, Tel Aviv, to Haim Farhi, February 1943.

8. Hilberg, p. 719.

9. Ibid., p. 720. For Department of State hesitation on Jewish rescue, see Arthur D. Morse, *While Six Million Died: A Chronicle of American Apathy* (New York: Random House, 1967), pp. 3-99.

the plan. The German foreign office also rejected it because of the anti-Nazi propaganda it would create and Arab sentiments against Jewish immigration. Filov agreed to reject the Swiss proposal on "technical grounds"; meanwhile the British were preparing for the admission of Eastern European Jews into Palestine. Oliver Stanley, the colonial secretary, arranged for 4,000 Rumanian, Hungarian, or Bulgarian children and 500 adults to obtain visas.[10]

Filov was afraid to reject the British request outright because of the probable adverse effect on world public opinion and Allied retaliation through bombing (until this time there had been no major air strikes on Bulgaria). The government told the Swiss that they could not supply the trains for transport (while at the same time they were arranging the transport of four times this number in the opposite direction) and that they did not want to separate the children from their families.[11]

At the beginning of March, Lord Halifax, the British ambassador to the United States, told a rally of the American Jewish Congress that 4,000 Jewish children and 500 adults would leave Bulgaria shortly and that a total of 29,000 Jews from all over Europe would emigrate to Palestine by the end of the month. The Sofia newspaper *Zora* reported this, and the Germans mistakenly thought that Bulgaria had arranged a secret "deal" with Great Britain. Bulgaria explained that the rumors arose from the Swiss request for 5,000 Jews.[12] At the same time in early March, 150 Jewish children from Rumania were scheduled to travel through Bulgaria. The RSHA wished Sofia to impede their passage.[13]

Through the spring and summer the Germans continued to be con-

10.   Foreign office press report (on Stanley statement), February 13, 1943, T120, serial K782, roll 4201, frame K207309; Beckerle, report, February 4, 1943, ibid., frame K207315 (many of the German documents are duplicated and filed in various serials, e.g., the documents listed here can be found in serial 1952 [Inland II geheim, Jewish Return; Jewish Travel to Palestine], roll 1079, as well as K782; for simplicity, I refer only to the latter listing); Hahn to Eichmann, February 8, 1943, ibid., frame K207313; Bergmann, Büro RAM, to Beckerle, February 13, 1943, ibid., frames K207311-12; Hahn to Eichmann, February 18, 1943, ibid., frame K207308; Filov, "Diary," entry for February 17, 1943, *Naroden Sud*, no. 3, p. 2.

11.   Beckerle, report, February 16, 1943, T120, serial K782, roll 4201, ibid., frame K207372; Beckerle, report, February 27, 1943, ibid., frames K207370-71; Hoffmann, report, April 5, 1942, T120, serial 2330, roll 1305, frames 486316-21; Pausch, foreign office, report, April 7, 1943, ibid., frame 486322.

12.   Press report, March 2, 1943, T120, serial K782, roll 4201, frame K207360; Rademacher to German embassy in Sofia, March 2, 1943, ibid., frame K207361; Beckerle to foreign office, March 4, 1943, ibid., frame K207342.

13.   Letter to Hahn (signature illegible), March 3, 1943, T120, serial 7708H (Inland II geheim, Feldscher Aktion [exchange of Jewish children]), roll 3237, frame E548808.

cerned about Jewish emigration without their knowledge. They believed, incorrectly, that George Earle, the former American minister to Sofia, was in Istanbul for the purpose of helping Jews emigrate.[14] (He was actually working for the Office of Strategic Services.) The Germans also became alarmed by radio reports from Cairo broadcasting that Jews, including young men who had joined the British army and girls who had entered the health corps, had left Bulgaria for Palestine. The rumors said that four groups had emigrated from Bulgaria to Palestine by March 13.[15] Indeed, individual Jews who could buy their way out made their exit from Bulgaria even in March 1943. We have seen how Iako Baruh helped prominent Bulgarians obtain visas for their friends.[16] Furthermore, Manfred von Killinger, the Reich's ambassador in Bucharest, reported that a group of Jews on their way to Palestine went through Bulgaria on March 14, 1943; and after that a few children with Chilean passports passed through Svilengrad.[17]

Beckerle reassured Berlin and supported the Bulgarian explanations. Franz Rademacher, the foreign office Jewish expert, informed other Axis capitals that Beckerle "had the impression" that Bulgaria would refuse the Swiss request for Jewish emigration. Rademacher wrote further that Germany with its allies must determine a unified policy on Jewish emigration. He stressed the effect of emigration on other matters including propaganda, military danger, and the hostility of the Arabs.[18]

The isolated emigrations continued, including Jews from Rumania and Hungary who passed through Bulgaria. An SS officer in Bucharest learned from a "well-informed" Jewish businessman, the president of the Rumanian capital's community, that Bulgaria planned to send 32,000 Jews to Palestine over a four-month period.[19] (This report was unfounded.) The Germans also heard that the Bulgarians were allowing Rumanian children through their country, even providing them with Red Cross aides. Killinger, the ambassador in Bucharest, wanted

14. Beckerle, report, March 10, 1943, T120, serial K782, roll 4201, frame K207343.

15. Beckerle, report, March 13, 1943, ibid., frames K207358-59.

16. Berry, reports, January 25 and February 22, 1943, Department of State, National Archives record group 59, doc. nos. 874.00/675 and 874.00/700; and later reports in the same series throughout 1943.

17. Killinger, report, April 30, 1943, T120, serial 5784H (Inland II geheim [Jewish travel to Palestine]), roll 2721, frame E421083.

18. Rademacher to German embassies in Budapest, Bucharest, and Rome, March 1943, T120, serial K782, roll 4201, frames K207354-55.

19. Stelzer, chargé d'affaires, report, Bucharest, March 17, 1943, T120, serial 2330, roll 1305, frame 486324.

Berlin to force Bulgaria to stop future transits;[20] however, Beckerle did not recommend this tactic. Although the Bulgarians denied knowledge of the specific incidents of passage through their country with which the Germans confronted them, they implied that there was some truth in the matter by arguing that if Berlin could not prevent Rumania and Hungary from allowing the emigration of Jews, Sofia should hardly take the blame in the eyes of world opinion for thwarting it. Beckerle also assured the foreign office that rumors of large-scale emigration from Bulgaria reported on Cairo radio were groundless, as were rumors of the planned emigration of 32,000 Jews. The Bulgarians, he said, were taking every step to stop even minor emigration by foreign citizens. On the question of Rumanian children Filov assured Beckerle late in March, about two weeks after the ambassador tried to relieve pressure from Berlin on the Bulgarians in the matter of transit visas, that the Bulgarians would take every step to prohibit Jewish travel through Bulgaria. Nevertheless, the prime minister cautioned, some Jews might get through.[21]

Staatssekretär (for Inland II: SS and police) Horst Wagner, who had succeeded Luther, remained unimpressed with Beckerle's assurances. At the beginning of April he suggested that the Bulgarians might talk strongly about refusing emigrations for the Jews while they allowed them to go on. He was also dissatisfied with the Bulgarian deportations to Poland and suspicious both of Earle's presence in Turkey and of the Bulgarian negotiations with the Swiss. The Staatssekretär stated that the Swedish ship *Oresund* was carrying Bulgarian Jews to Palestine. Beckerle denied it.[22] On April 4 Killinger reported that seventy-four Jewish children were to go through Bulgaria on their way to Palestine. Wagner wanted Sofia to revoke the visas issued by the Bulgarian embassy in Bucharest. Dimitur Shishmanov, the general secretary of the Bulgarian foreign office, told Beckerle that Bulgaria would invalidate

20. Killinger, reports, March 24 and April 30, 1943, T120, serial 7708H, roll 3237, frames E548802-03 and serial 5784H, roll 2721, frames E421083-85; Wagner to Beckerle, April 14, 1943, T120, serial K783, roll 4201, frame K207316 (Nuremberg doc. no. NG-1805).

21. Beckerle, reports, March 13 and 16 (2), and April 15, 1943, T120, serial K782, roll 4201, frames K207358-59; T120, serial 7708H, roll 3237, frame E548804; T120, serial K787 (Inland II geheim, A/B-1943-1944, II, Jews in Bulgaria), roll 4202, frame K208490; and T120, serial 1952, roll 1079, frame 436803; Pausch, foreign office, report, March 26, 1943, T120, serial K782, roll 4201, frame K207137; Hilberg, p. 504.

22. Wagner, enclosure C (unsigned) to report, March 3, 1943, T120, serial 2330, roll 1305, frame 486323; Beckerle, report, April 14. 1943, T120, serial K781 (Inland II geheim, Jews, general), roll 4201, frame K206942.

the visas, and the Ruse police would refuse passage. (A Rumanian lawyer pleaded with the Bulgarian authorities to no avail.) They would continue to refuse in the future. The Rumanians and the International Red Cross persisted in trying to get the Jews through. Wagner wired Sofia to disregard the Red Cross efforts and deny passage. Jews of armsbearing age, he said, must be stopped at all costs.[23]

In March 1943 the Bulgarian Jews commanded the attention of the major leaders of the West. At a meeting in Washington attended by Roosevelt, British Foreign Secretary Anthony Eden, Secretary of State Cordell Hull, Undersecretary of State Sumner Welles, Halifax, Harry Hopkins (the president's advisor), and William Strang (assistant undersecretary of state in the British Foreign Office), Hull raised the question of the Bulgarian Jews. He knew of their danger and asked the British foreign secretary if anything could be done to bring them to Palestine. Eden said that the Allies must approach questions of Jewish emigration from Europe skeptically because promising to rescue the Jews from one country would raise demands elsewhere. Transportation problems alone would embarrass the Allies if the Nazis accepted proposals to grant refuge to large numbers of Jews. Eden said that the British were ready to take 50,000 Jews into Palestine, but that the leaders should not make rash public statements about proposals regarding the Jews because failure to fulfill their promises would have a bad effect.[24]

On March 25 an unidentified member of the Subranie went to the American legation in Istanbul and asked for help for the Jews. He informed officials there of the anti-Jewish activity inside Bulgaria and said that nothing could help the Jews then in the occupied territory, but that the entire Bulgarian community was also threatened. Gabrovski, he said, was the chief promoter of the German demands. He also told Consul Burton Y. Berry about the Subranie protest which had postponed the fate of the Jews and suggested that, since the United States had great prestige in Bulgaria, a vigorous protest by the Americans through the Swiss embassy might help cancel the operations

23. Killinger, report, April 4, 1943, T120, serial K782, roll 4201, frames K207379-80; Wagner to Beckerle, April 8, 1943, T120, serial 1952, roll 1079, frames 436793-94; Beckerle, reports, April 10 and 20, 1943, T120, serial K782, roll 4201, frame K207391, and serial 1952, roll 1079, frame 436790; Eberhardt von Thadden, foreign office (Inland II, Jews), to Eichmann, June 12, 1943, T120, serial K782, roll 4201, frame K207423.

24. Berry, report, March 23, 1943, Department of State, National Archives record group 59, doc. no. 874.4016/68; Robert E. Sherwood, *Roosevelt and Hopkins: An Intimate History* (New York: Harper Bros., 1948), p. 717; Hilberg, pp. 720-21.

against the Jews by strengthening the hand of those people in the cabinet opposed to this activity. According to a former president of the Bulgarian Agricultural Cooperative Bank and a well-known Bulgarian lawyer, also in Istanbul on behalf of the Jews, and also unidentified by Berry, no more than 5 percent of the nation supported Nazi anti-Semitism. In fact, these Bulgarians told Berry, only 5 percent supported the Axis alliance and the remaining overwhelming majority of Bulgarians was sympathetic to the cause of the United Nations. The Bulgarian church and the faculty of Sofia University, they said, opposed the government's Jewish policy. Berry thought that the wartime circumstances made a direct protest by the United States impossible, but the Americans could get the point across through protests of the American Red Cross, the Federal Council of Churches, the Roman Catholic church, the Institute of International Peace, the Columbia Broadcasting System, and the National Broadcasting Company.[25]

In fact Hull sent a letter to Filov through the Swiss requesting that the Bulgarians allow the Jews to emigrate to a neutral country. The Swiss would not deliver the American note, because of their experience with the British request of February. The State Department gave the message to Ambassador Georgi K'oseivanov in Berne. The ex–prime minister answered the American note by blaming Belev exclusively, stating that he (the commissar) "had been forced to resign." (This latter was not true.)[26]

Ankara paid great attention to the American and British debate over permission for immigration to Palestine since Turkey would be a way station. The Americans in Turkey, led by Ambassador Laurence A. Steinhardt, a Jew, succeeded in convincing the British to send to Sofia a joint protest and a request for 30,000 Bulgarian Jews to leave the country. However, the plan called for temporary camps in Turkey before resettlement in Palestine. The Turkish foreign office rejected the plan. They agreed to allow the Jews to travel through to Palestine, but not to have a camp, even a temporary camp, on their soil. First of all, material for such a camp was in short supply because of the Turkish mobilization. Secondly, there was a housing and food shortage in the country, and even though the Americans and British were planning to feed the immigrants, the Turkish population would resent seeing the

25. Berry, report, March 25, 1943, Department of State, National Archives record group 59, doc. no. 874.4016/69.
26. Hull to Berry, March 27, 1943, ibid.; Leland Harrison, American minister at Berne, reports, April 1, 9, and 11, 1943, doc. nos. 874.4016/71, 874.4016/74, and 874.4016/75.

Bulgarians, as they would regard the Jews, being fed while they went hungry. Thirdly, there were sure to be a number of Axis agents among the emigrants, which would mean a large Turkish guard, detrimental to Turkish and Allied war interests if Ankara entered the war.[27]

In May the Germans foiled any attempt at large-scale emigration from Southeastern Europe to Palestine. German efforts to gain support among the Arab community in British-controlled areas in part determined their attitude toward emigration. For this reason they were very reluctant to offend Grand Mufti of Jerusalem Amin el Husseini who had sent a personal request to Ribbentrop through the Italians asking him not to permit emigration from the Balkans. The mufti also followed these requests with a number of messages of concern over the many rumors in the spring and summer of 1943.[28]

The Allies had finally convinced the Turkish foreign minister to agree to allow some Jews to stay a short time in Turkey. Although reluctant, the Turks believed that the efforts to obtain the release of the Jews would not be successful so they did not press the issue.[29] The British and Americans also persuaded the Turks to ask Bucharest about the use of two Rumanian ships—the *Transylvania* and the *Bessarabia*—for transporting the Jews to Istanbul. The Rumanians under German pressure refused.[30] The Bulgarians also refused to accede to Red Cross requests for a ship or to allow the Jews to pass through their country. The plans failed.[31]

27. Steinhardt, reports, March 29 and April 3 and 5, 1943, ibid., doc. nos. 874.4016/70, 874.4016/72, and 874.4016/73; draft of report for Hahn (unsigned), April 14, 1943, T120, serial K782, roll 4201, frames K207330-34; Wagner, May 19, 1943, T120, serial K784 (Inland II geheim, Feldscher Aktion), roll 4202, frame K207813.

28. Andor Hencke, political Unterstaatssekretär's office, report, May 12, 1943, T120, serial K782, roll 4201, frames K207420-21; Grand Mufti to Wagner, May 13 and June 10, 1943, ibid., frames K207418-19, K207454-56; Wagner, report, May 18, 1943, T120, serial 2330, roll 1305, frame 486337; Wagner, draft of report, June 17, 1943, T120, serial 1952, roll 1079, frame 436813.

29. Steinhardt, reports, May 1 and 26, 1943, Department of State, National Archives record group 59, doc. nos. 874.4016/80 and 874.4016/82; Hull to Steinhardt, May 18, 1943, doc. no. 874.4016/80.

30. Wagner, report, Sofia, May [sic] 1943, T120, serial 2330, roll 1305, frame 486336; Papen, report, May 10, 1943, T120, serial K784, roll 4202, frame K207819; Killinger, reports, May 12, 13, and 17, 1943, T120, serial 267, roll 225, frame 173908; T120, serial K784, roll 4202, frame K207818; T120, serial 5796 (Inland II geheim, Feldscher Aktion), roll 2723, frame E422439; Wagner to Beckerle, May 13, 1943, T120, serial 5796, roll 2723, frames E422442-43; Wagner to Killinger, May 19, 1943, T120, serial 5796, roll 2723, frame E422438.

31. Mohrmann, chargé d'affaires at Sofia, report, May 14, 1943, T120, serial K782, roll 4201, frame K207441; Killinger, report, May 25, 1943. T120, serial K782,

Bulgaria may have maintained contacts with the Allies on Jewish emigration through the spring. In May new rumors of projected deals circulated in Berlin. The Germans heard that the Swiss were arranging fifteen hundred visas for transit through Bulgaria. If the report was true, the plan never materialized. Another rumor had the Bulgarians preparing to exchange eight thousand Bulgarian Jews for eight thousand Bulgarians in South America. Shishmanov declared the rumor unfounded, and Beckerle supported him.[32]

The efforts of the Allies on behalf of the Jews of occupied Europe were halfhearted, tardy, and at times almost wholly absent. Yet once the tide of war turned, the Allied pressure on Sofia to cease anti-Semitic actions had its effect. The Bulgarians, whose fate was still bound to Berlin, attempted the difficult task of avoiding a clash with either Berlin or the Allies on the subject of the Jews. Their best policy, it appeared, was to avoid any new actions concerning the Jews until international trends became clearer.

Attitudes on Deportation (Spring 1943)

Through March and April of 1943 Bulgarian society continued to discuss the Jewish problem. The fate of the Jews from the new territories and the danger to the Bulgarian community caused great concern among Bulgarians with anti-Axis or pro-Western feelings. One of the most significant men holding these feelings was Metropolitan Stefan of Sofia. Not only he, but the entire Bulgarian church, led by the Holy Synod, opposed the government's Jewish policy, as they had opposed it since 1940. The individual churchmen and the Holy Synod as a body sent messages of protest and delegations to King Boris, Filov, and Gabrovski. On April 15 Boris held an audience with three of Bulgaria's leading clerics—Stefan, Kiril, and Bishop Neofit of Vidin. Filov was present. Boris explained to the bishops that the Jewish question in Bulgaria was connected to the European solution of the question. Stefan and Neofit, according to Filov, seemed most anxious to protect Jews who had con-

roll 4201, frames K207429-30; Thadden, draft of report, June 25, 1943, T120, serial K784, roll 4204, frame K206810.

32. Beckerle, report, May 31, 1943, T120, serial K782, roll 4201, frame K207427; Thadden to Eichmann, May 28 and June 1, 1943, T120, serial 5784H, roll 2721, frame E471090 and serial K782, roll 4201, frame K207426; Eichmann to Hahn, May 4, 1943, ibid., frame K207416; Wagner, report, May 13, 1943, T120, serial 2330, roll 1305, frame 486338; Mohrmann, report, May 14, 1943, ibid., frame 486339.

verted to Christianity. On this matter the government and church leaders agreed. Filov told the bishops that despite the recent scandal in the Subranie, the parliamentary body stood firmly with the government on the Jewish question. There was some uncomfortable discussion at the audience about a pamphlet by Neofit and one of Stefan's circulars condemning the king. The former excused himself, saying that he had expressed the view of the synod rather than his own. Filov felt that the government had taken the offensive at the meeting, forcing the bishops to retreat.[33]

At this time the government leaders solidified their anti-Semitic views. At no other period during the war years were official government pronouncements so similar to the anti-Jewish propaganda of the Reich. This was undoubtedly part of the process of rationalizing the deportations and should not be regarded as the normal attitude of the government leaders and the monarch (Gabrovski perhaps excepted).

Furthermore, the spring of 1943 was a time of crisis for Bulgaria as well as the Axis. The critical battle of Stalingrad and the Soviet victory there, the threatened invasion of Bulgaria by Turkey or of the Balkans by the Allies left the Bulgarian government, in fact the entire country, in a state of great tension. Up to now the war had not had much impact on Bulgaria: its soldiers were not at the front, and the Allied air raids had not yet begun. Now, however, partisan military activity led by the Communists greatly increased inside the country. The streets of Sofia were sometimes scenes of pitched battles. From February to May 1943 a series of assassinations disrupted the capital. In February Violeta Iakova, a famous Jewish partisan, killed General Lukov, former minister of war and leader of the right-wing Legionaires.[34] The king attributed the murder to Turkish agents; but Filov accused the Communists,[35] and Gabrovski agreed to use the assassination as an excuse to start an anti-Semitic campaign in the press.

On April 15 a partisan named Nikola Draganov broke into Deputy Sotir Ianev's office and shot him. Ianev was a former Socialist but a

33. Filov, "Diary," entry for April 15, 1943, *Naroden Sud*, no. 3, p. 3; interview with B. Piti, January 1966, Jaffa, Israel (this information has subsequently been published under the title *Te, spasitelite* [They, the rescuers] [Tel Aviv: n.p., 1969]); Arditi, *Yehudi Bulgariyah*, p. 202.

34. Mitka Grubcheva, *V imeto na naroda* [In the name of the people] (Sofia: BKP, 1962), pp. 187-94.

35. Report (unsigned), Sofia, February 14, 1943, T120, serial 267, roll 225, frames 173816-17. Beckerle, report, February 14, 1943, ibid., frames 173818-19; Filov, "Diary," entries for February 17 and April 15, 1943, *Naroden Sud*, no. 3, pp. 2-3.

government supporter in the Subranie.[36] In May assassins killed Col.
Atanas Pantev, the former police chief.

The assassination which most raised the government's public indignation, however, was that of a radio operator, Kuncho Ianakiev, a German agent. Unlike the other cases, the police apprehended the assassin—a Jew, Menahem Papo. Papo was a member of the Workers' Youth Union, a Communist front organization, and of a partisan group—*Al'osha*. His arrest, trial, and subsequent execution became a *cause célèbre* in Bulgaria. To the Communists, partisans, and Jews, he was a martyr, just as Leon Tadzher had been in 1941. For the government leaders, Papo and his group became the visual expression of their enemies.[37]

Despite the "hard line" now taken by the Filov regime, those Germans most interested in the deportation of the Jews mistrusted the Sofia government's motives and plans. Some of this is reflected in the controversy over emigration to Palestine. In late February of 1943—after the Dannecker-Belev agreement—Sofia expressed concern about the eastern front (Stalingrad). Beckerle, however, received the impression that the German reversal here would not affect "the still secret design for the radical solution of the Jewish question." In evidence, the ambassador pointed to the agreement as a sign of Bulgaria's faith in an ultimate Axis victory.[38]

At first the Germans generally expressed satisfaction over the success of the deportations from the new territories. The German consul at Skopje, Artur Witte, declared that the Macedonian Jews had been behind information leaks to the Allies and that these would now end. Also, the consul reported, in a matter of days after the deportation, black market prices on milk, eggs, meat, and lard dropped as much as 50 percent. He went on to report that the deportations brought expres-

36. Grubcheva, pp. 198-200; Filov, "Diary," entry for April 15, 1943, *Naroden Sud*, no. 3, p. 3.

37. Mohrmann, report, May 15, 1943, T120, serial 267, roll 225, frames 173911-12; enclosure to report for Thadden (author's signature illegible), May 17, 1943, T120, serial 2330, roll 1305, frames 486344-45; Hoffmann to RSHA, June 7, 1943, ibid., frames 486350-56 (Nuremberg doc. no. NG-2357). Beckerle, report, October 11, 1943, T120, serial K787, roll 4202, frames K208530-32; Gabrovski, statement to newspaper *Zora*, May 15, 1943, quoted in Natan Grinberg, *Dokumenti* [Documents] (Sofia: Central Consistory of Jews in Bulgaria, 1945), p. 187; Central Consistory of Jews in Bulgaria, *Evrei—zaginali v antifashistkata borba* [Jews—killed in the anti-Fascist battle] (Sofia: Natsionalen Komitet na Otechestveniia Front, 1958), pp. 108-15.

38. Beckerle, report, February 25, 1943, T120, serial 267, roll 225, frames 173837-38.

sions of satisfaction from the Macedonians. Beckerle's reports supported the consul's undoubtedly exaggerated opinions.[39]

Yet even in March a note of disappointment began to appear in Berlin's reports concerning Bulgaria and the Jews.[40] The parliamentary delegation led by Peshev worried the Germans. In April Hoffmann suggested that Gabrovski stopped the deportations from the old territorial boundaries of Bulgaria after receiving "a nod of approval from the highest place" (presumably meaning the throne). Rumors circulated in the German foreign office that Bulgarian leaders, especially Gabrovski, had deliberately deceived the Germans and had no intention of deporting Jews from Bulgaria proper. Beckerle did not believe this. The Bulgarians simply did not have the same racial attitude toward the Jews that the Germans had. They were interested primarily in confiscations. Thus they readily deported the Jews from the new territories, but feared public opinion too much in the case of the others. Beckerle concluded that the Bulgarians would with some prodding and despite the "usual Balkan weakness" come around.[41]

The foreign office, in particular Wagner, preferred Beckerle's moderate reports to Hoffmann's. Yet the undercurrent of dissatisfaction still remained. The March deportations were only 56 percent successful (under 11,500 of a planned 20,000)—not a very notable achievement. The 51,000 Jews still present in Bulgaria behind German lines disturbed the RSHA. In April a foreign office report, surveying the results of the Macedonian deportations, questioned why the doctors in the Skopje camp were released. As intellectuals, the report said, these were the most dangerous Jews.[42] This German concern had support among the right-wing extremists in Sofia. The Legionaires distributed a pamphlet castigating the government and Subranie for deporting only the Jews from the new territories.[43]

In April King Boris visited Hitler in Berlin. While there, he also met

39. Witte, draft of report, March 18, 1943, T120, serial 2330, roll 1305, frame 486309-13; Beckerle, report, March 21, 1943, ibid., frame 486314.

40. Witte, draft of report, March 18, 1943, ibid., frames 486309-13; Beckerle, report, March 21, 1943, ibid., frame 486314.

41. Hoffmann and Beckerle, report, April 5, 1943, ibid., frames 486316-21.

42. Unsigned enclosure C to Pausch report, April 3, 1943, ibid., frame 486323; SS Hauptsturmführer Bosshammer, RSHA, to Thadden, May 27, 1943, ibid., frames 486341-43.

43. Beckerle, report and enclosure (Union of Bulgarian National Legions, "Who Protects the Bulgarian Jews" [no date]), May 13, 1943, T120, serial K783 (Inland II geheim, Settlement of the Jewish question in Bulgaria), roll 4201, frames K207626-28.

with Ribbentrop. Boris told the foreign minister that in his opinion only the Jews from Macedonia and Thrace should be deported, as the Dannecker-Belev agreement maintained. Of course, these Jews had already been deported, but the agreement was intended to be a prelude to the deportation of all Jews in Bulgaria and Bulgarian-controlled areas. Boris was apparently having second thoughts about the German plans in light of the changing world situation and the disturbances within Bulgaria. They would deport "Communist elements" among the Jews, but the remainder of about 25,000 (a figure which indicates that Boris planned to interpret "Communist" very loosely) Bulgaria would intern in concentration camps and use for public works labor. Ribbentrop remained noncommittal. He said that the Germans believed that the only correct solution to the Jewish question was the radical one proposed at Wannsee. The RSHA felt that Boris was only seeking excuses and that the foreign office should continue to insist on deportations. For emphasis one SS report repeated a rumor that in one labor camp 2,000 Jews loafed most of the time and lived comfortably while Greeks nearby worked a twelve-hour day.[44]

New Attempts at Deportation and Expulsion from Sofia

Commissar Belev was not privy to the events and decisions of March 9 which curtailed arrangements for the deportation of Jews from the old territorial boundaries of Bulgaria. When informed of this news, he reacted with extreme anger, harassing the employees of the KEV as an outlet for his chagrin.[45] However, although the commissar was angry, he did not despair. Gabrovski had postponed the operations against the Jews in Bulgaria; he had not cancelled them. Belev called together his chiefs and proceeded to draft a new plan. By the new operation Belev intended to deport to Poland all Jews in the kingdom except those with foreign citizenship (Jews from Germany or German-occupied lands would be included in the deportations), Jews married to non-Jews, Jews whom the government had mobilized or the state needed, and those who were seriously ill. He hoped the KEV would carry out the plan by September 30, 1943.

Belev's new plan divided the Bulgarian Jews geographically, Sofia

44. Ribbentrop to Beckerle, April 4, 1943, T120, serial 267, roll 225, frames 173890-91; Bosshammer to Thadden, May 17, 1943, T120, serial 2330, roll 1305, frames 486341-43.
45. Sofia, Protocols of People's Court No. 7, II, 359-62 (testimony of Liliana Panitsa).

Jews (25,000) and those in the provinces (23,000). The KEV would deport the Jews from Danube stations by steamship through Vienna at the rate of 16,000 a month. As the two chief departure points Belev designated Lom and the small village and river station of Samovit (near Pleven), but other river stations would handle local populations. Belev planned that Bulgarian guards would accompany the ships to Vienna.

To facilitate the operation and to prevent pressure on the government by the Sofia Jews, similar to that of March, as a first step the government would transfer the Jews in the capital to the provinces. Government officials dealing with the Jewish question had previously considered this idea of moving Jews from Sofia. Article 23 of the ZZN forbade Jews to move into Sofia and gave the police the right to limit residence there as well. Article 29 of the decree-law of August 26, 1942, stated that the Jews of Sofia were subject to expulsion into the provinces or beyond the borders of Bulgaria. The article also provided for the immediate expulsion from the capital of unemployed Jews.

Excluding Sofia Jews who were temporarily or permanently not liable for deportation (mobilized, married to Christians, etc.) and Jews who worked in labor gangs, the number subject to evacuation into the provinces was approximately 16,000. Belev's plan called for 8,000 Jews to leave Sofia during each of two weeks. The KEV assigned temporary residences for these Jews in cities in the kingdom's eight administrative regions (excluding the new territories) as follows:

Region	Number of Jews
Burgas	3,000
Pleven	1,500
Plovdiv	1,500
Ruse	2,000
Shumen	1,500
Sofia	2,000
Stara Zagora	1,500
Vratsa	3,000

Belev emphasized that the evacuation into the provinces was only a step leading to the ultimate deportations into Poland, and he reassured the regional directors and regional police chiefs that the Jewish influx into their areas was only temporary.

Once the Sofia Jews were in the provinces, the KEV could carry out deportations on twenty-four hours' notice. Belev's plan mentioned the possibility of deportation operations beginning May 30. The police could assemble the Jews in the provinces, both local Jews and those from Sofia, and take them to schools. From there they would be sent to the staging centers in Lom and Samovit and then to Vienna. The operation would also include Jews liable to deportation, but who remained in the capital. The Bulgarian State Railways would transport the Jews (about 10,000 a week) to the staging areas, taking care to have sufficient numbers at the centers to utilize steamships at maximum efficiency. Security at the staging centers and disposition of remaining Jewish property in Bulgaria would follow the rules established for Thrace and Macedonia. At any one time there was room in Lom for only 5,000 Jews, in Samovit and Rahovo (a small supplementary area) for 2,000.

At the conclusion to these plans Belev included an interesting aside concerning his statement on the capacity of the staging areas. "At Tsibur [a stream a short distance east of Lom] there are not [proper] conditions for a temporary camp. If the deportation [operation] were not decided [upon], at Tsibur it would be possible to construct a permanent camp."[46]

Belev does not explain this remark "if the deportation [operation] were not decided [upon]." In particular, there is no indication as to whether he meant cancellation or further postponement of the operation. By the time the commissar drew up his new plan, presumably in May, there was a possibility that the government might reconsider the deportation plans. We should also consider as a hint of this change the statement that Boris made to Ribbentrop on his April visit to Berlin.

Dannecker, Hoffmann, and Gabrovski reviewed Belev's plan. Dannecker suggested that they divide the deportation proposals into two possibilities: first, Belev's plan for deportation of the Jews to Poland for reasons of state security (plan A) and second, if this were unacceptable, at least the expulsion of the Sofia Jews into the provinces (plan B). The Germans hoped that the latter at least would be a first step to eventual deportation. On May 20 Gabrovski presented the plans to the king. Boris immediately accepted plan B, but not plan A. The climate had changed. Boris was more wary of deportations than he had been in March. Nevertheless, the Jews were not yet out of danger. Plan A might still follow.[47]

On May 19, the day before Gabrovski's audience, the general public

46.   Belev, report (no date), in Grinberg, *Dokumenti*, pp. 185-87.
47.   Hoffmann, report, June 7, 1943, T120, serial 2330, roll 1305, frames 486350-56.

in Sofia learned of the new crisis for the Bulgarian Jews. Radio Berlin announced on that day that Bulgaria would shortly deport its Jews. Furthermore, Liliana Panitsa informed Dr. Levi of the scheme. On May 19 Leon Farhi, a member of the consistory and the Jewish aid society, called into his office about a score of Jewish leaders. Here Levi gave them the information Miss Panitsa had relayed, and the group decided once again, as they had in March, to ask leaders of Bulgarian society to intervene for the Jews with the government and the king. According to Benjamin Arditi, who attended the meeting, they also agreed to try to calm the Jewish community and mobilize it for a demonstration before the government and state leaders.[48] The next day the Jews obtained in advance an authentic copy of the order for their expulsion from Sofia from a contact in the government printing office. Rumors spread through Iuch Bunar. The Jews feared a general pogrom and a midnight police raid on the ghetto. One rumor circulating among the Jews held that Belev had taken over all police units in the capital for the coming operation. The community believed that the plan intended not merely expulsion from the capital, but deportation into German hands. The Jews did not know the king's rejection of plan A that same day.

On May 21 the cabinet approved a decree (not to be published in *Durzhaven Vestnik*) ordering the Jews out of Sofia. The decree excluded spouses of non-Jews, seriously ill persons, Jews who had converted to Christianity by August 29, 1942, and mobilized Jews. Belev had written in an early report that the KEV would deport "all Jews in Bulgaria outside the boundaries of the country." In a later report he wrote only of "the deportation of the Jews of Sofia and other cities of the kingdom" without mentioning where. (Jews from some other strategic cities were also to be expelled.)[49]

On the twenty-first the Sofia Jews began to receive orders to leave the city within three days for areas in the provinces. The KEV sent the leaders of the community instructions regarding the transfer of keys for homes of the evacuees. Despair and frustation, misery and bewilderment ruled the Jewish quarter. The beginnings of panic even affected the leadership of the community, who placed their hope on remaining calm. Bulgarian friends were unable to use their influence. Filov and Gabrovski could not be found. Nonetheless, the Jews redoubled their

48. For a day-by-day account of activities in the Jewish community at this time, see Arditi, *Roliata*, pp. 45-50. See also his *Yehudi Bulgariyah*, pp. 207-17. Sofia, Protocols of People's Court No. 7, IV, 1500 (testimony of Buko Levi).

49. Bulgaria, Council of Ministers, 70th decree, 74th protocol, May 21, 1943, Grinberg, *Dokumenti*, p. 187. Belev, reports (no date), pp. 188-89.

efforts to find people to intervene on their behalf. Levi, Colonel Tadzher, and others sought their acquaintances at court, in the military, in the government, and in Bulgarian society to try to prevent what seemed to them ultimate disaster.

On May 22 the capital Jews learned of feverish activity in Lom. Puntev was buying large quanties of food and clearing the schools. Many empty river steamships were docking at the port. Poland loomed even larger in the thoughts of the Jews. Iuch Bunar grew more chaotic as great numbers of peasants came into the quarter in order to buy Jewish goods being sold very cheaply. The Jews and Bulgarians continued to have no success in reaching the high officials of the court and government. Yet Arditi reports that the Jews knew most of the ministers were still in the capital.

By May 23, most of the Jews in Sofia already had orders to leave the capital. Many families would be divided. Some managed to use bribes to change their destinations in order to be with relatives or to gain an extension of the time of departure. Some even obtained these advantages by request without bribes as the KEV showed unusual leniency in what many thought were the Bulgarian Jews' last hours. The leaders of the consistory and welfare association met constantly but had no success in changing the plans. Then encouragement came. A group of Bulgarian opposition leaders headed by Col. Damian Velchev sent a letter of protest on behalf of the Jews. The protesters included Mushanov, Dimo Kazasov, Kimon Georgiev, the Agrarian Nikola Petkov, the Nationalist Atanas Burov, and others.[50] The action of prominent Bulgarians like these turned the tide in favor of the Jews.

Jewish contacts had finally borne results. Geron met with an influential Macedonian leader, Dr. Konstantin Stanishev. Buko Levi spoke to Dr. Handzhiev, a dignitary close to the king. Handzhiev promised to give Levi a positive and presumably hopeful statement on the fate of the Jews the next day. Ekaterina Karavelova, the widow of one of Bulgaria's first prime ministers and called by the Bulgarians "the mother of the court," promised to speak to the king on behalf of the Jews, while Metropolitan Stefan said that the Holy Synod would protest the deportation.

However, in his latest statements, Filov continued to maintain that the government would deport the Jews. Belev issued a statement that the fate of the Bulgarian Jews was already determined. Even though

50. Interview with B. Piti, January 1966, Jaffa, Israel. See also Arditi, *Roliata*, pp. 48-49.

May 24 was an important Bulgarian holiday, the day of Sts. Cyril and Methodius marked by parades and celebrations in the capital, the king left the city on the twenty-third. That afternoon Jews of all ages gathered in the small courtyard of the central synagogue in the east end of the ghetto. They decided to reconvene there the next day to march in demonstration on the palace. Communists and other members of the Fatherland Front inside and outside Iuch Bunar also called for demonstrations and the mobilization of the Jews in self-defense.[51]

May 24 was the day scheduled for the first expulsions. The citizens of Sofia planned to celebrate the holiday with parades, especially by children and adolescents. Fear of clashes with young nationalists— members of the state-organized Brannik clubs—caused the consistory leadership, on the advice of the security officer Mois Madzher, to reverse its earlier plans for a demonstration and to order the sexton to close the central synagogue. The initiative for action now fell to a curious figure in the Jewish community—Rabbi Daniel Tsion.

The Bulgarian Jewish community regarded Tsion, a mystic and student of comparative theology, with high esteem for his knowledge, but with some suspicion because of his interest in non-Jewish religions. In 1942 he had been president of the Jewish Religious Court and the foremost rabbi of the Sofia community, Josef Geron and other consistory leaders accused him of embracing Dunovism, an occult Christian sect native to Bulgaria, which included adoration of the rising sun as part of its daily service. Tsion insisted that although he knew many Dunovists, he himself, as a nonmember, merely studied the group's beliefs.

In the fall of 1942, while Rabbi Tsion had been interceding for the Jews with dignitaries whom he knew in the capital, he had heard, he believed, a message from God with a specific warning against persecution (the Jews were not mentioned by name in the message) which Tsion was to give to the leaders of the Bulgarian state and government. Tsion typed the message and duplicated a number of copies on a cyclostile apparatus. He gave the message to important officials in the capital, including the minister of finance, Bozhilov, with whom the rabbi was

---

51. "Appeal to the Jewish Population" (Communist pamphlet from May 1943) from "Moreshet" documents (unnumbered); Vladislav Topalov, "L'opinion publique bulgare contre les persécutions des juifs (octobre 1940-le 9 septembre 1944)," Études Historiques à l'occasion du XIIe Congrès Internationale des Sciences Historiques—Vienne, août-septembre, 1965, 2 (Sofia: BAN, 1965), p. 486. The present Bulgarian president and first secretary of the Bulgarian Communist party, Todor Zhivkov, was at that time the party secretary of the third Sofia district in the Jewish ghetto.

acquainted; the director of police; and Metropolitan Stefan. According to the rabbi's own account of his actions, the officials accepted the circular and treated him with respect. The metropolitan, who had long opposed the government's anti-Jewish measures, told the rabbi that the words surely came from God. Tsion gave a copy of the message to the chancellor of the court with a personal letter addressed to the king. He also gave copies of the message and the letter to the king's private chaplain, and a few days later the chaplain told the rabbi that Boris had assured him that the Jews would not be sent outside the borders of Bulgaria. (Tsion correctly understood that the decree-law of August 26, 1942, implied this danger.)

Boris, like his father Ferdinand, was very superstitious, and he very well might have seen some supernatural intent behind the rabbi's action. However, whether Boris intended to keep this promise if he had indeed made it and whether he had the ability or courage to deny deportation under all forms of Nazi pressure are questions which cannot be answered simply and which also have a bearing on any interpretation of the king's promise to Tsion.

In any case the leaders of the consistory, when they heard of Tsion's activities, declared that they in no way supported his actions, which they regarded as abnormal, and relieved the rabbi from his position on the religious court (with a pension).[52]

In the subsequent crisis of May 1943 Tsion's friendship with the Dunovists helped the Jews. Many of the people at court, perhaps even the king himself, belonged to the sect. Boris's sister Eudoxia was a member, as was also one of the king's most trusted advisors, the pro-Western Liubomir Lulchev. On May 24 at five in the morning Tsion and Menahem Mushanov, a Zionist leader, went to the Dunovist prayer grounds in eastern Sofia. Here they asked Lulchev for his advice, and he suggested that the planned demonstration go on.

When Tsion returned to the central synagogue to lead morning prayers, he found the gate locked. Agitated Jews crowded the street in front of the building. Tsion led them to the Iuch Bunar synagogue several blocks away on Princess Klementina (now Aleksandur Stamboliiski) Street. A large group had already gathered there. Tsion made a comforting speech to the throng, and Sofia's chief rabbi, Asher Hananel, also spoke.

52. For an account of these events see Rabbi Daniel Tsion, *Pet godini pod fashistki gnet* (*Spomeni*) [Five years under fascist terror (memoirs)] (Sofia n.p., 1945), pp. 34-54. Interview with Josef Geron, Pardis Katz, Israel, December, 1965.

At this time Mushanov told Tsion that Metropolitan Stefan was ready to help. Both rabbis, Tsion and Hananel, followed by a small group of others, went to see him. The streets of the capital were filled with crowds awaiting the beginning of the day's festivities, and the square before Aleksandur Nevski Cathedral was especially full—with young people who would participate in the parade and with worshipers.

The Jews greeted Stefan as he was leaving his house, and the metropolitan invited Hananel and Tsion in to hear their complaint. Stefan, upset by both the action against the Jews and the desecration by the government of the holy day, told the rabbis to wait in his home while he went to the palace. Boris was not there, but the metropolitan told the head of the king's chancellery, Pavel Gruev, to advise the king to change the orders at once. He also prepared for the king a letter in the style of Ecclesiastes, warning him not to persecute the Jews, lest he himself be persecuted. God, he said, would judge him by his own acts. Gruev promised to send the letter to the king. Returning to his home, the metropolitan told the rabbis and the assembled Jews the results of this conference.

According to Tsion, Stefan informed them that the king in the presence of the prime minister had promised not to deport the Jews. Either this statement referred to an earlier meeting, perhaps that of April 15, or Rabbi Tsion misinterpreted the metropolitan. At any rate the rabbi told this to the Jews in Iuch Bunar.

Rabbi Hananel in 1945 recalled that the metropolitan had at the time advised him to visit the court personally to intercede for the Jews, and that he and several leaders of the Sofia Jewish community had visited Mme Karavelova. Under her direction the delegation wrote a letter to the king asking for his aid. They wrote that they were prepared to make sacrifices for Bulgaria, but within its borders, not outside them. Mme Karavelova signed the letter. Other persons close to the court supported the petition, including the king's sister Eudoxia. Jewish leaders also appealed to the papal nuncio in Sofia, as well as to the Roman Catholic priests attendant on Queen Giovanna.

While the Jewish delegation was at the palace, Metropolitan Stefan addressed the crowds in front of Aleksandur Nevski cathedral. He lamented the absence of Jewish students at the holiday traditionally celebrated by all Bulgarians and said that the persecutions, which were also contrary to Bulgarian traditional tolerance, marred the festivities. Later Stefan spoke to Filov but was unable to extract a commitment to stop the deportations. Filov told him that the operation was politically necessary and that Stefan should no longer trouble himself about it, especially that he should stop disturbing the king. Stefan objected that he opposed the action on moral, not political, grounds. After the day ended, the metropolitan wrote a report on its events for the benefit of the king. He sent protests to government officials and demanded on official investigation. Stefan also told the Holy Synod to reexpress their opinion against persecutions. Boris acknowledged the receipt of the letter and the complaint and attributed the anti-Jewish policies solely to the German union. After his actions on behalf of the Jews in May, the KEV and some other Ratnitsi began to harass Stefan, but he was beyond their reach. However, Stefan heard rumors that the government was planning to try him for antigovernment activity. He could get neither Filov nor Boris to deny or confirm this, but no trial took place.

While the rabbis and other leaders spoke with Stefan and Mme Karavelova, more militant Jews began a demonstration march to the palace along Klementina Street. It did not reach further than Paissi Street, well within the ghetto. Since Gabrovski and Belev had expected trouble, the commissar sent a mixed group of police and KEV agents under the authority of Iaroslav Kalitsin, to break up the crowd and arrest the demonstrators. The officials tried to avoid a melee, but they did not treat the demonstrators leniently. Trucks and motorcycles blocked the route of the marchers. The police subdued the crowd with drawn pistols, machine guns, and whips. The officers singled out the youths among the demonstrators and forced them into the trucks. Police agents raided Jewish homes. Some accounts of the events state that Bulgarian friends helped some of the Jews, but extensive displays of Bulgarian support were scarcely possible, as the demonstrators did not even leave the ghetto.

After putting a stop to the demonstration, the KEV and police arrested those Jews scheduled for expulsion on the twenty-fourth and transported them out of the capital. They were especially eager for the seizure of the leaders of the Jewish community. After a day full of arrests, during the night the commissariat sent the most important leaders to the concentration camp at Samovit. Several Bulgarians helped the leaders at this time. Dimo Kazasov, for instance, hid the family of his colleague and friend, Menahem Faionov. The authorities had some difficulty in finding the rabbis, Hananel and Tsion, because, as we know, they were not in the ghetto. Tsion was arrested when he returned home after the conference with Stefan. Despite advance warning, he decided not to hide, and the authorities sent him to Samovit the same day.

The police found it harder to locate Hananel. The chief rabbi spent most of the day outside the ghetto gathering support for the community. Before he returned home, he called his wife and learned of his impending arrest. She advised him to stay away. The rabbi went to his mother's house, but the police arrested him the next morning and took him to the first precinct's headquarters. Hananel remained under guard that whole day. In the evening the police took him to the KEV building. Miss Panitsa escorted the rabbi into Belev's office, and immediately the commissar subjected him to a torrent of verbal abuse for pleading with the king and the bishop. "Don't you know that we are the crown and the church, that we do not do anything without the crown?" Belev was particularly abusive toward Stefan, whom he told the rabbi he hated and whose views he would disregard. However, the commissar in exasperation also told the rabbi: "You should be thankful that you have support, powerful support behind you; if this were not so, I would lock you and your entire spiritual community up this evening and send you to Germany, not Poland."

Belev placed Hananel under house arrest and ordered him not to talk to anyone except the commissar. We can surmise from Belev's statement that the court had intervened to modify the action against the Jews. Belev was correct when he told the rabbi that he did not do anything without the crown; however, this was not always what he wished to do. While returning home, the rabbi learned that Radio Sofia had announced a change in the deportation orders to prevent Communist demonstrations, but that the Jews were still to be sent out of the capital. The rabbi was not sent to Samovit because as a holder of the Cross of St. George, a military decoration, he had the right to remain in Sofia.[53]

Arrests followed for several days after May 24 although deportation to Poland was no longer an immediate concern. Before the permanent camp at Samovit was constructed, the prisoners underwent a harsh regime in the town's school building. The Jewish leaders, most of whom were among the first inmates of the camp, naturally did not know what the KEV had planned, and many of them assumed that this was the first step to deportation. From their camp at Samovit they could see the empty barges moored ominously at the Danube station.

In Sofia the expulsions continued through the following weeks. The Jews had one and a half days to obey their evacuation orders or face forced expulsion. German reports indicate that 90 percent of the Jews under orders left the capital voluntarily. In all, the government desig-

53. Sofia, Protocols of the People's Court No. 7, III, 805-17 (testimony of Dr. Asher Hananel).

nated about twenty cities to receive the evacuees, for security reasons avoiding cities along the border (with the exception of the Danube). The Sofia Jews were thrust into the limited space occupied by the resident Jews and were thrown on the charity of the local consistories and their welfare funds. At first the government housed some in empty schools, but this ceased with the end of the spring vacation. The government put the property of the Jews up for auction and gave their homes to the poor.

However, despite the reality of expulsion, the protest by prominent Bulgarians, particularly that by Metropolitan Stefan, against the government's proposed Jewish measures had forced Boris and Filov to reconsider their policy of deportation. It was no longer a feasible solution to the Jewish problem in Bulgaria, and would not be unless German successes in the war outweighed the forces of internal resistance at home. Hoffmann put his faith in the feeling that the increase of Jews in the countryside would cause the peasants, whom he counted on as more anti-Semitic than the capital residents, to demand the deportation of the Jews. Somewhat illogically, he argued that since the Jews always had money, the black market caused by their presence would drive up prices and cause further discontent; in actuality the impoverished and robbed Sofia Jews were in less of a position to affect prices than the German army stationed in the kingdom. Furthermore, the police attaché counted on a security risk in the cities with an expanded Jewish population to force the Bulgarians to reconsider deportations.[54]

Events of the Summer of 1943

In his report of June 7, Hoffmann wrote that Belev had again requested that the Reich supply one small and five large ships for the

54. For Hoffmann's views see his report of June 7, 1943, T120, serial 2330, roll 1305, frames 486350-56. For the events of May 24 and the following days, see Tsion, pp. 55-62; Metropolitan Stefan, letter of memoirs, October 17, 1950, BAN, Ebroistika, doc. no. 90; Hashua Davidov Sabetai, memoirs, September 16, 1948, doc. no. 35; Jewish Anti-Fascist Committee to Central Consistory, Sofia, 1945, doc. no. 149; Sofia Protocols of People's Court No. 7, III, 746-48 (testimony of Menahem Faionov); III, 774-79 (testimony of Isak Francis, commissar for Jewish questions after September 9, 1944); III, 804 (testimony of Daniel Tsion); III, 804-11 (testimony of Asher Hananel); IV, 1500-02 (testimony of Buko Levi); IV, 1546-49 (testimony of Mois Madzhar) (these are the most important of numerous testimonies in the protocols concerning the events of May 1943); Mohrmann, report, May 25, 1943, T120, serial 2330, roll 1305, frame 486346. See also the June 7 report of Hoffmann mentioned above; Arditi, *Roliata*, pp. 49-50, and *Yehudi Bulgariyah*, pp. 214-17.

transfer of 25,000 Jews in three months' time. The ships cost 20,000 leva ($243) a day, but the commissar announced that Bulgaria would reimburse the Germans from the Jewish community fund if any delay occurred or if there were damage to the ships from any source. Belev also indicated that the expulsion from Sofia was almost complete, but several thousand Jews still remained, having used personal influence to avoid inclusion in the operation. The commissar promised to try to expel them. Filov and Gabrovski especially were damaging the Jewish program, Belev complained, but Hoffmann noted in the report that Filov had constantly assured Beckerle that the government agreed with a solution in the German sense. The major difficulty, the police attaché wrote, was that this was not a simple question for Bulgaria (*"dass die bulgarische Regierung diese Frage nicht einfach über das Knie brechen kann"*). Matters of internal and foreign politics demanded attention. Hoffmann compared Bulgaria's position to that of Hungary, whose leaders were also reluctant to deport Jews in 1943. He reassured Berlin that the Bulgarian government could be trusted, but that its desire to prevent adverse foreign propaganda certainly was understandable. As evidence of Bulgarian good faith, he referred to Filov's arguments with the Swiss ambassador, justifying the deportation of the Macedonian Jews to Poland. Furthermore, a leading anti-Semite in the Subranie, Dimitur Andreev, told Belev that after the assassination of Sotir Ianev (in which, by the way, no Jews were implicated), the representatives felt that the Jews must be deported. (This was surely an exaggeration.) Hoffmann's conclusion was that Bulgaria was nevertheless committed to deportations and that there was no way it could get out of its commitment.[55]

Beckerle sent a report of his own on the same day, confirming this position. Both Boris and Filov, however, for the present insisted on the need for Jewish labor in Bulgaria. Contrary to the report of Hauptsturmführer Bosshammer, the government expressed satisfaction with the quality of the Jewish laborers; in fact, they wished there were additional workers available. Belev's statements against the government, Beckerle said, were untrustworthy. The commissar was part of an opposition movement against the king and cabinet. Beckerle himself had second thoughts about the commissar's proposals. He assured Berlin of Filov's and the entire government's honesty in this matter, but urged the Germans to consider the Bulgarian mentality—its lack of ideological strength —and in particular the fact that since the Bulgarians had grown up with

55. Hoffmann, report, June 7, 1943, T120, serial 2330, roll 1305, frame 486350-56.

Armenians, Greeks, and Gypsies, they had no innate prejudice against the Jews as did the people of northern Europe. The Bulgarian Jews, unlike Jews in northern Europe, Beckerle continued, were mostly lower-class artisans and "diligent workers." (This was tantamount to an admission that anti-Semitic propaganda in Bulgaria stemmed from false premises.)

Beckerle concluded that Berlin should not press Sofia on this matter, for such pressure might alienate the Bulgarians. The government at least recognized that the Jews were allies of their enemies, the Western powers and the Communists; and deportations might be forthcoming in the immediate future. Now that the technical difficulties of resettlement in the country had been met, some problems were cleared up. The ambassador felt that the rash of assassinations at the beginning of the year would spur the government to action. In addition, Beckerle insisted that the question was related to German victories in the war.[56]

In his last point Beckerle had correctly assessed the German problem. The war had turned against the Reich, and Bulgaria would not really consider deportation again until this reversal had ceased. The moderation of Beckerle's statement reflects his tact and diplomacy. He also assured the Germans he would continue to urge the Bulgarians to begin deportations.

In August Horst Wagner wrote to Beckerle about the Bulgarian situation. The RSHA reported that the resettlement, contrary to expectation, had not increased anti-Semitism in the villages. The RSHA insisted that the Jews were spies for the Communists and the West, maintaining secret radio stations, spreading rumors and news reports from the BBC and the radio station "Hristo Botev" in the Caucasus. The Jews would certainly present a danger behind the lines if there were an Allied invasion of the Balkans. Furthermore, every day their influence in high state and church circles increased. Because of these factors, the SS desired the immediate deportation of the Bulgarian Jews. They assumed Bulgaria was ready to comply.

Beckerle in his answer tried to cool Wagner and the RSHA's urgency. It was less hopeful than his replies of June. He confessed that every effort to impress the Bulgarian government with the need for deportation had failed. He included a detailed report in answer to the points Wagner raised. The resettlement, Beckerle claimed, had indeed pro-

56. Beckerle, report, June 7, 1943, ibid., frames 486357-59 (Nuremberg doc. no. NG-2357); Hoffmann reiterated this position later in the month, report, June 24, 1943, T120, serial 267, roll 225, frames 173953-56.

duced anti-Semitism in the villages. (Although there were incidents of anti-Semitism, especially later on after Allied bombing raids began, there is no evidence that this was widespread.) Beckerle had approached the minister of war on the question of further Jewish resettlement, but he had refused to involve the military.

Beckerle traced the origins of the difficulties to April when Boris had raised objections with Ribbentrop. The Bulgarians concerned themselves too much with the impression that the deportations would make abroad. The ambassador compared this to Bulgaria's refusal to publicize its downings of American planes flying to and from the Ploesti raids of August 1943 and its censorship of anti-Communist propaganda. Beckerle traced all of Bulgaria's actions to a terrifying fear (*Angst*) of Allied air raids. He said that the Bulgarians admitted that they were trying to create a false picture of the internal political situation until Germany could prevent such attacks, which had not yet begun against Bulgaria. Sofia also raised the question of the lack of deportations from Rumania and Hungary.[57] Beckerle concluded with the belief that only a German victory in the war could force the Bulgarians to change their minds. It was unprofitable and even dangerous for the Reich to put pressure on Sofia at this time, but the foreign office might try discussing the matter with the Bulgarian embassy in Berlin.[58]

The new German victories never materialized, and the RSHA's despair in August over the loss of the Bulgarian Jews proved to be justified. After May 1943 Berlin's attempts to induce the Bulgarians to send their Jews to Poland were fruitless. Indeed, as the war for Bulgaria drew to a close in the following months, the Germans stopped requesting deportations. Other more urgent matters connected with their retreat from the Soviet Union demanded Berlin's attention. While the protests of the Bulgarian community in March and May were the initial factor in preventing the destruction of the Bulgarian Jewish community, it was the

57. The Hungarians resisted deportations until March 1944, when a government with extreme anti-Semitic tendencies came to power. The Rumanians vacillated between carrying out the Final Solution with excessive enthusiasm and refusing to implement it at all. The Rumanians actually maintained their own extermination center in Podolia, where barbarism exceeded that of the Germans in Poland, even if the number of the victims did not. The Jews who were killed there came from territory Bucharest took from the USSR in 1941. However, the Rumanians never did send Jews to Poland. See Hilberg, pp. 485-554, and below, pp. 196-97.

58. Wagner to Beckerle, August [15], 1943, T120, serial K780, roll 4201, frame K206527; Beckerle, reports, August 18 and 19, 1943, ibid., frames K206528-33. See Wagner to Kaltenbrunner, chief of the RSHA, August 31, 1943, ibid., frames K206542-47 (Nuremberg doc. no. NG-3302).

increased victories of the Allies which sustained the government's decision not to hand the Jews over to the Nazis.

Rescue Attempts During the Summer of 1943

Meanwhile, in the summer of 1943, rescue operations originating in the West went into a new, if still only halfhearted, phase. Through the Swiss the British government sent Berlin another message that it would allow 5,000 Jewish children from Poland and other occupied eastern territories into Palestine. Persons living in the Allied and neutral lands and interested in the fate of the Bulgarian Jews tried to arrange for their migration to Palestine as well. These persons included Jaques Asseov; Stephen Wise; Rabbi Marcus Ehrenpreis of Stockholm, the former chief rabbi of Bulgaria; G. M. Dimitrov, leader of the Agrarian Union—"Aleksandur Stamboliiski"; and others. In July Rabbi Freedman, chairman of the Propalestine Committee in Jerusalem, a Zionist organization, sent a telegram to Churchill and Eden asking that Bulgarian Jews be permitted into Palestine. The Action Juive asked that a number of Jews larger than the British quota of 5,000 be permitted to leave German-held lands. In addition, Red Cross officials asked the German embassy in Ankara to permit one thousand Bulgarian Jews to sail to Haifa.

The Germans answered the British request by refusing permission for the Jews' emigration to Palestine because of the injustice it would do the Arab inhabitants, but they stated that the Germans would be willing to send the Jews to Great Britain in exchange for German prisoners of war. The Reich counted on the House of Commons to refuse the influx of so many unwanted persons into England. Berlin told Sofia and other governments which had received similar requests to follow the same course. The Germans were convinced that the British would never accept the proposal, but in the event that London did, they prepared to permit the emigration. The British rejected the plan, arguing that they did not want to exchange German prisoners for persons who were not citizens of the British Empire.

A second proposal of 1943, originating with Marshal Antonescu of Rumania, to exchange Jews for ransom payments, the United Nations similarly rejected. Nevertheless, pressure in the Allied countries to rescue the Jews, despite some official reluctance, spurred the governments to increase their efforts to force the Axis powers to comply in the latter half of 1943 and 1944. In October 1943 the Swiss, on behalf of the

British, once again asked the Sofia government to permit 5,000 Jews to leave for Palestine. The Bulgarians had continued their tactics of the spring—refusing on technical grounds and managing to avoid an unqualified denial which would cast them in a bad light. The Allies, however, were losing patience with delaying tactics. The Bulgarians said that they were quite ready to make use of the German exchange solution if the Allies would accept. From the other side, Berlin put counterpressure on the Bulgarians not to permit the emigrations.

As a result, mass emigration from Bulgaria did not occur, but toward the end of 1943 and especially through 1944, the Bulgarians did not hinder individual emigration of Jews. In fact, exit visas soon became rather easy to obtain, and the major problem for the prospective emigré was obtaining a British entry visa to Palestine. (London, while ready to permit mass migration, made things difficult for the single traveler.) The stream of emigrants through Istanbul, which actually never completely stopped even in the early days of 1943, became a strong and steady flow.[59]

The Death of King Boris III

In August of 1943 King Boris III suddenly died, ending almost a decade of semidictatorial rule. This abrupt change in the hierarchy of the state placed a new strain on Bulgaria's wartime leaders and gravely affected the course of the country in the months that followed. Furthermore, the suddenness of the king's death raised a number of rumors that he had been murdered. Because some of these rumors are related to Bulgaria's Jewish policy, we may with some profit review the circumstances of the monarch's death and the crisis which ensued.

The events of August must be considered in the light of the course of the war, not only the collapse of Mussolini, but also the advance of the Red Army. In July the Allies invaded Sicily and by the end of the month Mussolini resigned as head of the government. Marshal Badoglio began negotiating a truce with the Allies. The Italian collapse disturbed Axis authority on the Balkan peninsula, and Hitler now needed Bulgaria to

59. Wagner, Vortragsnotiz, July 21, 1943, T120, serial 2330, roll 1305, frames 486362-68; Papen and Torerezu, report, Ankara, July 13, 1943, T120, serial K784, roll 4202, frame K207809; Thadden, Vortragsnotiz, December 20, 1943, ibid., frames K207740-41; enclosure to above, October 28, 1943, ibid., frames K207744-45; Hilberg, p. 721; Arditi, *Yehudi Bulgariyah*, pp. 314-17. For reports of Jewish emigrés from Bulgaria, see various consular reports from Istanbul in Department of State documents, National Archives record group 59, under number 874.4016.

take over more of the military requirements there. On August 9, Beckerle informed the king that Hitler wanted to see him for the third time that year at his headquarters (the Wolfsschantze).[60] Besides Boris's visit of April to Berchtesgaden he had traveled to the Wolfsschantze in June to discuss the possibility of a Balkan front which did not materialize.[61] The Bulgarians were extremely sensitive about publicized German interference in their country's affairs, and the king especially did not like the unfavorable impression caused by his frequent visits to Hitler. Both in April and June he had traveled incognito. Again in August Boris requested the strictest secrecy regarding the visit. His secretary, Stanislav A. Balan, asked that the führer's pilot Hans Bauer wear civilian clothes, as he had been recognized at the airport in June, and the news of the king's trip then had leaked out.[62] Boris and Filov were troubled over the suddenness of the German request. They feared Hitler would ask for more Bulgarian participation in the war, perhaps action on the Russian front. They decided that Bulgaria could expend more troops in the Balkans, if necessary.[63]

In order to avoid traveling on the thirteenth, Boris decided to leave August 14. He returned the day after. Hitler apparently did not ask the Bulgarian monarch to send troops into Russia. Boris told Filov that the journey was not satisfactory, but that they had discussed only an expanded role for Bulgaria in the Balkans. The Germans still believed that an Allied invasion there was forthcoming. With Italy in confusion and the Germans in retreat in the East, Hitler asked Bulgaria to supply two divisions to fight in northern Greece and eventually in Albania—essentially backing up German troops. Boris promised only one. He now had little confidence in the German ability to stop the Russians or in that of the Western powers to stop the spread of communism into the Balkans after the war. The journey had made him very weary and downcast.[64]

60. Filov, "Diary," entry for August 9, 1943, *Naroden Sud*, no. 5, p. 3; Beckerle, report, August 9, 1943, T120, serial 267, roll 225, frame 174013.

61. Filov, "Diary," entries for May 30, June 5, and June 10, 1943, *Naroden Sud*, no. 3, p. 4; Beckerle to Ribbentrop, May 29, 1943, T120, serial 267, roll 225, frame 173923.

62. Ribbentrop to Beckerle, August 10, 1943, T120, serial 267, roll 225, frame 174014; Beckerle to Ribbentrop, August 10, 1943, ibid., frame 174015; Beckerle, reports, August 11 and 12, 1943, ibid., frames 174021-22.

63. Beckerle to Ribbentrop, August 11, 1943, ibid., frames 174017-19; Beckerle, report, August 14, 1943, ibid., frame 174025; Filov, "Diary," entries for August 10 and 14, 1943, *Naroden Sud*, no. 5, p. 3.

64. Beckerle to Ribbentrop, August 6, 1943, T120, serial 267, roll 225, frame 174011; Filov, "Diary," entry for August 15, 1943, *Naroden Sud*, no. 5, p. 3.

After his return from the führer's headquarters, the king went for a week's holiday to Cham Koria, his retreat in the Rila mountains; on one day he climbed Mousalla—the highest peak in the Balkans. Boris returned to Sofia on Monday the twenty-third. That evening he had a heart attack, and five days later he died.

Iordan Sevov, the enigmatic advisor of the king, informed Filov of the king's illness only on August 25.[65] The Germans learned of it on the twenty-third, the night of the attack, although Beckerle's telegram on the subject of the illness reached Hitler only on the twenty-fourth. Colonel von Schönebeck, the air attaché, had informed Göring the day before.[66] Hitler was very disturbed that Göring had received the news first; and Beckerle, who did not get along with the air attaché anyway, insisted that Schönebeck be dismissed from Sofia. It is doubtful, however, that this conflict between the führer and his air force chief had significance in the death of King Boris.

Three leading German physicians came to the king's side to help the Bulgarian physicians. The king rallied a few times in his five-day ordeal and occasionally was conscious, but he never recovered. During the whole time the public was unaware of his illness. Only on August 27 did Reuters News Agency publish a first report released by the government under pressure of rumors.

As soon as the news of the king's illness and death appeared abroad, rumors of assassination spread throughout the world. The *New York Times* told a bizarre story of a police inspector shooting Boris in the Sofia railway station. A more sober, if still incredible, story has developed since. Hitler is supposed to have ordered the assassination of Boris, to occur on his return home from their stormy meeting of the fourteenth. Scanty memoirs and statements charge that during his return journey, the Nazis gave the king a poison gas through his oxygen mask and that this induced his heart attack. The king's lack of a history of heart disease, supporters of this account say, makes a natural attack seem unlikely.[67]

This story of an unidentified poison which induces a heart attack a

65. Filov, "Diary," entry for August 25, 1943, *Naroden Sud*, no. 5, p. 3.
66. Ribbentrop to Beckerle, September 1, 1943, T120, serial 267, roll 225, frames 174132-33; Beckerle to Ribbentrop, September 2, 1943, ibid., frames 174142-44; report (unsigned), September 8, 1943, ibid., frames 174236-43.
67. The most important of these statements supporting the assassination theory and implicating the Germans is Prince Kiril's testimony before the People's Court in January 1945. See the London *Times*, January 15, 1945, p. 3; *New York Times*, January 13, 1945, p. 4. For a discussion of the king's return flight, see Helmut Heiber, "Der Tod des Zaren Boris," *Vierteljahrshefte für Zeitgeschichte*, 4 (October 1961), pp. 392-93.

week after its administration leaves one somewhat skeptical. Furthermore, the questions of both motive and culprit cannot be answered with satisfactory proof. Since, according to Filov, the discussion between Hitler and Boris involved the use of Bulgarian troops only in the Balkans, not in the Soviet Union, the king's refusal to break off relations with the latter seems to have little to do with a motive. It is also doubtful that an argument over the use of one division in the Balkans would have provided Hitler with sufficient motive to have Boris assassinated. Furthermore, there is no evidence that Hitler planned this alleged assassination. In fact, all things point to the contrary: that he was surprised by the king's death.

Nevertheless, the German physicians believed that poisoning was a possibility. They admitted so to Beckerle, although they were reluctant to give a scientific opinion without an autopsy. Beckerle instructed the doctors not to mention this possibility to anyone, presumably because of the current Allied propaganda trying to link the Germans with the king's death. Beckerle in his dispatch regarding the conversation wrote that the doctors thought Boris had been poisoned, but he did not give his own opinion.[68] If the Germans did indeed poison Boris, there is one possible motive: the fear in Germany, in particular within the RSHA, that Boris was planning to pull out of the war. Mussolini's government had fallen on July 25. The Badoglio government did not actually sign a separate peace until September, but as a partner Italy was lost. Bulgaria, the country that had been the first to make peace in World War I, could, the Germans believed, be next.

At the beginning of August, Sevov went to Ankara; a few days later K'oseivanov, the former prime minister, reported to the king from Berne. There is no doubt that both men were in contact with the Allies, although in the American documents reports of this are lacking. Shortly thereafter a rumor arose in German circles, especially among the RSHA, that a government less friendly to the Axis would replace Filov's. K'oseivanov's name was first mentioned; but on August 16 the RSHA told the foreign office of a rumor that a government officially headed by Mushanov and Bagrianov and controlled in reality by Sevov and the moderate Agrarian Konstantin Muraviev was about to be formed. Muraviev and Mushanov were anti-German. The RSHA reports also sug-

68.   Beckerle, report, August 29, 1943, T120, serial 267, roll 225, frames 174094-96. In 1965, Beckerle stated his belief that Boris had been poisoned but was reluctant to say who he thought had assassinated the king. Interview with Adolf-Heinz Beckerle, Frankfurt-am-Main, Germany, November 1965.

gested that the government change would foreshadow an armistice with England.[69]

Whether the rumors were true or not, they could have motivated an assassination by the RSHA without Hitler's knowledge. Nevertheless, without more definite evidence it is difficult to give full credence to the assassination hypotheses. The consensus of historians currently writing in Bulgaria is that Boris died of natural causes. One thing is clear: the Nazis would not have murdered Boris for his refusal either to send troops into the Soviet Union or to deport the Jews to Poland.[70]

After the king's death the immediate political problem for Bulgaria was the determination of a regency council for the king's heir, six-year-old King Simeon. Berlin desired that someone who would follow Boris's pro-German policy should become supreme leader of the country. If in addition it was someone whom they could control better than they had the wily Boris all the better. Direct German interference and pressure primarily influenced the ultimate selection.

Article 27 of the constitution provided that a Great Subranie, a special congress with twice the membership of the legislative Subranie, select the three regents of the council. The constitution required that the regents themselves be former ministers or judges. Relatives of the king were by strong implication not likely candidates. (This implication, in fact, had been a factor in the struggle between crown and Subranie in

---

69. Dietrich von Jagow, Budapest, report, August 11, 1943, T120, serial 267, roll 225, fr. 174016; Obergruppenführer Ernst Kaltenbrunner, Chef SP und SD, RSHA, to Himmler and Wagner, August 16, 1943, T120, serial 2320H, roll 1305, frames 485661-62. Also duplicated in T120, serial 267, roll 225, frames 174027-28.

70. For the king's illness and death, in addition to those items mentioned in the preceding notes, see Filov, "Diary," entries for August 25, 26, 27, 28, 1943, *Naroden Sud*, no. 5, p. 3; and Beckerle, reports, August 24, 25, 26, 27, and 28, 1943, T120, serial 267, roll 225, frames 174042, 174044-49, 174054, 174063, 174067, 174072-73, 174078-80, and 174083-84. Queen Giovanna of Bulgaria wrote a memoir of her husband's death but declared that she did not know whether or not he had died of natural causes. See Giovanna di Bulgaria, "Svelo per la prima volta i retroscena della morte misteriosa di mio marito" [I reveal for the first time the intrigue behind the mysterious death of my husband], *Oggi* (Milan), September 7, 1961, pp. 54-55, 57, and 59. Heiber has the most complete account, although at times it seems to take on the character of a polemic exonerating the Germans. He does not think the RSHA could have committed the assassination alone (p. 415). See also N. P. Nikolaev, *Le regne et la morte de Boris III roi des Bulgares 1894-1918-1943* (Uppsala: Ulmqvist and Wiksells, 1952), pp. 82-96; Bulgarian Academy of Sciences, *Istoriia na Bulgariia* [History of Bulgaria], ed. D. Kosev et al. (Sofia: "Nauka i izkustvo," 1962-64), III, 405 (hereafter cited as BAN, *Istoriia*); Ilcho Dimitrov, "Smurtta na Tsar Boris III" [The death of King Boris III], *Istoricheski pregled* [Historical review], 24, no. 2 (1968), pp. 40-59.

the 1880s.)[71] Constitutionally Boris could have selected a regency council, subject to the approval of the Great Subranie, before he died, but
he had not done so.

In late August and early September the highest Bulgarian political
circles proposed many persons with varying views for the regency:
among them Mushanov; K'oseivanov; Hristo Kalfov, president of the
Subranie and a member of the Military League; Nikola Georgiev, chief
justice of the administrative court; Sevov; Muraviev; Tsankov; and Kimon Georgiev.[72] Filov discussed the matter with friends of the government and the opposition alike, including the ex-premiers Mushanov,
Tsankov, and Kimon Georgiev.[73] The right wing of Bulgarian politics,
especially the military, favored General Nikola Zhekov, a hero of World
War I and now head of the Legionaires, or General Ivan Vulkov, minister of war in the twenties and afterward ambassador to Rome, who
had IMRO connections.[74] The Germans were not satisfied with most of
these candidates although some would have been acceptable. Kalfov,
who at one time had been a Tsankovite, was too much identified with
Italy. Sevov was too mysterious and unknown. He was the head of Boris's
espionage bureau, and Beckerle and Ribbentrop distrusted him.[75]

Both Filov and the Germans, as well as such other Bulgarian leaders
as Tsankov, thought it unwise to convoke a Great Subranie because
the resultant political disputes would disturb internal stability in wartime. They concluded that a regency proposed by Filov's cabinet would
have to be approved by the ordinary Subranie.[76] Furthermore, even

71. C. E. Black, *The Establishment of Constitutional Government in Bulgaria*
(Princeton, N.J.: Princeton University Press, 1943), pp. 250, 311-14.
72. Filov, "Diary," entries for August 29 and 31, September 1 and 6, 1943,
Naroden Sud, no. 5, pp. 3-4; Beckerle, reports, August 30 and September 6, 1943,
T120, serial 267, roll 225, frames 174023-24; Gustav A. Steengracht von Moyland,
Staatssekretär in charge after April 1943, to Franz von Sonnleithner, Büro RAM,
August 30, 1943, ibid., frames 174113-16; Günther Altenburg, foreign office, and
Beckerle to Ribbentrop, August 31, September 1, 2, and 6, 1943, ibid., frames
174127-29, 174138-40, 174145-46, and 174193-95; Steengracht and Jagow to Ribbentrop, Budapest, September 6, 1943, ibid., frames 174203-07.
73. Filov, "Diary," entry for September 1, 1943, *Naroden Sud*, no. 5, p. 3.
74. Steengracht to Sonnleithner, September 6, 1943, T120, serial 267, roll 225,
frames 174189-91.
75. "Kniaginiata Evdokiia risuva portretite na tsarskite suvetnitsi (Iz pokaz-
aniiata na Kniaginiata)" [Princess Eudoxia depicts portraits of the tsar's advisors
(From the testimony of the princess)], *Naroden Sud*, no. 2, p. 5; Beckerle, reports,
August 31, September 2 and 9, 1943, T120, serial 267, roll 225, frames 174122-23,
174153-55, 174249-51; Altenburg and Beckerle to Ribbentrop, September 3, 1943,
ibid., frames 174159-60; Steengracht, Sofia, report, September 5, 1943, ibid., frames
174178-81; Jagow, report, September 9, 1943, ibid., frame 174248.
76. Filov, "Diary," entry for September 1, 1943, *Naroden Sud*. no. 5, p. 3;

during those several days before the king's death, Berlin thought that it would serve the Nazi purpose if the king's brother Kiril was the chief regent. Ribbentrop had the impression that Kiril was popular among military circles and very pro-Nazi. Beckerle advised him that the prince, unlike his brother, was completely apolitical, enjoyed little popularity with any large segment of the Bulgarian population, and was one of the most notorious roués in Europe. Nevertheless, the foreign office thought that he would comply with German wishes and would represent a continuation of Boris's government. They definitely wanted him for the regency. The Bulgarians objected that this was illegal under Bulgarian constitutional law. Berlin advised Sofia that Bulgarian law had been broken many times since 1934, and that one more irregularity would not matter. German lawyers helped their Bulgarian colleagues find loopholes. So, although the leaders whom Filov consulted did not think Kiril a good choice, he was to be a regent. The dowager queen gave her approval.[77]

The Germans also wanted Filov as a regent.[78] Filov, whom the king had chosen as prime minister for his lack of both political experience and independence, had proven to be loyal to the German cause in the past years. Filov agreed to enter the regency council, but this created new problems. Filov wanted to run the government with Kiril, although officially the first regent, subordinate to him and the third regent also a weaker personality. The Germans and Filov agreed on General Mihov, the minister of war, a pro-German officer without notable political ambitions.[79] The depleted cabinet would now not only require a new prime minister but at least new ministers of foreign affairs and war as well. The Germans toyed with the idea of establishing a Ratnik or

---

77. Filov, "Diary," entries for September 1 and 6, 1943, *Naroden Sud*, no. 5, pp. 3-4; Steengracht to Beckerle, August 27, 1943, T120, serial 267, roll 225, frame 174050; Beckerle, reports, August 27, September 1 and 8, 1943, ibid., frames 174051, 174135-37, 174227-29; report (unsigned), Sofia, August 28, 1943, ibid., frames 174076-77; von Brandenstein, chairman of the German-Bulgarian Trade Committee, report, Berlin, August 30, 1943, ibid., frames 174117-18; Beckerle to Ribbentrop, August 31, 1943, ibid., frames 174125-26.

78. Beckerle, reports, August 31 and September 2, 1943, T120, serial 267, roll 225, frames 174119-20, 174148-50; Altenburg and Beckerle to Ribbentrop, September 3, 1943, ibid., frames 174159-60; Steengracht, report, Sofia, September 5, 1943, ibid., frames 174178-81.

79. Beckerle, reports, September 9 and 10, 1943, ibid., frames 174249-51, 174258; Altenburg and Beckerle to Ribbentrop, September 9, 1943, ibid., frame 174252.

Legionaire government but rejected it.[80] The Nazis kept an eye upon IMRO leader Ivan Mihailov, who was living in Zagreb as a guest of Ante Pavelich.[81] Beckerle did not think much of Tsankov although he had champions in Berlin, led by Ribbentrop. For one thing, the ambassador now said, his signing of the Subranie protest against Jewish deportation was against him, even though in March Beckerle had suggested that this was not a serious gesture. Tsankov at any rate was unpopular in the country at large because of his leadership of the 1923 *coup d'état* against Stamboliiski.[82] If Tsankov was unacceptable, then Berlin wanted Gabrovski as prime minister.[83]

The names of Bagrianov, another ghost from the past, and K'oseivanov also circulated frequently in pregovernment rumors. K'oseivanov in fact, became a most serious candidate, first for a position on the regency and then for the premiership. Filov, who had been K'oseivanov's minister of education, did not object unconditionally to Boris's ex–prime minister, but Berlin thought him to be completely unsuitable for its purpose. The Germans put pressure on Sofia not to consider his candidacy.[84]

Filov preferred a weak prime minister, so that he himself could control affairs in Bulgaria, and the Nazis agreed. The outgoing premier insisted that the new cabinet should not include Gabrovski—the most likely person to form an opposition faction to Filov in the government.[85] On September 7 in spite of the insistence of the opposition, led

80. Beckerle, reports, August 30 and September 2 and 8, 1943, T120, serial 267, roll 225, frames 174108-09, 174148-50, 174234-35; Ribbentrop to Altenburg and Beckerle, September 8, 1943, ibid., frames 174223-24.

81. Feine, Southeastern Europe division of the political section foreign office, report, August 13, 1943, ibid., frames 174023-24; Altenburg and Beckerle to Ribbentrop, September 9, 1943, ibid., frame 174256.

82. Altenburg and Beckerle to Ribbentrop, August 31, 1943, ibid., frames 174127-29; Ribbentrop to Beckerle, September 1, 1943, ibid., frame 174131; Ribbentrop to Steengracht, September 5, 1943, ibid., frames 174182-83.

83. Altenburg and Beckerle to Ribbentrop, September 6, 1943, ibid., frames 174193-95; Ribbentrop to Altenburg and Beckerle, September 8, 1943, ibid., frames 174223-24.

84. Ribbentrop to Beckerle, September 1, 1943, ibid., frames 174138-40; Ribbentrop to Steengracht, September 5, 1943, ibid., frames 174182-83; Steengracht to Sonnleithner, September 6, 1943, ibid., frames 174189-91; Ribbentrop to Altenburg and Beckerle, September 8, 1943, ibid., frames 174223-24; Beckerle, report, September 8, 1943, ibid., frames 174225-26; Altenburg (Athens) to Ribbentrop, September 11, 1943, T120, serial 284 (Office of Staatssekretär, Bulgaria, vol. 6, September 11, 1943, to February 29, 1944), roll 241, frame 181107.

85. Filov, "Diary," entry for September 12, 1943, *Naroden Sud*, no. 5, p. 4; Sonnleithner to Steengracht, September 6, 1943, T120, serial 267, roll 225, frames 174187-88; Beckerle, report, September 6, 1943, ibid., frames 174198-202; Steen-

by Mushanov and Stainov, that the proper procedure, the calling of a Great Subranie, be followed and their protest of the motion, the Subranie accepted Kiril, Filov, and Mihov as regents.[86] A few days later a new cabinet was announced. The prime minister was the senior member of the departing cabinet, Minister of Finance Dobri Bozhilov. The new foreign minister was a professional diplomat, Sava Kirov, who at that time represented the kingdom at Ankara. The incoming minister of internal affairs was Docho Hristov, one of the leading anti-Semites of the Subranie, a friend of Gabrovski. However, Subranie member Dr. Ivan Beshkov, an Agrarian, became minister of agriculture, and Ivan Vazov became minister of trade. Both these men had signed the protest against the deportation of the Jews. The Germans pronounced the new cabinet satisfactory—K'oseivanov was not included. Yet, in reality, although committed to a pro-German policy, the new government was the most moderate since January 1940.[87]

The cabinet change led to one important immediate result for the Jews. With Gabrovski out of the government, the protective cover on the Vatev corruption case was removed. Agent Lazanov after his dismissal from the commissariat had joined Sofia's police force. In the fall of 1943 he told his superiors of the Vatev affair in the commissariat. The chief of criminal police took the matter up with the public prosecutor. The case was not brought to trial because of the connections of the persons involved, but rumors of corruption in the KEV were now public. In October the government asked Belev to resign, although he had not been involved in Vatev's dishonesty. Belev took a new post in the Ministry of Internal Affairs—chief of the Central Directorate of Control. This was not really a demotion; Belev chose the position for himself. The cabinet appointed as the new commissar for Jewish questions Hristo Stomaniakov, an assistant procurator in the Sofia appellate court. Unlike Belev, he was not a professional anti-Semite. The government asked for Belev's resignation, not because its Jewish policy had gone through

---

gracht and Jagow (Budapest) to Ribbentrop, September 6, 1943, ibid., frames 174203-07; Altenburg (Athens) to Ribbentrop, September 11, 1943, T120, serial 284, roll 241, frame 181107.

86. Filov, "Diary," entry for September 1, 1943, *Naroden Sud*, no. 5, p. 3; Beckerle, reports, September 8 and 9, 1943, T120, serial 267, roll 225, frames 174227-29, 174257.

87. Filov, "Diary," entries for September 1, 6, and 9, 1943, *Naroden Sud*, no. 5, pp. 3-4; Altenburg and Beckerle to Ribbentrop, September 10, 1943, T120, serial 267, roll 225, frame 174260; Beckerle to Oberkommando der Wehrmacht (OKW), September 14, 1943, T120, serial 284, roll 241, frame 181118; Beckerle, reports, September 14, 1943, ibid., frames 181119-27.

a dramatic change, but because of public scandal. However, his replacement reflected the change which the Jewish policy had undergone in 1943. The German influence and, to a degree, interest in this area had decreased. The Bulgarians now considered the question strictly a legal matter and would treat it in that manner. Without their admitting it, a quite astonishing transition had already taken place.[88]

The KEV Under Stomaniakov

The new minister of internal affairs was one of the country's leading anti-Semites, but the commissar was not one at all, and the atmosphere of tension for the Jews lessened greatly at the end of 1943 and throughout 1944. The position of the Jews froze as the legal restrictions remained but did not worsen, and for the most part, discussion of the dreaded deportations stopped. In one of his first acts pertaining to the Jews Hristov ordered those who had been expelled from the capital to liquidate their movable property. The Nazis, as well they might, interpreted this as an act confirming the Sofia ban on Jews. The Jews were allowed to return for ten days in November to dispose of their property.[89]

During these months the Jews lived crowded into the homes of other Jews in provincial towns, or, in the case of most of the men of working age, separated from their families in permanent work detachments. In the provinces, the Jews lived under a rigorous regime, restricted in movement, in work, etc. The series of provincial restrictions which had been applied after August 1942 remained in force. Only a small minority were in the concentration camps at Pleven (Tabashko Cheshma and Kailuka Park) and Samovit, which had become short-term prisons for the infractions of regulations established by the Jewish laws. Other concentration camps in Bulgaria, larger and more numerous, were used principally for imprisoning Communists and partisans. Some Jews, who fought with the partisans or who were members of the BKP, found themselves incarcerated in these.

The Jews confined in the special concentration camps endured the worst conditions. Life in these camps was depressing; the food and

---

88. Svetoslav P. Nikolov, report (no date—after September 9, 1944); Iordan Karelov Lazanov, two reports (no date—after September 9, 1944) (all of these are found in BAN, Ebroistika, doc. no. 55); Sonnleithner to Altenburg, October 27, 1943, T120, serial 284, roll 241, frames 181241-46; Beckerle, report, October 13, 1943, T120, serial K787, roll 4202, frame K208532.

89. News release, October 7, 1943, T120, serial K787, roll 4202, frame K208534; German embassy in Sofia, report, November 8, 1943, ibid., frame K208536.

housing were poor. Men, women, and children lived in the same barracks under a regulated regime.

Authorities abused the inmates in a number of ways—threats of deportation, anti-Semitic speeches, severe restrictions of movement and activity, confiscation of property, etc. Rabbi Daniel Tsion wrote in his memoirs that he was slapped by a guard after he complained to a superior about this guard's physical and mental abuse. This indicates that excessive anti-Semitism and cruelty may not have come upon orders from above. There are some who thought that after Stomaniakov became commissar, the administration in the camps became more lenient. Fraternization between Jewish inmates and Bulgarian guards was not unusual, even with guards who could occasionally be cruel or appear to be, in the context of the times, anti-Semitic.[90]

Bulgarian Politics in Crisis

In the new regime, Filov, who had not previously distinguished himself as a politician, proved to be the leading personality. Berlin's hope of dominating Bulgarian politics at first appeared promising, but Filov under stress demonstrated his independence. Moreover as the Red Army advanced steadily westward, German influence in the kingdom lessened. Caught between opposing powers nearing the climax of their struggle, the Bulgarian government became very unstable.

The most serious issues confronting the government were the activities of Communist-led partisans and the demands of the Soviet Union. With the increasing Russian victories, the partisan campaigns began to take on the nature of a civil war, and the German and Bulgarian military had to help the police. Sofia asked Berlin for increased military supplies to fight the guerrillas.[91] Communists also infiltrated the army, causing a shake-up of the general staff in May 1944.[92]

90.   For the best description of life in Samovit, see Tsion, pp. 60-77. Also see Sofia, Protocols of People's Court No. 7, II, 746-48 (testimony of Menahem Faionov); II, 799 (testimony of Zhak Natan); and II, 977-78 (testimony of Mrs. Eliazer Alkalai), among others, Rabbi Avram Hegan, statement ("Episode from Samovit"), BAN, Ebroistika, doc. no. 31; Albert Adrori, statement ("My Experience at Samovit"), doc. no. 31; Hashua Davidov Sabetai, statement, September 16, 1948, doc. no. 35; lists of persons sent to concentration camps, doc. no. 45.

91.   Sonnleithner to Altenburg, October 25, 1943, T120, serial 284, roll 241, frames 181241-46; Beckerle, report, November 13, 1943, ibid., frame 181289; Altenburg and Beckerle to Ribbentrop, March 10, 1944, T120, serial 76 (Office of Staatssekretär, Bulgaria, vol. 7, March 1 to August 31, 1944), roll 73, frames 57583-84; Beckerle, reports, April 28 and May 15, 1944, ibid., frames 57694, 57745.

92.   Sonnleithner to Altenburg, October 25, 1943, T120, serial 284, roll 241,

The most important area of partisan activity was Macedonia, where Josef Broz-Tito's forces had acquired control over all Communist guerrillas. (The Bulgarians also collaborated with the Greek equivalent of the Fatherland Front [EAM] and its army [ELAS].) To achieve better security the Germans considered setting up some sort of autonomous Macedonia under Mihailov, the IMRO leader, or placing Macedonia under Serbian administration. The Bulgarians were wary of any authority given to IMRO, and told Beckerle that they preferred the latter suggestion, most likely with the idea that after the war they would still be able to annex Macedonia.[93]

Soviet demands on the kingdom began in January 1944. Ambassador Aleksandr Lavrishchev protested that the Bulgarians were violating their neutrality by allowing the Germans to build ships in Varna harbor. The Soviets intimated a threat along with the protest by telling Bozhilov that the Allies at Tehran had asked Stalin to declare war against Bulgaria. Moscow had refused, but Sofia was to understand that such a declaration was not beyond possibility.[94] Although Bozhilov denied it, Lavrishchev's accusation was true, and the prime minister consulted Beckerle on the matter. The ambassador supported Bozhilov's denial as the best course of action, but Ribbentrop in Berlin sent advice to Sofia that the Bulgarian government should not answer the Russian protest at all and, if the Russians persisted in their inquiry, should tell them that it was none of their concern. The German-Bulgarian debate over this became quite heated, and Beckerle blamed the impasse on Bozhilov's stubbornness.[95]

By May Russia increased its demands, asking not only that Germany cease shipbuilding in Varna, but that the Bulgarians allow the Russians

---

frames 181241-46; Hermann Neubacher, special minister plenipotentiary, southeast, report, Belgrade, November 19, 1943, ibid., frame 181300; Ribbentrop, report, March 12, 1944, T120, serial 76, roll 73, frames 57592-94.

93. Neubacher, report, Belgrade, November 19, 1943, T120, serial 284, roll 241, frame 181301; Beckerle, reports, November 22, 23, 27, and December 11, 1943, ibid., frames 181302-05, 181309-13, and 181332-33; Altenburg to Beckerle, December 9, 1943, ibid., frame 181328; Neubacher to Ribbentrop, December 12, 1943, ibid., frame 181334; Neubacher, report, Athens, May 21, 1944, T120, serial 76, roll 73, frame 57768-69. See also Nissan Oren, "The Bulgarian Communist Party, 1934-1944" (Ph.D. diss., Columbia University, 1960), pp. 306-38.

94. Beckerle, report, January 24, 1944, T120, serial 284, roll 241, frames 181474-76; Beckerle, report, April 22, 1944, T120, serial 76, roll 73, frames 57688-90.

95. Beckerle, reports, January 24 and February 2 and 11, 1944, T120, serial

to reopen their consulate there, along with two additional consulates in the ports of Burgas and Ruse. The alarmed Germans advised the Bulgarians to break diplomatic relations with Moscow completely, but by this time Germany was clearly on the road to defeat. (The Red Army by May 9 had all but cleared the Wehrmacht from the Soviet Union.) It was all that the government could do to deny the Russians the consulates.[96]

The Bulgarians also began to take a more circumspect attitude toward the Western Allies. An official of the Auswärtige Amt in October 1943 attributed the lessening of public propaganda against the Jews to fear of American and English censure. Beckerle agreed and flatly ascribed Bulgaria's unwillingness to follow up on further anti-Semitic action, including deportations, to fear of Allied condemnation.[97]

Bulgaria had expected and feared American and British bombings long before the first planes attacked in November 1943. Over one hundred bombers destroyed the Sofia railroad station and part of the Sofia-Plovdiv line. The planes also bombed a number of residences, leaving over one hundred fifty casualties.[98] Further attacks followed. On January 11, 1944, an especially heavy raid over Sofia hit the Subranie building while the body was in session, and a number of members were injured. Raids occurred over provincial cities as well—Plovdiv, Pleven, Varna, Burgas, etc.[99] General panic gripped the inhabitants of the capital. Schools closed in January, and the Ministry of Education scheduled their reopening for August. Some groups asked the government to declare Sofia an open city. This was not done, but a general evacuation began and by January 26 a large part of the city was cleared. The foreign

284, roll 241, frames 181476-78, 181487-88, and 181529; Ribbentrop to Beckerle, January 29 and February 9, 1944, ibid., frames 181487-88 and 181529; Altenburg to Beckerle, February 15, 1944, ibid., frame 181549.

96. Beckerle, reports, May 3, 4, and 12, 1944, T120, serial 76, roll 73, frames 57697-704, 57717-18; Ribbentrop to Hencke, May 6, 1944, ibid., frames 57707-09; Ribbentrop to Beckerle, May 18, 1944, ibid., frames 57751-54; Altenburg to Beckerle, May 14 and 15, 1944, ibid., frames 57731 and 57733.

97. Sonnleithner to Altenburg, October 25, 1943, T120, serial 284, roll 241, frames 181241-46; Beckerle, reports, October 29 and December 16, 1943, ibid., frames 181259-60 and 181353-54.

98. Beckerle, reports, October 29 and November 19, 1943, ibid., frames 181259-60 and 181298-99.

99. Beckerle, reports, November 27, 1943, January 12 and February 11, 1944, ibid., frames 181314, 181441-45, and 181540-41; Argel, military attaché at Sofia, report, January 26, 1944, ibid., frame 181479.

community, the various ministries, the court, even the KEV established new offices outside the capital. The Subranie began meeting secretly.[100] Ironically the Bulgarians of Sofia were forced from their homes just as the Jews had been some eight months earlier. A few Germans wanted to send German women and children to Berlin, but Beckerle advised against it for the sake of the alliance although some evacuation did take place. Berlin sent air-defense experts to aid the Royal Bulgarian Air Force.[101] The Germans had known of the planned attacks on Bulgaria through documents given to Minister Franz von Papen in Ankara by the famous spy Cicero, but the foreign office had deemed it in their best interest not to inform Sofia.[102]

The Germans felt that the attacks were an attempt to drive Bulgaria into the arms of the Soviet Union. It seems clear that the bombings were intended to put pressure on Bulgaria, which the Allies regarded now as a weak link in the Axis chain. Furthermore, although the raids caused some anti-American and anti-English feeling, the government did begin to explore peace overtures with the West.[103]

The German embassy reports from these months are full of suspicions and inquiries about special Bulgarian missions to countries where the government could have contact with the Allies. The American documents are silent about this, but no doubt such contacts took place. We have see that there may have been some as early as the summer of 1943. In December a Mr. Kujumdzhiiski, a Jew born in Bulgaria, but by then an American citizen, tried to establish contact with Sofia for negotiations. Minister Dimitur Shishmanov, who had replaced Kirov in Octo-

100. Beckerle, reports, December 18 and 23, 1943, January 11, 12, 21, and 26, and February 11, 1944, ibid., frames 181370-73, 181383-85, 181398-99, 181446-48, 181460-62, 181480-82, and 181540-41; Altenburg to Beckerle, January 23, 1940, ibid., frames 181470-72.

101. Schönebeck to Field Marshal Wilhelm Keitel (OKW), November 14, 1943, ibid., frame 181290; Ribbentrop to Beckerle, January 22, 1944, ibid., frames 181463-64; Dr. Drechsel, Landesgruppenleiter in Bulgaria, to Beckerle and Ernst Bohle, Gauleiter für Ausland Deutsche, January 22, 1944, ibid., frame 181467; Beckerle to Ribbentrop, January 23, 1944, ibid., frames 181468-69; Altenburg to Stein, February 1, 1944, ibid., frame 181499; Dr. Karl Ritter, ambassador for special purposes, foreign office, to Beckerle, February 6, 1944, ibid., frames 181515-17; Steengracht, report, February 9, 1944, ibid., frame 181535.

102. Franz von Papen, "Postscript," in L. C. Moyzisch, *Operation Cicero* (New York: Coward-McCann, 1950), p. 208.

103. Beckerle, reports, December 24, 26, 27, 1943, January 12, and February 16 and 23, 1944, T120, serial 284, roll 241, frames 181388-89, 181393-94, 181398-99, 181446-48, 181557-61, and 181582-83; Kaltenbrunner to Wagner, February 23, 1944, ibid., frames 181576-79.

ber 1943, assured Beckerle that Sofia was not interested.[104] In January 1944 Filov sent Sevov to Turkey. German opinion as to whether this trip was for negotiation was divided. Beckerle insisted that Sevov was not seeking a peace opening, but Papen reported that the architect was empowered to come to terms with the Allies if Bulgaria could keep Dobrudzha, Macedonia, and Thrace. At any rate nothing came of it.[105]

The war crisis, the internal instability, the weakness of Bozhilov's cabinet, pressure from Berlin and from the Allies all conspired to topple the government in the spring of 1944. The Wilhelmstrasse, frustrated in its attempts to dominate absolutely the Sofia regime, once again searched the disreputable areas of Bulgarian fascism for a replacement for Bozhilov. However, neither Zhekov nor Kantardzhiev, Tsankov nor Mihailov, was strong enough nor capable enough to lead a cabinet.[106] Filov for his part wished to establish another government which he could control, but in the end this was also impossible. On May 24 in a surprising move the regents asked the former minister of agriculture, Ivan Bagrianov, to form a government. Bagrianov was closer to the court circles than Filov and would rival him for the real leadership of the kingdom. Furthermore, Bagrianov, who served without portfolio, selected as minister of foreign affairs, Purvan Draganov, another powerful political figure close to the crown, whom Sofia gossip declared to be an illegitimate son of the deposed King Ferdinand. In the summer of 1942 Boris had removed him from his post as ambassador to Berlin because of his ambition, and for the following two years he had served in a ministerial post at Madrid.[107] Except for General Rusi H. Rusev, the minister of war, everyone in Bagrianov's cabinet was new.[108]

104. Beckerle, reports, December 23, 1943, January 12, and February 10, 1944, ibid., frames 181381-82, 181446-48, and 181536.

105. Beckerle, reports, February 17 and 24, 1944, ibid., frames 181562-63, 181580-81; Papen, March 7, 1944, report, T120, serial 76, roll 73, frames 57576-77.

106. Sonnleithner to Altenburg, October 25, 1943, T120, serial 284, roll 241, frames 181241-46; Ribbentrop to Beckerle, December 29, 1943, ibid., frame 181400; Beckerle, report, December 31, 1943, ibid., frames 181410-15. For rumors of cabinet changes in 1944 see Beckerle, reports, February 8, 9, and 12, 1944, ibid., frames 181522-28, 181531-32, and 181565-70; Beckerle, reports, March 2 and April 14, 1944, T120, serial 76, roll 73, frames 57560-61 and 57682-83; Filov, "Diary," entries for April and May 1944, Naroden Sud, no. 8, pp. 3-5.

107. Beckerle, report, July 8, 1942, T120, serial 286, roll 244, frame 182001. For a secret German report defaming Draganov, Bagrianov, and the royal family, see Beckerle, report, August 22, 1944, T120, serial 76, roll 73, frames 578048-50.

108. Filov, "Diary," entries of May 24 to June 2, 1944, Naroden Sud, no. 8, pp. 5-6; Beckerle, reports, May 31 and June 1, 1944, T120, serial 76, roll 73, frames 57793-800.

The majority of the members in the new government still leaned toward Germany. The minister of internal affairs, Dr. Aleksandur D. Stanishev, a noted surgeon, was the president of the Sofia branch of the German-Bulgarian association (*Deutsch-Bulgarische Gesellschaft*), a Macedonian leader, and a personal friend of Beckerle. The German ambassador regarded him as the "strongest" personality in the new cabinet—meaning the one on whom the Reich could most rely.[109]

Nevertheless, the course of the war in 1944 pulled the Bulgarians further away from the Axis. Just as the king's pro-British sympathies could not prevent Boris from leading his country into the German alliance in the years before 1941, so now Bagrianov's pro-German feelings could not prevent him from following a path divergent from the Reich. In the summer of 1944 Bagrianov and Draganov, both politicians, looked for a way to save their own country and its monarchy and let Hitler look after himself.

Still clearly in the German orbit, the new government immediately showed a conciliatory attitude toward the Allies. Bagrianov hoped as much as possible to prevent Communist influence in Bulgarian affairs after the war was over, to maintain the position of the Saxe-Coburg dynasty, and to hold on to all or part of the annexed territory. Upon taking office, the prime minister addressed the nation by radio. His speech contained hints that his government would be more moderate and propitiatory to the West.[110] By mid-August the hints had become more obvious, and even Beckerle began seeking radical solutions to the Bulgarian crisis, such as an outright German invasion of Bulgaria and the establishment of a government of right-wing elements—Ratnitsi, Legionaires, Tsankovites, etc.[111]

The Wilhelmstrasse was upset with the Bagrianov-Draganov government from the start. Ribbentrop continued without success to ask Beckerle to have Tsankov installed. He advised the embassy in Sofia to watch the cabinet very carefully.[112] The major problem for the new government remained the Soviet demands concerning the three major

109. Beckerle, reports, June 2, 1944, T120, serial 76, roll 73, frames 57807-08, 57815-18.

110. Transcript of Bagrianov's radio speech of June 3, 1944, ibid., frames 57829-30; Altenburg to Beckerle, June 15, 1944, ibid., frames 57854-56; Beckerle, report, June 16, 1944, ibid., frame 57861; Ribbentrop to Beckerle, June 19, 1944, ibid., frame 57876.

111. Beckerle, reports, August 10 and 19, 1944, ibid., frames 57999-58001 and 58034-40.

112. Altenburg to Beckerle, June 8 and 9, 1944, ibid., frames 57836-39; Beckerle, report, June 20, 1944, ibid., frames 57879-80.

Bulgarian ports. Berlin pressed for a severance of relations, but its influence over Bulgaria continued to dwindle.[113] On July 28 the government reopened the Russian consulate at Varna and extended its jurisdiction to Ruse and Burgas.[114] Before this the Bulgarians had asked the Germans to pull out of Varna, and Berlin had reluctantly agreed.[115] The Bulgarians also strictly regulated anti-Soviet propaganda, even trying to limit that which emanated from the German embassy.[116] They sought and obtained German acquiescence to a request to keep Russan prisoners of war out of Bulgaria, after the USSR had demanded that Sofia free these prisoners.[117]

The new government's moderation with respect to the Jews became apparent almost immediately. Bagrianov and General Rusev, the minister of war, made contact with several prominent Jewish leaders including Col. Avram Tadzher, Josefico Levi, and Vitali Haimov. Bagrianov assured the Jews that there would be a new policy under his government for the Jews in general, although for the present the Bulgarians still had to move cautiously because of their positions vis-à-vis the Germans. In the meantime, Stomaniakov appointed Colonel Tadzher, whom both Jews and Bulgarians highly esteemed, president of the central consistory.[118]

On August 17, 1944, Bagrianov addressed an extraordinary session of the Subranie to indicate the possibility of Bulgaria's pulling out of the war. In one part of his speech he said: "The government declares that it understands the will of the Bulgarian people and firmly resolves to eliminate everything which impedes the devotion to peace of this

113. Beckerle, reports, June 14, 17, 19, and 29, 1944, ibid., frames 57849-50, 57863, 57870-72, 57898-99, and 57901-03; Slavcho Zagorov, ambassador to Germany, to Andor Hencke, Unterstaatssekreiär for politics, June 28 and July 1, 1944, ibid., frames 57897 and 57911; Ribbentrop to Beckerle, July 2, 1944, ibid., frames 57912-13.

114. Beckerle, report, July 28, 1944, ibid., frames 57963-64.

115. Ritter, report, June 22, 1944, ibid., frames 57882-83; Ritter to Beckerle, June 29, 1944, ibid., frame 57904; Beckerle, reports, July 3, 1944, ibid., frames 57914-15; Ribbentrop to Beckerle, July 8, 1944, ibid., frames 57928-29; report (unsigned), July 12, 1944, ibid., frames 57936-37.

116. Beckerle, reports, July 21 and August 1, 1944, ibid., frames 57950-51 and 57968-69; Schellenberg to Ribbentrop, July 30, 1944, ibid., frame 57966.

117. Bulgarian foreign office to German embassy and German embassy to Bulgarian foreign office (verbal notes in Beckerle, report, July 21, 1944, ibid., frames 57950-53).

118. Eli Baruh, Iz istoriiata na bulgarskoto evreistvo [From the history of the Bulgarian Jews] (Tel Aviv: n.p., 1960), pp. 159-61; interview with Josefico Levi, Tel Aviv, Israel, February 1966. Levi and Tadzher had served as officers with Bagrianov in the same unit during World War I.

national will, (loud and continuous applause) including even the [German] army of occupation and the Jewish problem. (Applause.)"[119]

During the summer of 1944 Ira Hirschmann, a special representative of President Roosevelt's War Refugee Board, visited Turkey to see what he could do on behalf of the Balkan Jews. He spoke to Sofia's ambassador, Nikola Balabanov, in Ankara in July. After conferring with Sofia, Balabanov answered Hirschmann as follows:

> There is no doubt that the new Bulgarian government regrets exceedingly all the anti-Jewish measures taken by our country and that it does not in the least approve these measures.
>
> I have the impression that the government intends to abolish the present laws regarding the Jews at an opportune moment. However, for the present it has firmly decided to do away with arbitrary methods in the application of these laws, as well as with all restrictive measures not provided by such laws.[120]

Reports that Bulgaria had rescinded its Jewish laws began prematurely on August 16, the day before Bagrianov's speech. By that time the government had decided to abrogate the laws and pull out of the German alliance, but was taking no action until terms of surrender became clearer. A Bulgarian delegation, led by Stoicho Moshanov, had gone to Turkey seeking peace earlier in August. On August 31 the cabinet abrogated restrictive legislation affecting the Jews, both in the ZZN and the decree-law of August 26, 1942, as well as in other minor and supplementary legislation. Jews were allowed the same freedom of travel as Bulgarians, the same civil and political rights. They did not have to wear stars or have signs on their homes. They could use whatever name they chose. Formerly illegal Jewish organizations, institutions, and activities were revived. Jews were allowed the economic freedom of other Bulgarians; special taxes were abolished. In short, the legal situation prior to January 29, 1941, was restored. The government also promised to return confiscated Jewish property. The KEV became a record-keeping institution charged with aiding the return of pre-1941 conditions and subordinated to the Ministries of Justice and Finance.[121]

119. Bulgaria, Narodno Subranie, *Dnevnitsi,* 25th ONS, 7th extraordinary sess. (August 1944), p. 8.

120. Ira Hirschmann, *Lifeline to the Promised Land* (New York: Jewish Book Guild of America, 1946), p. 158. Hirschmann writes about Bulgaria on pp. 152-64. See also his *Caution to the Winds* (New York: David McKay, 1962), pp. 152-68.

121. Mohrmann, report, August 25, 1944, T120, serial 76, roll 73, frame 58057; *DV,* no. 193 (September 5, 1943), p. 3.

The war in Bulgaria was lost. The next few days Moshanov continued to negotiate in Egypt for surrender. At first, the Bulgarians wanted the Allies to agree to their retaining Macedonia and Thrace, but this was not possible and Sofia was not in a position to argue. Although they were not yet at war with Bulgaria, the Soviets, who were seeking an excuse to invade the kingdom as they approached the Danube, had a say in the terms. The Allies asked for a withdrawal of the declarations of war of 1941, the right to march through Bulgaria, the expulsion of German soldiers, and a new cabinet including Nikola Mushanov and Stainov and without the most obvious fascists and Germanophiles.[122]

Ribbentrop ordered the German embassy to cease political and military conversations with the Bulgarians.[123] Draganov asked the Germans to withdraw their forces.[124] On August 29 the German embassy began carrying out a general evacuation and ceased operations two days later. Bulgarian forces attempted to disarm retreating Germans and in some cases engaged them in battle. As a last hopeless gesture, Berlin flew Ivan Mihailov to Skopje to establish an independent Macedonia. He had no chance of success.[125]

Aftermath

On September 2 the regency council replaced Bagrianov's government with one definitely oriented toward the West, led by the Agrarian Konstantin Muraviev.[126] Members of the former legal opposition dominated the new cabinet. The leaders of the centrist BZNS—"Vrabcha 1" —Dimitur Gichev (without portfolio), Vergil Dimov (internal affairs), and Muraviev (foreign affairs) himself—were most prominent; but two important Democrats, Nikola Mushanov (without portfolio) and Alek-

122. Mohrmann, report, August 26, 1944, T120, serial 76, roll 73, frames 58066-67; Schellenberg, reports, August 27, 1944, ibid., frames 58075-81; Beckerle, report, August 29, 1944, ibid., frames 58102-03. Robert Lee Wolff, *The Balkans in Our Time* (Cambridge, Mass.: Harvard University Press, 1967), pp. 245-46.

123. Ribbentrop to Mohrmann, August 26, 1944, T120, serial 76, roll 73, frame 58068.

124. Mohrmann, reports, August 24 and 26, 1944, ibid., frames 58053-54 and 58066; Beckerle, report, August 29, 1944, ibid., frames 58091, 58096, and 58110-11.

125. Steengracht, report, August 30, 1944, ibid., frames 58113-17; Timmler, foreign office, to Beckerle, August 31, 1944, frame 58118 (Nuremberg doc. no. NG-3912). For German military activity against the Bulgarians after September 1944 (Operation Hundsohn), see the war diaries of Army Group E in captured German records, T311, serial 65030, roll 178; serials 65721/1 and 65722/2, roll 182; serial 66135/1, rolls 190 and 191; serial 66135/2, roll 191.

126. *New York Times*, September 3, 1944, p. 22.

sandur Girginov (finance) and the Nationalist leader Atanas Burov (without portfolio) also entered the government. Muraviev invited some members of the Fatherland Front to join, but without success.

The Soviet Union was not satisfied with the new government, even though it declared a position of "strict neutrality." *Izvestiia* and the radio station "Hristo Botev" accused the Muraviev government of protecting German soldiers who were fleeing the Red Army in Rumania and of continuing to allow the Nazis to use Burgas and Varna as submarine bases to raid Russian ships. Only a radical new government, which among other conditions would declare war on Berlin, could satisfy Moscow. In reality the USSR would accept only the Fatherland Front.

The Muraviev government, overwhelmed by external factors, could not begin to cope with Bulgarian problems. Indeed, the Germans still operated on Bulgarian territory, for the most part trying to evacuate their forces. The Bulgarians could not prevent evacuation from Rumania through their country in any case and could only disarm the German troops by force. Generally, officials of the Boris-Filov regime remained at their posts. Therefore, in the provinces royalist soldiers and police continued to fight Communist and republican partisans. Conditions in general were chaotic. The Western powers, whom Filov and Muraviev were most anxious to conciliate, remained noncommittal, while Stoicho Moshanov continued to press the government's case in Cairo.

The Muraviev period was also a time of flux for the Jews. Officially the restrictions ceased, but the government issued only very few orders of significance to promote a complete return to pre-1941 conditions. On September 7 the government granted amnesty to Jews indicted under ZZN and other anti-Semitic legislation.[127] Many Jews began to return to Sofia.

On September 5 the USSR had declared war on Bulgaria Filov resigned his position, and Muraviev declared war on the Reich.[128] For a few days the kingdom whose leaders had struggled in vain to keep it neutral found itself at war not only with England, America, and the Soviet Union, but with Germany as well. Fatherland Front forces, the Communist-led partisans, seized control in some cities in the provinces, replacing old officials. On the ninth the Fatherland Front revolutionaries succeeded in taking the capital. Many members of the Sofia gar-

---

127. Topalov, p. 488.
128. The sequence of these events is taken from BAN, *Istoriia*, III, 474.

rison and the police force by that time had gone over secretly to the OF. Others decided to remain neutral. In a matter of hours the Muraviev cabinet was arrested and a new enlarged government led by Kimon Georgiev and composed exclusively of OF members took its place. The OF arrested also the regency council and replaced it with Venelin Ganev (independent), Tsvetko Boboshevski (Zveno), and Todor Pavlov (BKP).[129]

The Western Allies and the USSR recognized the new government, but Berlin established a government-in-exile under Aleksandur Tsankov. The Red Army agreed to an armistice, the OF joined the United Nations in the war against the Nazis, and the Bulgarian occupation force in Yugoslavia joined the Red Army in expelling their former allies from the Balkans into Austria. This was the only frontline action that Bulgarian forces saw during the entire war. The Georgiev government readily accepted the terms of surrender which the Allies presented to them, although they had fruitlessly hoped to retain part of Thrace. Bulgaria, according to the terms of the armistice signed in Moscow on October 28, 1944, placed its armed forces at the disposal of the United Nations under Soviet command. Likewise the USSR took control of Bulgarian industry, transport, utilities, fuel, press, radio, theater, etc. for the Allies. The armistice also required the Bulgarians to cooperate with the war-crime tribunals and disband all fascist organizations inside their country. Article V of the terms specified that Bulgaria must release from captivity persons imprisoned for siding with the Allies, regardless of their citizenship or nationality, as well as people held for "religious or social reasons." The same article required that all discriminatory legislation be ended. The armistice placed Bulgaria (until German defeat) under an Allied Control Commission.[130]

The members of the Fatherland Front had no serious objections to these provisions. As regards the Jews, the Bagrianov government had

129. Oren, pp. 344, 355; BAN, *Istoriia*, III, 429-33, 473-86; Wolff, pp. 246-47; Marin V. Pundeff, "Bulgaria's Place in Axis Policy" (Ph.D. diss., University of Southern California, 1958), pp. 470-80; Hugh Seton-Watson, *The East European Revolution*, 3d ed. (New York: Frederick A. Praeger, 1956), pp. 96-97; *New York Times*, September 12, 1944, p. 8.

130. United Nations, *Armistice Agreement between the United States of America, the Union of Soviet Socialist Republics, and the United Kingdom and Bulgaria, together with Protocol Signed at Moscow October 28, 1944, Effective October 28, 1944, and Related Papers* (Washington, D.C.: Government Printing Office, 1945); Wolff, pp. 247-48; Tass, October 30, 1944, press release, London, Wiener Library Archives, file of press clippings for Bulgaria, file number 3[11] and 3[12]; *New York Times*, October 30, 1944, p. 5; London *Times*, October 30, 1944, p. 30.

already abrogated the discriminatory legislation, and the OF now implemented the return to pre-1941 conditions. On September 23 Dimo Kazasov, minister of propaganda, announced that the government would return the Jews' property. This matter, however, was extremely complicated. Much of the property was lost or destroyed. The Bulgarian economy was ruined. Records were confused. In the meantime, the Jews were impoverished.

David Ben-Gurion visited Bulgaria late in 1944 and promised to obtain aid for the Bulgarian Jews, since as a German ally Bulgaria in general was not eligible for UN relief. In March 1945, a law authorizing the return of Jewish property was published in *Durzhaven Vestnik*. Jewish land now owned by peasants and property now owned by the government was not to be returned, but the ex-owners would be compensated. The government set the value of property at 1943 levels. The law promised that the government would restore pharmacies and other shops still in existence. It voided compulsory stock sales. The government would return rents collected on Jewish property and pay compensation in the amount of 30 million leva ($364,000) for unreturned property.[131] However, the government was unable to return all of the property and money confiscated; and even when it could, the KEV statements of value of liquidated businesses, which the government used in its calculations, were lower than the actual worth. Furthermore, as time went by and the BKP's position in the Fatherland Front became stronger, nationalization of industry and business eliminated the possibility of return for much of the expropriated Jewish property. The Jewish Joint-Distribution Committee did send relief to the impoverished Jews.[132]

The restoration of pre-1941 conditions was one aspect of the government's program as regards the Jews. Another was the trial of those responsible for the anti-Semitic policy in the years 1940-1944. The government tried not only the persons specifically connected with the KEV but all important officials of the governments of those years. The OF courts tried and executed Filov, Prince Kiril, Mihov, Bozhilov, and

131.   Jewish Telegraph Agency (JTA) news releases, Washington, D.C., September 23, 1944; London, December 1, 1944; Tel Aviv, December 21, 1944, all in YIVO; Cairo release, March 8, 1945, Wiener Library, file no. 3[11] and 3[12].

132.   JTA news release, Sofia, January 22, 1945; *Joint-Distribution Committee News*, January 24, 1945; New York *Herald Tribune*, July 12, 1945; JTA news releases, Sofia, January 28, 1946; March 10, 1946; June 13, 1946; January 1, 1947; all in Wiener Library, file no. 3[11] and 3[12]. Peter Meyer, "Bulgaria," in *The Jews in the Soviet Satellites*, ed. Peter Meyer (Syracuse, N.Y.: Syracuse University Press, 1953), pp. 575-79.

Bagrianov for war crimes. The government also sentenced to death twenty-six ministers, including all in Filov's and Bozhilov's cabinets, and all but four in Bagrianov's. The king's advisors and staff, Sevov, Lulchev, Balan, and Gruev, among others, suffered the same fate. The courts sentenced many others to prison terms. All except Gen. Ivan Marinov, minister of war, in Muraviev's cabinet received sentences ranging from six months to life.[133]

Sixty-eight members of the twenty-fifth Subranie were sentenced to death. One member who because of his position was a prime candidate for the death sentence escaped the firing squad—Dimitur Peshev. As vice-president of the Subranie, he was regarded by the OF as one of the chief architect's of the government's programs. That he aided the Jews in their hour of need was irrelevant. In fact, the government executed for war crimes Ivan V. Petrov, the government representative who had consistently spoken up for the Jews in the Subranie. Yet it was Peshev's protest on behalf of the Jews that helped save his life in 1945. Joseph Iasharoff, a Jewish lawyer selected by the consistory, defended Peshev before the People's Court. Iasharoff did not base his defense solely on Peshev's 1943 action, but also on the fact that this was the second time the Kiustendil representative had risked his career for a moral principle. On the first occasion in 1936, as minister of justice, he had refused to sign the execution order for Damian Velchev, forcing the king to commute his sentence. In 1945 Velchev was the Fatherland Front's minister of war. The court still sentenced Peshev to fifteen years at hard labor.[134]

KEV officials faced trial before People's Court No. 7, which opened in March 1945. Other defendants at this trial included leaders of Jewish labor battalions; anti-Semitic writers, such as Aleksandur Pudarev; local officials involved in deportations; and liquidators of Jewish property. The court sentenced Belev, who had escaped from Bulgaria, to death in absentia—the only capital sentence. Three others on trial in absentia were sentenced to life imprisonment—Boris Tasev, chief of agents; Spas Stoianchevski, a clerk in the commissariat office; and Marko V. Mehlemov, a writer and announcer for Radio Donau. It would seem that the severity of the sentences was in part prompted by the absence of the defendants, for, although Tasev was one of the chief executioners of

133. Wolff, pp. 292-93; *Naroden Sud*, no. 5, pp. 1-2.
134. *New York Times*, February 2, 1945, p. 3, and February 3, 1945, p. 6; interview with Joseph Iasharoff, Tel Aviv, Israel, February 1966; *Naroden Sud*, no. 5, p. 2.

the commissariat's work, others who were apprehended and who were more responsible for anti-Semitic activity than Stoianchevski and Mehlemov received lesser punishment. (A five-member judicial board consisting of both professional jurists and laymen determined the verdicts.) Kalitsin received fifteen years' imprisonment. The court sentenced Zahari Velkov to ten years and Pencho Lukov to eight. The second commissar, Stomaniakov, was sentenced to six years. Iliia Dobrevski and Atanas Ovcharov were each sentenced to two years. The court acquitted twenty of those on trial, including Maria Pavlova, Liliana Panitsa, Dr. Ivan Popov, Dr. Iosif Vatev, Aleksandur Pudarev, Peiu Draganov, and Colonel Mumdzhiev of the labor service, as well as most of the leaders of the Jewish labor groups.[135]

The most critical question for the Bulgarian Jews after September 9 was not the return of their confiscated property nor the punishment of their former persecutors, but whether they would remain in Bulgaria or move to Palestine. Almost at once after the Fatherland Front takeover, as the Jews were again allowed freedom of expression and organization, the Bulgarian community split into factions—one led by Zionists advocating migration to Palestine and seeking help from the World Zionist Organization, and the other led chiefly, but not exclusively, by Communists, urging that the Jews remain in Bulgaria. The former had by far the greater allegiance. Zionist groups and other Jewish organizations reestablished themselves or came out of hiding, and a varied Jewish press once again appeared in Bulgaria.

After the seizure of power by the OF, David Ieroham, who was not a Zionist, replaced Colonel Tadzher as president of the central consistory, and Tadzher, who was not readily identified with any particular faction in the Jewish community, became chairman of the Jewish Committee of the Fatherland Front. This latter group encompassed both Zionist and non-Zionist organizations. The Bulgarian Jews also formed a Jewish Anti-Fascist Committee, which was close to the Fatherland Front and soon dominated by the Communists.

The various groups of the OF, both Bulgarian and Jewish, also divided on the Zionist question. The BKP and Zveno urged the Jews to remain in Bulgaria. The Social Democrats, whose Jewish section identi-

135. Sofia, Ministry of Justice, people's prosecutors Boris Burov et al., *Bill of Indictment* before People's Court No. 7, Petko Petrinski presiding, February 1945; Sofia, Ministry of Justice, Petko Petrinski, President of People's Court No. 7, et al., *Sentence Pronounced by People's Court No. 7*, April 2, 1945, BAN, Ebroistika, doc. no. 42; JTA press release, Sofia, April 6, 1945, Wiener Library file no. 3[11] and 3[12].

fied with Zionist socialism and who extolled the socialist virtues of the kibbutzim in Palestine, sympathized with emigration.[136]

In September 1944 Kazasov, as minister of propaganda, announced that the Fatherland Front government looked favorably upon Jewish emigration to Palestine. Prime Minister Georgiev repeated this the next month.[137] However, statements by leaders of the new ruling circles soon after indicated that their position was not so certain. A Jewish Telegraph Agency release of November 26, 1944, stated that emigrating Jews would not be allowed to take their property with them and that only Jews who were not eligible for military service could leave the country. Children would be allowed to leave the country only with their parents.[138] The Jewish Communists especially tried to convince the community to remain in Bulgaria. Zhak Natan, a leading Marxist economist, denounced the Zionists as chauvinists before People's Court No. 7.[139] The pro-Communist *Evreiski Vesti* (*Jewish News*) also deprecated the Zionists. The Jews in the Communist youth association asked their counterparts in the Jewish youth organization, Hachalutz, to give up their nationalist program (migration to Palestine) and join in a single group under the auspices of the Fatherland Front. At the very same time that this request was made (May 1945) there were many Zionist demonstrations in Bulgaria to mark the Allied victory in Europe as well as to demand a Jewish homeland in Palestine. The Ministry of Agriculture, which was in the hands of the BZNS and more sympathetic than the Communists toward the Zionist aims, agreed to allow the Jews to use government land to train youth who wished to work on the kibbutzim in the Holy Land.[140]

Once again in July Prime Minister Georgiev supported the basic prin-

---

136. Consistorie Centrale des Juifs en Bulgarie, "Exposé sur les situations économiques, politiques et culturelles du judaïsme bulgare," mimeographed report, January, 1947; Joint-Distribution Committee, New York, report, July 25, 1946, Wiener Library, file no. 3[11] and 3[12]. For the Jewish Anti-Fascist Committee, see BAN, Ebroistika, doc. no. 149. Copies of the *Biuletin na evreiskata sektsiia*, BRSDP [Bulletin of the Jewish section, Bulgarian Workers' Social Democratic Party], are found in doc. no. 6.

137. JTA news releases, Sofia, September 24, 1944 (YIVO); Jerusalem, October 24, 1944, Wiener Library, file no. 3[11] and 3[12].

138. JTA news release, London, November 26, 1944 (YIVO).

139. Sofia, Protocols of People's Court No. 7, III, 798-99 (testimony of Zhak Natan).

140. JTA news releases, Sofia, September 28, 1944; May 13, 1945; June 18, 1945; *JTA Bulletin*, 26 (August 30, 1945), pp. 1-2; JTA news releases, Sofia, August 16, 1945; October 7, 1945; January 7, 1946; January 27, 1946; February 25, 1946; and February 27, 1946; all in Wiener Library, file no. 3[11] and 3[12].

ciple of a Jewish homeland, but he went on to qualify his statement by implying that able-bodied Jews might not be allowed to leave the country.[141]

After the war, as relations between Great Britain and the Soviet Union worsened, the BKP opposition to Jewish emigration lessened Along with the World Zionist Organization, the Communists condemned the British white-paper policy which limited Jewish immigration to Palestine.[142]

In the meantime the BKP gained complete domination over the Fatherland Front. In 1945 and the beginning of 1946 independent Social Democrats and Agrarians lost their influence in the government. In September 1946 a plebescite ended the monarchy and established a republic. In October, after a Great National Subranie began to meet to consider a new constitution for Bulgaria, the former Comintern secretary general and BKP leader Georgi Dimitrov replaced Kimon Georgiev as prime minister. Throughout 1946 and 1947 Jews left Bulgaria for Palestine. The white paper of course limited Jewish immigration; but Bulgaria, like all states in Moscow's orbit, supported a Jewish homeland and the United Nations division plan of 1948. When the Zionists proclaimed the sovereign state of Israel, Sofia extended recognition; and the Dimitrov government permitted free emigration to Israel beginning in May 1948. Forty thousand Jews left Bulgaria, moving into various areas of Israel which had been vacated by the Palestinian Arabs—Jaffa, Ramle, Acre, etc.[143]

The reasons for this decisive permission to emigrate after earlier vacillation (and continued doubt on the side of the Jewish Communists in Bulgaria) are not easy to ascertain, nor are they necessarily within the scope of this work. Perhaps permission for emigration was one manifestation of support for Israel and a source of embarrassment for Great Britain. Also, the emigration lessened the obligation of the Sofia government to return the confiscated property of the Jews. Many of the emigrés renounced their rights of return of property, even though in some cases requests for reimbursement continued from Israel. Furthermore, the

---

141. *JTA Bulletin*, 26 (July 6, 1945), pp. 1-2, Wiener Library, file no. 3[11] and 3[12].

142. *JTA Bulletin*, 26 (August 30, 1945), pp. 1-2. JTA news releases, Sofia, September 28, 1945; November 11, 1945; November 22, 1945; in Wiener Library, file no. 3[11] and 3[12].

143. Interview with B. Piti, January 1966, Jaffa, Israel.

emigration from the viewpoint of the Bulgarians could have been part of a program to create a more homogeneous citizenry in Bulgaria. Beginning in 1950 the government forced many Turks of Bulgarian citizenship to leave the country, although even after the emigration Turks, Jews, Gypsies, and Armenians still lived in Bulgaria.[144]

144. Huey Louis Kostanick, *Turkish Resettlement of Bulgarian Turks, 1950-1953*, University of California Publications in Geography, vol. VIII, no. 2 (Berkeley, Calif.: University of California Press, 1957).

6

Conclusions

The Crown and the Jews

Speculation about the intent and actions of King Boris with respect to the Jews during the war has created a great controversy among both Bulgarians and Jews.[1] One group of authors claims that the king was the single person responsible for preventing the deportation of the Bulgarian Jews to Poland. They say that he never intended to deport these Jews and that he carefully outwitted the Germans, leading them to believe he would give up the Jews while actually conspiring to foil the Reich's plans. There are popular theories that Hitler had Boris assassinated partly or entirely because he would not deport the Jews. A Bulgarian survivor gave as one of the arguments in support of this hypothesis the simply negative reason that Boris could have deported the Jews if he had wanted to.[2] On the other hand, there arc those who believe that the king was ultimately responsible for the entire program in Bulgaria bearing on the Jewish question, that he was a confirmed anti-Semite and pro-Nazi, and that only political pressure prevented him from deporting the Jews.

This controversy has taken on the character of political debate rather than historical investigation. Quite often it is an indirect debate over the merits or shortcomings of the present Bulgarian regime.

King Boris gave an audience to the British ambassador, Sir George Rendel, shortly before Bulgaria joined the Three-Power Pact, in order to explain the necessity of his joining the Axis. At this meeting the king told Rendel that he hoped nothing would happen to the Bulgarian

1. See, for example, the works of Benjamin Arditi, Natan Grinberg, and Haim Keshales, and other articles, both scholarly and popular, published in Bulgaria and abroad.
2. Interview with Josef Geron, Pardis Katz, Israel, December 1965.

Jews.[3] This expressed well enough Boris's attitude. He *hoped* nothing would happen to the Jews—an admission that their fate was really out of his hands. The king himself was neither a Nazi nor an anti-Semite; but by February 1941 Bulgaria already had an anti-Semitic program in progress, as well as an anti-Semitic campaign in the nation's press. Although it is clear that the king on his own initiative would neither have killed the Bulgarian Jews nor have sent them out of the country, his role, if any, in preventing this from happening depends on his actions. To be given credit for saving the Jews, he must have played an active, not a passive, role.

Boris had the political ability to ingratiate himself with all kinds of people. Along parade routes he would habitually greet peasants whom he had met before. He also impressed people with knowledge of their own favorite interests and respect for their opinions.[4] Boris's politics were the politics of compromise—appearing to be all things to all men—not the politics of conflict inherent in Nazi racial theories.

This ability to compromise, his greatest political asset, was also the source of his greatest political weakness—his vacillation. He wished to please as many groups as possible, to be above the factionalism of parties; therefore many of his own convictions were lost in the background. When he faced insurmountable problems, he lacked the fortitude to meet them head on and shied away.

Political objectivity gave him shrewd powers of observation and capabilities of incisive analysis. Yet Boris also sought reassurance and feared competition for his political power. The king, as had his father, had begun his reign under the domination of a powerful premier. Like his father, he was also determined to be master of his own house. After 1934, when Boris obtained dictatorial powers in Bulgaria, his tolerance for opposition decreased even further. Friend and foe alike—Bagrianov, K'oseivanov, Draganov, Mushanov, Georgiev, Velchev, etc.—were eliminated from positions of influence as their influence became too great. Initiative and independence in Bulgarian politics became a handicap. Because the king still wanted to rule his country legally, he reestablished a parliament, but when he could not control that parliament, he dismissed it.

The German alliance, including a solution to the Jewish question,

3. Interview with Sir George Rendel, London, October 1965.
4. For a good description of Boris's personality, see George Rendel, *The Sword and the Olive: Recollections of Diplomacy and the Foreign Service, 1913-1954* (London: John Murray, 1957), pp. 146-53.

exposed the flaw in the king's political personality. In 1941 Boris reasoned that he had no other logical choice but to align himself to the Reich. (Personally he was undoubtedly closer to England.) Despite the alliance, Boris knew the Germans were in a precarious position; and after the USSR and the United States came into the war, he was convinced that Hitler would ultimately lose. From the alliance, Boris realized the national aspirations of Bulgaria in Dobrudzha, Macedonia, and Thrace; from defeat he expected the communization of Bulgaria and the deposition of the house of Saxe-Coburg.

Part of the insurmountable problem of the Axis alliance was the fate of the Bulgarian Jews. The Jewish community became a pawn in the king's international maneuvers. If alliance with the Reich meant an anti-Semitic law, Boris knew that Bulgaria must have such a law, although he tried to make it as mild as possible. When the German demands in regard to the Jews turned to deportation and execution, Boris's problem became insoluble. To save the Jews, the king thought that he would have to break the alliance. This meant possible invasion of Bulgaria or a Nazi-sponsored coup against his rule. Under these circumstances, as much as King Boris disliked the alternative, the Jews were expendable.

He put the matter out of his hands. The cabinet and, to an even greater degree, the KEV handled the details of the Jewish question. After June 1942 there was really no need for Boris to involve himself at all. Occasionally he intervened, as did many other Bulgarian officials, on behalf of individual Jews, or tried to find some new delay or escape for the Jews by methods such as insisting on the need for their labor in Bulgaria, but he did not put up much resistance and allowed the commissariat to do its work.

The RSHA attaché in Sofia, Hoffmann, thought Boris was behind the halting of deportation plans in March 1943. He wrote that Gabrovski stopped the transport of the Bulgarian Jews after he received "a nod from the highest place." Actually, although Boris approved Filov's action, it was the prime minister who halted the transport in response to the Subranie protest. Both Filov and Gabrovski intended this only as a postponement, not a cancellation. When Filov spoke to Boris about this a few days later the king told him to be "firm," even though the king himself hardly seemed firm in these matters.

On May 24, 1943, when the Jewish question reached its second crisis, Boris was out of Sofia. The ultimate decision not to deport the Jews after May had to come from the king, and it did; but again it was a response to pressure rather than a decision taken on his own initiative. A change in the pressure could have caused him to reverse this decision.

It is true that if Boris had desired to deport the Jews he could have, but it is not true that any desire to prevent deportation would succeed. His opposition did not save the Jews of Macedonia, Thrace, and Pirot. The champions of the king argue that in regard to these Jews he was hopelessly under the control of the Germans; but pressure from Germany for Jewish deportations was not greater in the new territories than it was for the first-designated eight thousand deportees from the old territorial boundaries of Bulgaria. Also, it cannot be logically argued from the evidence that the king sacrificed the Jews in the occupied lands to put off the Germans and save the Bulgarian Jews as was the case in France.[5] There is no record of such a scheme, and the manner in which the Bulgarian Jews avoided deportation indicates that if the Subranie had not protested the deportations, the Bulgarian Jews would have gone to Poland with those from Macedonia and Thrace. Finally the deportation operation in the occupied territories was the work of Bulgarian officials and soldiers, not Germans.

The members of the Bulgarian court certainly disliked the Nazis' Jewish policy and disapproved of the deportations, but they could not always effect change in political policies. Queen Giovanna; her confessor, Father Romano; the king's sister Princess Eudoxia; the king's secretary Balan; Mme Karavelova; and the king's advisors Liubomir Lulchev and Pavel Gruev all, at one time or another, acted on behalf of the Jews—either for individuals or for the entire community. The influence of the circles at court certainly helped to persuade Boris to change his mind about deportations—one of the times that the court did effect change—but only in conjunction with pressure from elsewhere and in circumstances favorable to change.

Some questions remain: Could King Boris have done any more than he did to save the Jews? Could he possibly have saved the Jews from the occupied territories? Since the Bulgarian Jews were not sent to Poland, it would seem that perhaps the answer to these questions is yes. Boris, acting under pressure, was able to delay the transport of the Bulgarian Jews without a German invasion. Therefore, could he not have stopped these deportations on his own initiative, if he had been determined to do so? The king's defiance, however, of the Germans would have to have occurred in the fall of 1942, not in May 1943, especially if the Jews in the occupied lands were to be saved. Defiance at that time could conceivably have been more likely to bring on a German invasion

5.   For an attempt to compare the Final Solution in Bulgaria with that of France see Jacques Sabille [Philippe Hoission], "Le sauvetage des juifs burglares pendant la deuxième guerre mondiale," in *Le Monde Juif*, no. 30 (March 1950), p. 5.

or a German-inspired coup which would have led to the deportation of the entire Jewish community. Whether Boris could have saved the Jews on his own initiative cannot therefore be readily determined. In any case, despite these qualifications and the fact that the Bulgarian Jews were not deported, Boris's role in the Jewish question in his country was clearly not an active one.

The Church and the Jews

No other institution with comparable influence so consistently opposed the government's anti-Semitic policy as did the Holy Synod of the Bulgarian Orthodox church. No other man with comparable influence so opposed the government's anti-Semitic policy as did Metropolitan Stefan. Stefan was openly pro-British and because of this an embarrassment to the government. It was under his direction as chairman that the Holy Synod sent letters of protest to the government against the ZZN and the deportation of Jews in March 1943.[6]

The other metropolitans of Bulgaria, particularly Kiril of Plovdiv and Neofit of Vidin, followed Stefan's lead. Kiril was especially vehement in his protests of the government's actions with regard to the Jews. In 1938 he had written a brochure "Faith and Resolution," which condemned anti-Semitism. He participated in the protests of the Holy Synod and issued his own personal condemnations of the government leaders as well.

The first concern of the Bulgarian church was for Christians who because of their ancestry or because they had converted from Judaism fell within the definition of "Jew" established by Bulgarian legislation. However, the churchmen based their opposition to the legislation on moral principles, and thus they put pressure on the government on behalf of the full Jews also. Roman Catholic clerics in Bulgaria intervened on behalf of the Jews as well.[7]

6. For Stefan's role see also the memoir he sent to the consistory in 1950 in Bulgarian Academy of Sciences, Institute for Balkan Studies, Section for Hebrew Studies archives, doc. no. 90 (hereafter cited as BAN, Ebroistika).

7. One of the Roman Catholic clerics who spoke out on behalf of the Bulgarian Jews was Angelo Roncalli, apostolic delegate to Turkey and Greece, and the future Pope John XXIII. Roncalli had been apostolic visitator to Bulgaria from 1924 to 1934. In the crisis of 1943 he wrote to King Boris urging him to protect the Jews (Arthur D. Morse, *While Six Million Died: A Chronicle of American Apathy* [New York: Random House, 1967], pp. 320-21). Rome advised Roncalli not to concern himself with such political matters. Meriol Trevor, *Pope John* (Garden City, N.Y.: Doubleday, 1962), p. 178.

On September 27, 1942, Stefan caused a flurry of excitement and scandal in Sofia by preaching against the anti-Semitic policy in his Sunday sermon. This was at a time just after the KEV had begun its operation and had secretly started to draft plans for deportation. The essence of Stefan's sermon was that God had punished the Jews for the rejection of Christ, and man therefore had no right to persecute them. Bulgarians were bound to accept as brothers especially Jews who had received Christianity. This sermon disturbed Berlin, but the government was unable to control the errant cleric.[8]

Stefan's protests and his upbraiding of the government continued over the next months. We have seen how in May 1943 at the request of Rabbis Tsion and Hananel, he took up the cause of the Jews. He warned Boris that the persecution of the Jews could put his soul in mortal danger. Boris apparently was very much affected by these warnings, and Stefan's exhortations in May were a very influential factor in Boris's rejection of deportations as a solution to the Jewish question. Bulgaria's right-wing extremists attacked the Bulgarian metropolitan as a traitor. There were occasional rumors that the government might press charges against him.[9]

One incident from those days perhaps best describes the metropolitan and his attitudes. In June 1941 Stefan accosted the government censor, Danshev, at a private party in the home of a Sofia businessman. The metropolitan, who was inebriated, berated the censor for suppressing some antiwar articles he had written and also expressed some anti-Nazi sentiments. Stefan added, however, that he was an admirer of many Germans, naming Stefan Zweig, Thomas Mann, and Albert Wassermann. The conversation was in Bulgarian, and fortunately the Germans present did not understand what was said.[10]

The Subranie and the Jews

Without doubt Bulgaria's twenty-fifth Subranie deserves the label of "rubber-stamp parliament." With rare exception every bill the government put before it became law; with rare exception every government

8. Schellenberg to Luther, November 2, 1942, T120, serial 2330, roll 1305, frames 486242-48.

9. German report of pamphlet, July 1943, T120, serial K783, roll 4201, frames K207652-53. Stefan to central consistory, October 17, 1950, pp. 16-18, BAN, Ebroistika, doc. no. 90.

10. Schellenberg to Luther, June 13, 1941, T120, serial 2320H, roll 1305, frames 485510-13.

proposal was approved. Non-government-sponsored legislation had no chance for success. Yet it was essentially the Subranie, or rather the parliamentarians who sat in it, that first began the series of events which prevented the Jewish deportations. Furthermore, it was mainly parliamentarians belonging to the government faction who were responsible for this prevention.

Political parties were illegal, and officially there were none in the Subranie. The body was divided into two groups: those who declared their support for the government; and those who did not, constituting an opposition. The government faction had about 120 of 160 representatives, but the government's real support varied with each issue. However, it could always count on an overwhelming majority. The opposition group claimed men who had belonged to many of the old parties —Democrats, Agrarians, Social Democrats, Communists, etc., and they did not necessarily work in unison.

Although all manner of conservatives, chauvinists, and fascists (often closer to Italy than to Germany) sat in the Subranie, the representatives of the government faction were generally not anti-Semites, but followed the government's lead in supporting anti-Jewish legislation. One important government supporter, Ivan Vasiliev Petrov of Teteven, consistently opposed the government's anti-Semitic program. Nevertheless, it was a group of government representatives who led the attack on the Jews—a symptom of their extremism, and this extremism really placed them outside of the mainstream of the government's attitudes. These men included the pro-Nazis Mitakov and Kostov, and members of the nationalist Young Bulgaria group: Docho Hristov, Ivan Batemburgski, Dr. Atanas Popov, and Dimitur Andreev. (Even though Young Bulgaria apparently worked closely with Gabrovski, and Hristov himself became minister of internal affairs in September 1943, there is evidence that Boris and Filov distrusted the group.)[11]

The champions of the Jews in the Subranie were limited mainly to Mushanov, Stainov, Petrov, the Communist representatives, and some others. Purges of the Subranie after June 1941 reduced these ranks. A small opposition with even fewer committed to reversing the government's policy regarding the Jews could not be an effective nucleus for changing that policy. The authors of the government programs knew what to expect from this quarter, and they knew that there was nothing to fear. For the Subranie to introduce an effective protest, that protest had to originate in the government faction, not the opposition.

11. Filov, "Diary," entry for March 21, 1942, *Naroden Sud*, no. 2, p. 3.

The March protest did emanate from the government faction, and was put forward by one of the government's leaders. A delegation led by Mushanov or Stainov would not have convinced Gabrovski to halt the deportations, but he had to listen to a delegation led by Peshev. There was, however, neither a dramatic reversal of the government's policy nor a sudden determination by the signers of Peshev's protest on behalf of the Jews in March 1943. Peshev himself saw his action through, but Filov rather easily forced most of the protesters to reaffirm their loyalty to the government. The Subranie's effectiveness served only to delay, but it was the first of a series of reversing actions which saved the Bulgarian Jews. The Subranie alone would not have been able to stop the deportations permanently.

Peshev's power derived from his position as vice-president in the Subranie. His protest was unexpected. For Peshev personally the act required great moral courage. One of the reasons that the deportation procedures went so smoothly before March 1943 was that everyone did what was expected of him. The philo-Semites in the opposition protested, but the government carried on its work. Sociological, psychological, and political forces, whatever they may have been, determined the responses and limitation of action that each character would play in the drama. When Peshev exceeded the limit of his acceptable and expected actions, when he chose a response that was beyond the ordinary for him, he upset the scenario. Of course, once Peshev had acted, his role changed; and his influence was limited by quite another set of determinants and expectations. He became one of the opposition, so to speak; and his influence on the government's actions was over. Thus, although he initiated the abrupt change of policy, he could not lead the change to its completion.

The Bulgarian Nation and the Jews

The relative lack of anti-Semitism among the Bulgarian peasants and the active objections from large segments of Bulgarian ruling society contributed to the prevention of deportations. The tolerant atmosphere was not unique to Bulgaria, nor by itself was it decisive. Only through the channeling of popular discontent into political pressure could the political change required to eliminate deportations occur. Thus only if certain conditions prevailed would the various elements of the Bulgarian nation who opposed anti-Jewish measures be effective. First of all, the government would necessarily have to be responsible to these elements. Politically the king, who was the ultimate and actual leader of the Bulgarian government, was not really responsible to the public. On the contrary, the cabinet and packed parliament were more responsible to him. Nevertheless, despite the practical elimination of ministerial responsibility, the opinions of the public held some weight because Boris chose to take them into account and because he wished to continue the illusion of a representative government. Therefore, as long as the leaders had not personally committed themselves to the Final Solution, but had only followed Hitler's lead, there was the possibility that sentiments against the government's Jewish program would have effect.

Secondly, the degree of effectiveness of popular opinion depended upon the organization and influence of that opinion. Stefan and Peshev, protesting on behalf of the Jews, were more effective than a parish priest or a local official. The Holy Synod and a large section of the Subranie protesting on behalf of the Jews were more effective than Stefan and Peshev alone. The defenders of the Bulgarian Jews included many prominent individuals, but organization (with the exception of the church) was generally lacking. Political organizations which did defend the Jews had little influence with the government even if they had support from the public.

Not all of the Bulgarian nation unconditionally opposed the Jewish legislation. Much of the country was indifferent. There were small groups of ardent pro-Nazis and anti-Semites—the Ratnitsi, the Legionaires, etc. In addition there were those Bulgarians who supported the government simply because it was the government. This group included military organizations, trade societies, patriotic student groups, business associations, etc. On the other hand, opponents to the Jewish policy included groups of professionals and intellectuals. Furthermore, many members of the political opposition undoubtedly also protested the government's Jewish policy because it was a political issue. In short, Bulgaria was divided on this point.

Many of the government's supporters had moral misgivings about the Jewish program, and opponents of the government sometimes used the Jewish issue to embarrass it. Aleksandur Tsankov, although close to Berlin, signed the Subranie protest. It was more the usual pattern for right-wing opponents of the government to reproach Boris and Filov for not going far enough in achieving the Final Solution in Bulgaria. The old Zveno group, as well as the legal opposition, stood on the side of the Jews both because of the merits of the issue and because of their opposition to the government. The two outlawed parties—the Agrarian Union —"Aleksandur Stamboliiski" and the Bulgarian Communist party—included in their lists of complaints against the royal regime the oppression of the Jews.

Agrarians in exile, such as G. M. Dimitrov, Kosta Todorov, and Dimitur Matsankiev, used Allied radio stations to speak out against the government's Jewish policy. Dimitrov spent much time in Palestine broadcasting into Bulgaria over Radio Haifa. The exiled Agrarians were also in contact with their comrades inside Bulgaria, asking them to act against the anti-Jewish measures. They sent instructions to their supporters among the masses to protest the government's Jewish actions.[12]

The Communists likewise campaigned from abroad and in Bulgaria against the government's Jewish policy. Georgi Dimitrov and Vasil Kolarov broadcast over the pirate radio station "Hristo Botev" condemnations of discrimination and deportation. Illegal presses inside Bulgaria issued appeals to the Jews to rise in revolt against the government and to Bulgarians to protest the anti-Jewish measures. Although the success of these appeals was limited, the Communists through the partisan movement presented an opportunity for the most militant method of fighting the government. Many Jews did join the resistance detachments, but there was no large-scale revolt within the Jewish community.

Some historians, journalists, and commentators maintain that the Bulgarian Communist party led the resistance to the anti-Jewish measures and inspired the popular resistance which prevented deportations.[13] While the BKP certainly led the general military resistance in Bulgaria during the war, there is little to support the claim that they were the most effective group in determining the fate of the Jews. Their very alienation from Bulgarian ruling circles prohibited influence on the government. Boris and Filov did not follow the advice of Dimitrov and Kolarov in 1943, and it is inconceivable that the BKP inspired Peshev and Stefan to their protests.

General Conclusions

The most significant conclusion to be derived from the Bulgarian experience with the Final Solution is the rather undramatic and matter-of-

12.   Interview with B. Piti, January 1966, Jaffa, Israel (this information has subsequently been published under the title *Te, spasitelite* [They, the rescuers] [Tel Aviv: n.p., 1969]); interview with G. M. Dimitrov, Washington, D.C., May 1967.

13.   See, for example, Natan Grinberg, *Hitleristkiiat natisk za unishtozhavane na evreite ot Bulgariia* [The Hitlerist pressure for destroying the Jews of Bulgaria] (Tel Aviv: "Amal," 1961). For BKP activity on behalf of the Jews information comes from interview with B. Piti, January 1966, Jaffa, Israel.

fact quality of the events. At first glance a statement of the facts is quite astonishing. The Jews of a small nation closely allied to the Nazi Reich survived the holocaust. It seems as if some drama must have been played out here to make Bulgaria different from the other nations—great and small—in Hitler's Europe. However, an investigation of the facts has shown that the survival of Bulgaria's Jewish community was not so surprising.

The overpowering image of Hitler dominating Europe and his fixation on the destruction of the Jews hides the actual diversity that existed in Nazi-dominated Europe. Despite Bulgarian claims that theirs was the only country in which all Jews survived, their experience was not unique. Denmark was more dramatic and courageous, Italy more persistent, Finland more thorough. The Bulgarian Jews, like a great many Rumanian and Italian Jews, and all of the Finnish Jews, were saved because these countries were allied to the Reich rather than defeated by it. (Berlin never concerned itself with Finland's two thousand Jews.)

The Final Solution was Berlin's plan—not Rome's, not Bucharest's, not Helsinki's, not Sofia's. The German Nazis wanted to destroy the Jews; the Bulgarians and the other allies of Hitler did not. The association of fascism with anti-Semitism is not verified by the facts. Italy's fascism, the model for Europe, enlisted Jewish Italians along with Christians. Fascist Italy and Francoist Spain protected their Jewish citizens from the Nazi net, indeed even went out of their way to protect Jews who were not their citizens. Also, Hitler's allies included governments which were neither fascist nor anti-Semitic. Bulgaria is a prime example.

While the Nazis administered the occupied lands, and hence the Jews there were doomed, they could reach the Jews of their allies only through the foreign office and diplomacy. Therefore it was in the allied countries where the Jews had the best chance for survival. Even though Denmark alone among the occupied lands was able to save its Jewish community by smuggling them to Sweden—it was over 90 percent successful—Denmark's characterization by Berlin as a model satellite gave it leeway for action similar to that of the allies.

In Yugoslavia the government defied Hitler in 1941. The country was overrun; and over 60,000 members of the Jewish community (1939 population—75,000) were destroyed, with help, it may be added, from the Bulgarians. In a similar situation in Bulgaria the government cooperated and the Jews survived—the irony of history manifest.

Perhaps we can gain some additional insight into the application of the Final Solution by examining the destruction process in Bulgaria's neighboring countries. The Wehrmacht occupied Serbia and Greece, and there the Jews fell under direct Nazi control. On the other hand, Rumania as an independent and diplomatic ally of the Reich held the same relationship to Germany as Bulgaria.

In Serbia and Greece the Nazis accomplished their grisly work without much difficulty or complication. In the former area they decimated the Jewish community by mass shootings even before the Wannsee conference. Anti-Jewish legislation on the German model went into effect in Serbia on May 30, 1941, shortly after the fall of Yugoslavia. In autumn of the same year the foreign office representatives in Belgrade wanted to send Jewish men from Serbia down the Danube into Rumania. Diplomatic complications made this suggestion impracticable, and the government did not implement the request. In any case beginning in October the Wehrmacht began a policy of executing Jewish and Gypsy men as reprisal for acts of resistance by Yugoslavs. In this manner the Germans killed from 4,000 to 5,000 Jews. At the same time, beginning in November the RSHA concentrated Jewish women and children (about 15,000) in a camp at Zemun near Belgrade. By June 1942 the SS had killed nearly all of these in mobile gas units disguised as Red Cross vans. The Nazis used both of these liquidation methods in the USSR before the establishment of the Polish extermination centers. Thus in Serbia about 20,000 of a total of 23,000 Jews perished before the summer of 1942.[14]

The Germans destroyed the Jewish community of Greece almost as thoroughly as that of Serbia, but in a different fashion, relying on the basic plan of the Wannsee conference. Most of Greece's 74,000 Jews— a total of 53,000—lived in Salonika. About 13,000 lived in areas controlled by Italians, and, as elsewhere in Europe, Rome went out of its way to protect them. By March 1943 the other Jews of Greece were already living under a strict regime including forced labor battalions. Beginning in that month the RSHA began deporting the community of Salonika and its environs. Because a German military governor administered this region, the Nazis did not have the diplomatic problems they had in Bulgaria. Enlisting the aid of Salonika's chief rabbi by telling him that the Jews were to be resettled in Poland, district by district from March to June the Nazis sent almost all of the Salonika Jews to Auschwitz. Jews from the remaining areas of Greece, including, after the fall of Mussolini, those from the Italian-administered sections as well as the

14. Raul Hilberg, *The Destruction of the European Jews* (Chicago; Quadrangle Books, 1961), pp. 433-42.

Albanian Jews, became subject to deportation after the Salonika operation. From the fall of 1943 to July 1944, the Wehrmacht and SS rounded up Jews from the mainland and Aegean islands and sent them to the extermination centers in Poland. In all, the Nazis deported over 60,000 Jews from Greece and Albania.[15]

Rumania, one of the most anti-Semitic countries in Europe, had one of the continent's largest Jewish populations. There were 800,000 Jews in Rumania in 1939, but after the Soviet annexation of Bessarabia and the Vienna Award only 350,000 remained within the borders of the country. Still, once the Rumanians reoccupied Bessarabia and Bukovina in 1941, 300,000 of the lost Jews again came under Bucharest's authority. Rumania did not need Germany to inspire anti-Semitic legislation. With the growth of native fascism in the thirties under the guise of organizations like the Iron Guard and A. C. Cuza's League of National Christian Defense, Rumania's Jews suffered some of the same restrictions that the Nazis introduced into Germany; but Rumania's laws were based exclusively on religion, not ancestry. Only in August 1940 as Bucharest approached the Axis alliance, did the Rumanian government introduce anti-Semitic legislation modeled on that of Nuremberg.

As in Bulgaria, Rumania's application of the Final Solution can be divided into two parts—the fate of the Jews in the Regat (old Rumania) and the fate of those in recaptured Bessarabia and Bukovina. For the most part the Regat Jews survived, while a significant number of those from Bessarabia and Bukovina perished. Also like the Bulgarians, the Rumanians eagerly confiscated property of Jews from all areas. However, there were some notable differences between the two neighboring kingdoms attributable in large measure to the presence of a genuine fascist movement and widespread anti-Semitism in Rumania. For one thing, in 1941 two large, unorganized pogroms occurred in Rumania, which, while not part of the systematic Nazi destruction process, were responsible for the deaths of thousands of Jews. In January in an attempted revolution by the Iron Guard the fascists cruelly murdered about a thousand Jews, and in June, in the wake of the invasion of the Soviet Union, Rumanian soldiers on a rampage killed over four thousand Jews in Iasi (in the Regat). Probably thousands more perished as the government evacuated the Jews of the city.

More significant than these pogroms, the Rumanians had the only

15. Ibid., pp. 442-53; Gerald Reitlinger, *The Final Solution: The Attempt to Exterminate the Jews of Europe, 1939-1945* (New York: Beechhurst Press, 1953), pp. 370-79.

government besides that of the Nazis which operated an extermination center. In the fall of 1941 Bucharest began the expulsion of Bessarabia's Jews across the Dniester River into concentration camps in the Podolia section of the Ukraine (between the Dniester and the Bug rivers). Already before this time the Rumanians had expelled thousands of Jews across the Dniester when that area was under German control and an *Einsatzgruppe* operated there. A great number of Jews had died at that time. After Rumanian control began, 185,000 Jews went to concentration camps in Podolia. Only ten thousand of these came from the Regat. Over one hundred thousand of these Jews were executed by shooting or starved to death in the camps.

Later, in August 1942 the Rumanians agreed to deport the Jews of the Regat to extermination centers in Poland, but as in Bulgaria, diplomatic entanglements and the changing course of the war prevented the fulfillment of these plans. In fact, no Rumanian Jews went to Poland (except, again as in Bulgaria, a few whom the Nazis caught outside the state). In 1943 the Rumanians relaxed their regime in the Podolia camps; they allowed Jews to leave the country for Palestine rather easily; and they ceased consideration for implementing the plans of the Wannsee conference in their country. The striking similarities between anti-Semitic Rumania and philo-Semitic Bulgaria emphasize the prominent role that the course of the war had in saving those Jews who survived in both countries.[16]

Just as the Jews of the collaborating countries had a better chance than those of the conquered, inside Bulgaria those who were close to the government were usually more effective champions of the Jews than those who were in opposition. It was not primarily through an enraged public or defiant anti-Nazis that the Jews escaped deportation, but first through the action of the government and its supporters. Anti-Nazis, such as Metropolitan Stefan, were instrumental in convincing the government to change its plans, but Peshev took the initial step in reversing deportations, and the government itself had to make the final decision.

The Jewish question in Bulgaria as elsewhere in the world concerned "political anti-Semitism" as opposed to "social anti-Semitism." As such, the key to behavior was alliance to Germany. Generally Hitler's friends and allies became anti-Semites; his foes became champions of the Jews, often despite their personal beliefs. There was a natural tendency to develop anti-Semitic attitudes as a process of rationalization. We have

16.   Hilberg, pp. 485-509; Reitlinger, pp. 394-411.

seen that this happened to Boris and Filov in the critical days of 1943. The implementation of the Final Solution, however, was a political action, not a social one.

Political forces determined the result of the Bulgarian Final Solution. Upon entering into the German alliance, the government had decided that the Jews were expendable. Its second thoughts on this matter were not decisive enough alone to prevent deportations, but they did leave the government in a state of ambivalence. Boris and Filov permitted Belev to prepare for the Jewish deportations, indeed, to carry them out in part, because Nazi political influence upon them was greater than the influence opposing deportations. When this latter influence increased noticeably in March 1943 with the addition of significant government supporters, Filov, with Boris's approval, intervened to delay the culmination of the operation. Yet the Germans were still in control, and the government did carry out deportations from the occupied lands. By May, when once again the Jews of Bulgaria were to be deported, German influence had lessened considerably because of reversals in the war. Bulgarian opponents to the Jewish policy were able to halt the procedures. Only a new period of prolonged Nazi success could again activate them. Although internal forces were still important, the Allied victories in Russia, Africa, and Italy were most decisive in halting the destruction of Bulgarian Jewry in Bulgaria. The Bulgarian Jews' escape of the Polish extermination centers certainly depended on the fortunate circumstances that their deportations were scheduled at this critical juncture of the war.

If the Germans had really determined to eliminate the Bulgarian Jews in the spring and summer of 1943, they probably could have done so, but at a cost to the war effort higher than they wanted to pay. The elimination of some forty thousand Balkan Jews was simply not worth that much to them. We must consider that on the one hand the Germans at this time were sending millions of Jews to Poland from all over Europe, and that on the other Berlin had difficulties in procuring not only the Bulgarian Jews, but the Rumanian and Hungarian as well. All things considered, the Reich thought that its best policy was to leave the implementation of the Final Solution in the hands of Sofia.

Within the year after May 1943 Germany's position in the war was too weak to counteract Allied pressure on Bulgaria not to carry out deportations, even on a regime—the regency—which the Germans had fashioned for their own control. The war continued to go badly for the Germans, and deportations never became a serious question for Bulgaria again. So the fate of the Jews depended on political pressures on a malleable government: on the one side, the Reich, and on the other, influential opinion inside Bulgaria uniting with the Allies.

It is just as significant that the non-anti-Semitic, non-Nazi government of Bulgaria deported over eleven thousand foreign Jews as that they did not deport those with Bulgarian citizenship. Bulgarian leaders were not men with a warped ideology. They were not the "pathological international gangsters" that Allied propaganda proclaimed the Nazis and their allies to be. The rulers of Bulgaria during the war were similar to statesmen all over Europe, with similar backgrounds and traditions. That the Nazi ideology corrupted Bulgarian statesmen, forcing them to participate in at least part of the Final Solution, is more revealing than that the Nazis elsewhere cooperated with members of extreme anti-Semitic groups. The Bulgarian experience was dependent largely on circumstances and could have happened anywhere. Nazi attitudes could have corrupted persons who were not ideological anti-Semites. Given the opportunity, persons who in fact did not do so could have saved all or part of their Jewish community. Certainly in many countries besides Bulgaria both these things happened—non-Nazis participated in the destruction of European Jewry, and other Jews were saved. Indeed, traditional diplomats and "normal" men—including many in the SS who were closest to the actual operations—carried out a large part of the application of the Final Solution even in Germany. Even the hardened anti-Semite Himmler had to steel himself to carry out the duties pursuant to Jewish annihilation.[17]

The critical question, then, "Who saved the Bulgarian Jews?" cannot be answered because it is not really a valid question. Those who planned to place the Bulgarian Jews in a situation which would have required their rescue, that is, deportation to Poland, never completed their plans. On a melodramatic level, heroes and villains can be found in the Bulgarian story, but the determining factors in the disposition of the Final Solution in Bulgaria were the political forces at work on the Sofia government.

17. Hilberg, pp. 218-19.

Appendices

Abbreviations Used in Text

Bibliographical Essay

Index

Jewish Consistories in Bulgaria

These statistics are collected from the following sources: Commissariat for Jewish Questions, "Svedenie za naselcnieto na evreiskite obshtini i biudzhetite na sushtite" [Information on the population of Jewish communities and the budgets for the same], from the private collection of Benjamin Arditi, Holon, Israel; Bulgaria, Direction Générale de la Statistique, *Annuaire Statistique du Royaume de Bulgarie*, 34 (1942), pp. 27–28; Yugoslavia, Pretsednishtvo Ministarskog Saveta–Opshta Drzhavna Statistika, *Prethodni rezultati popisa stanovnishtva od 31 marta 1931 godine u Kraljevini Jugoslaviji* [Presidium of the Council of Ministers–General State Statistics, Tentative results of the census of population from 31 March 1931 in the Kingdom of Yugoslavia] (Belgrade: Government Press of the Kingdom of Yugoslavia, 1931), pp. 21-22; Greece, Statistique Générale de la Grèce, *Annuaire statistique de la Grèce*, 9 (1938), p. 33; List of commissariat delegates, CDIA, fund 190, op. 1, arh. ed. 8850 (inventory list 1, archival unit 8850), pp. 3-4, Bulgarian Jewish Organization Archives, copies of CDIA documents, vol. II; Natan Grinberg, *Dokumenti* [Documents] (Sofia: Central Consistory of Jews in Bulgaria, 1945), pp. 172-80. Grinberg, writing about the events of March 1943 and using other KEV documents, has minor differences from the commissariat list concerning population, which apparently is for some cities only approximate, and spelling of some delegates' names. Since Grinberg's list is not complete, I preferred to use the list from the Arditi collection for population. I have corrected the totals that appear on the original documents, which are in error.

Obshtina	Jews (1943)	Total Population[a]	1943 Budget (leva)	KEV Representative
1. Berkovitsa	79	6,081	226,935	Nedko Vatsev Vuchev (district governor)
2. Bitola[b]	2,700	32,982[c]	1,126,816	Georgi Dochev Dzhambizov (secretary of district director)
3. Burgas	1,520	36,230	1,020,536	Nikola Gerchev Ivanov (district governor)
4. Chirpan	210	11,288	152,000	Ivan Atanasov (district police chief)
5. Dobrich[b]	312	27,845[d]	669,204	Vladimir P. Ivanov (police chief)
6. Drama[b]	500	29,339[e]	231,260	Gulub Dimitrov (district controller)
7. Dupnitsa	960	15,044	703,511	Kiril Nodov (asst. police chief)
8. Ferdinand	101	5,959	197,100	Pavel Lulchev Bozhkov (district governor)
9. Giumiurdzhina[b]	775	30,130[e]	578,410	Iordan M. Rainov (mayor)
10. Gorna Dzhumaia	210	9,977	165,000	Stefan Ivanov Stamboliev (district governor)
11. Haskovo	1,030	26,516	528,092	St. Petrov (asst. police chief)
12. Iambol	925	24,920	745,748	Stoian Mitev (mayor)
13. Kavala[b]	1,700	49,980[e]	520,076	Iosif Popov (police chief)
14. Karnobat	330	8,944	142,325	Peniu Todorov Karamanov (district governor)

Obshtina	Jews (1943)	Total Population[a]	1943 Budget (leva)	KEV Representative
15. Kazanluk	520	11,598	296,958	Asen Georgiev Ignatov (district governor)
16. Kiustendil	650	15,861	541,500	Georgi Efimov (mayor)
17. Ksanti[b]	500	33,712[e]	313,392	Dobri Petev (asst. mayor)
18. Kurdzhali	200	6,487	99,800	Todor Penkov Vluskov (mayor)
19. Lom	416	14,658	412,087	Slavi Puntev (not a public official)
20. Nevrokop	514	8,767	170,780	Vasil Kostov Manov (district governor)
21. Nova Zagora	102	9,552	154,500	Vasil Iliev Burodzhiev (district governor)
22. Pazardzhik	1,316	23,228	830,216	Atanas Iliev Popov (district governor)
23. Pirot[b]	200	11,238[c]	159,564	Georgi Pavlov Popov (district governor)
24. Pleven	860	31,520	768,776	Stefan pop Stefanov (police chief)
25. Plovdiv	5,092	99,883	2,835,622	Dimitur Velikov (asst. mayor)
26. Provadiia	153	7,905	149,317	Petur Mitov Trifonov (district governor)
27. Razgrad	99	15,730	205,120	Boncho Panov Chobanov (district governor)
28. Ruse	3,220	49,447	2,377,922	Ivan Dochev (lawyer— not a public official)

Obshtina	Jews (1943)	Total Population[a]	1943 Budget (leva)	KEV Representative
29. Samokov	410	11,035	248,725	Dimitur Hristov Karastoianov (mayor)
30. Seres[b]	500	29,640[e]	342,150	Mihail Bochev (police chief)
31. Shumen	540	25,486	635,294	Dimitur Hristov Chavdarov (police chief)
32. Shtip[b]	480	20,097[c]	286,790	Ignat Atanasov Motsev (district police chief)
33. Silistra[b]	205	15,089[d]	194,853	Vladimir Stoichev Ivanov (district governor)
34. Skopje[b]	4,050	64,807[c]	2,912,000	Ivan Zahariev Iliev (police chief)
35. Sliven	625	30,571	386,329	Petur Minchev Solarov (not a public official)
36. Sofia	27,289	287,095	13,931,520	Iaroslav Kalitsin (KEV official)
37. Stara Zagora	490	29,825	488,600	Hristo P. Dimitrov (asst. police chief)
38. Varna	2,050	69,944	1,267,122	Stoian Panaiotov Ivanov (police chief)
39. Vidin	1,445	18,465	983,600	Ivan Petrov Nedelkov (Subranie representative)
40. Vratsa	125	16,177	117,900	Nikola Slavov Nikolov (mayor)

Obshtina	Jews (1943)	Total Population[a]	1943 Budget (leva)	KEV Representative
Central Consistory	—	—	1,209,180	Pencho Lukov (KEV official)
Totals	63,403	1,273,052	39,326,630	

a. From Bulgarian 1934 census unless otherwise noted.
b. In areas added to Bulgaria after August 1940: Drama, Giumiurdzhina, Kavala, Ksanti, and Seres in Thrace; Shtip, Skopje, and Bitola in Macedonia; Pirot in Serbia; and Dobrich and Silistra in southern Dobrudzha.
c. From Yugoslav census of 1931.
d. From a special Bulgarian census of 1941.
e. From Greek census of 1928.

The Dannecker-Belev Agreement

[Copies of the Bulgarian version of the Dannecker-Belev agreement are located in Natan Grinberg, *Dokumenti* (Documents) (Sofia: Central Consistory of Jews in Bulgaria, 1945), pp. 14-16 (from which this translation is made); and in Bulgarian Academy of Sciences, Institute for Balkan Studies, Section for Hebrew Studies archives, doc. no. 38. The German version is not found among the captured foreign office documents in Washington or among the public Bulgarian sources.]

AGREEMENT

for the deportation of the first 20,000 Jews from the new Bulgarian lands Thrace and Macedonia into the German eastern regions
attained between
Bulgarian Commissar for Jewish Questions, Mr. Aleksandur *Belev*, on one side, and German plenipotentiary, Captain of the Defense Detachment [SS-Hauptsturmführer] Theodor *Dannecker*, on the other side.

1. After confirmation by the Council of Ministers, in the new Bulgarian lands Thrace and Macedonia* will be prepared 20,000 Jews— without regard to age and sex—for deportation.

The German Reich is ready to accept these Jews in their eastern regions.

2. Departure stations, passengers, and number of trains are established as follows:

    a)   in Skopje   5,000 with 5 trains
    b)   in Bitola   3,000 with 3 trains

* Belev crossed out the words "from the new Bulgarian lands Thrace and Macedonia" in the title and "in the new Bulgarian lands Thrace and Macedonia" in the text.

c)	in Pirot	2,000 with 2 trains
d)	in G. Dzhumaia	3,000 with 3 trains
e)	in Dupnitsa	3,000 with 3 trains
f)	in Radomir	4,000 with 4 trains

As complete accommodation of the last 12,000 Jews in the camps is possible only until 15 April 1943, the German plenipotentiary will procure these 12 trains—insofar as this will be possible according to technical conditions—to be prepared to depart in the time from the end of March to 15 April 1943.

The Jews concentrated in the cities Skopje and Bitola will be deported after 15 April 1943.

3. The Bulgarian Commissariat for Jewish Questions as an organ of the Ministry of Internal Affairs and National Health accepts on behalf of the German Reich the guarantee that the following basic conditions will be fulfilled:

a) The inclusion of Jews exclusively is permitted in the transports.

b) Jews in mixed marriages are not to be included.

c) In case the Jews being deported are not yet deprived of their citizenship, then this must occur at their departure from Bulgarian territory.

d) Jews with contagious diseases are not to be included.

e) Jews may not carry with them any arms, poisons, currency, precious metals, etc.

4. For each transport one list of persons included in the transport will be prepared; this list must contain the name, surnames, date and place of birth, last residence, and occupation of the Jews in three copies.

Two copies are to be transferred to the German guard accompanying the transport, and one to the German plenipotentiary in Sofia. The Bulgarian government will give according to arrangement the necessary food supplies for about fifteen days, counting from the day of traveling to the train, as well as the necessary number of water casks.

5. The question of the guard for the transport is still to be decided. Possibly a German guard command will take over the transports even in the departure station.

6. a) The amount of monetary compensation payable by Bulgaria, determined according to the number of deportees, will be decided with a special agreement. The carrying out of the transports in opportune time will not be affected by this.

b) The expenses for the transport from the departure station to the destination are the responsibility of Bulgaria.

7.   The Bulgarian State Railway and the German State Railway will agree directly on the schedule of the trains as well as on the disposition of the means of transport.

8.   In no case will the Bulgarian government ask for the return of the deported Jews.

9.   The present agreement will be prepared in two copies in the Bulgarian and German languages, each of these copies being regarded as an original.

Sofia, 22 February 1943

A. Belev   (signed)

T. Dannecker   (signed)

Warrant No. 127 of the Council of Ministers and Related Documents

[These documents are translated from Natan Grinberg, *Dokumenti* (Documents) (Sofia: Central Consistory of Jews in Bulgaria, 1945), pp. 41-44.]

One Hundred and Twenty-seventh Warrant of the Council of Ministers, accepted at its meeting of 2 March 1943, protocol No. 32.

For The Commissariat for Jewish Questions

On the basis of art. 1 of the law for charging the Council of Ministers to take all measures for solving the Jewish question and matters connected with it, the following is approved:

The Commissar for Jewish Questions is charged to deport from the borders of the country in agreement with the German authorities up to 20,000 Jews, inhabiting the recently liberated territories.

Attending ministers: Bogdan Filov, Petur Gabrovski, Boris Iotsov, Dobri Bozhilov, Nikola Mihov, Nikola Zahariev, Hristo Petrov, Engineer Dimitur Vasilev, Engineer Vasil Radoslavov.

The present warrant is not subject to promulgation in the *State Gazette*.

To His Honor the Chairman
of the Council of Ministers

Ministry
of Internal Affairs and
National Health

Sofia

March, 1943
Sofia

REPORT
of Petur Gabrovski
Minister of Internal Affairs
and National Health

Relating to: Charging the Commissar for Jewish Questions to deport from the borders of the country in agreement with the German authorities up to 20,000 Jews, inhabiting the recently liberated territories.

Grounds: Art. 1 of the law for charging the Council of Ministers to take all measures for solving the Jewish question and matters connected with it.

Mister Chairman:

According to the agreement attained between the Commissar for Jewish Questions and the German plenipotentiary Theodor Dannecker, it is intended that 20,000 Jews inhabiting the recently liberated territories are about to be deported outside of the boundaries of the country. For this purpose it is necessary to charge the Commissar for Jewish Questions to accomplish this deportation.

As we report to you above, Mister Chairman, please present to the esteemed Council of Ministers the proposal that, if they approve, they accept the following

WARRANT:

The Commissar for Jewish Questions is charged to deport from the borders of the country in agreement with the German authorities up to 20,000 Jews, inhabiting the recently liberated territories.

Concerns: The Ministry of Internal Affairs and National Health—The Commissariat for Jewish Questions

Minister: P. Gabrovski

To His Honor the
Chairman of the Council
of Ministers

The Ministry of
Internal Affairs
and   Sofia
National Health
No. . . . .
. . . . March 1943
Sofia

REPORT
of Petur Gabrovski, Minister
of Internal Affairs and National
Health

Relating to: Charging the Commissar for Jewish Questions to deport from the borders of the country in agreement with the German authorities up to 20,000 Jews, inhabiting the recently liberated territories and lodged in camps in the cities of Skopje, Pirot, G. Dzhumaia, and Radomir. [*sic*]

Grounds: Art. 1 of the law for charging the Council of Ministers to take all measures for solving the Jewish question and matters connected with it.

Mister Chairman:

Concerning the agreement achieved between the Commissar for Jewish Questions and the German plenipotentiary—Theodor Dannecker—it is intended that up to 20,000 Jews, without regard to sex and age, who inhabit the recently liberated territories and are lodged in the camps in the cities of Skopje, Pirot, Gorna Dzhumaia, Dupnitsa, and Radomir are about to be deported outside the borders of the country. For this purpose it is necessary to charge the Commissar for Jewish Questions to accomplish this deportation.

As we report to you above, Mister Chairman, please present to the esteemed Council of Ministers the proposal that, if they approve, they accept the following

WARRANT:

The Commissar for Jewish Questions is charged to deport from the borders of the country in agreement with the German authorities up to 20,000 Jews, without regard to sex and age, inhabiting the recently liberated territories and lodged in camps in the cities of Skopje, Pirot, Gorna Dzhumaia, Dupnitsa, and Radomir.

Concerns: The Ministry of Internal Affairs and National Health—The Commissariat for Jewish Questions.

Minister: P. Gabrovski

Signatories of the Subranie Protest of March 17, 1943

[The names are taken from a photostat of the protest letter supplied by the archives of the Kibbutz Lohamei HaGhetaoth. Some of the names are barely legible, but I believe that I have identified all of them through comparison with a roster of the members of the twenty-fifth Narodno Subranie. The representatives did not actually sign the letter with their own hands; rather apparently one person wrote all the names at the end of the letter. The names appear here in the order in which they appear on the letter. For convenience complete names and districts are given.]

Dimitur Iosifov Peshev	Kiustendil I
Georgi Zhelezov Svinarov	Provadiia II
Spas Marinov Popovski	Belogradchik
Aleksandur Gatev Krustev	Nikopol I
Todor Pavlov Kozhuharov	Sofia urban III
Petur Georgiev Mihalev	Kiustendil III
Ignat Iliev Haidudov	Pleven II
Marin Ivanov Tiutiundzhiev	Shumen I
Simeon Kirov Halachev	Omortag
Georgi Petrov Kenderov	Pazardzhik I
Sotir Ianev Drobachki	Dupnitsa I
Sirko Stanchev Petkov	Zlatograd
Doncho Dimov Uzunov	Gorna Oriahovitsa II
Dr. Ivan Kotsev Iotov	Pazardzhik II
Danail Zhechev Kunev	Kotel
Dr. Petur Ivanov K'oseivanov	Peshtera
Andro Hristov Lulchev	Nikopol II
Georgi Mikov Ninov	Pleven IV

Aleksandur Tsalov Tsankov	Sofia urban I
Nikola Stoichev Mushanov	Sofia urban II
Vasil Hristov Velchev	Novi Pazar I
Dimitur Nikolov Ikonomov	Dupnitsa II
Ivan Dimitrov Minkov	Stara Zagora III
Iliia Dimitrov Slavkov	Nevrokop
Georgi p. Stefanov Prodanov	Sredets
Stefan Stoianov Statelov	Gorna Oriahovitsa I
Ivan Vasilev Petrov	Teteven
Georgi Todorov Krustev	Plovdiv rural IV
Stefan h. Vasilev Karaivanov	Karlovo I
Tasko Stoichkov Stoilkov	Sveti Vrach
Aleksandur Simov Gigov	Breznik
Filip Dimitrov Mahmudiev	Gorna Oriahovitsa III
Dimitur Atanasov Arnaudov	Sliven I
Petur Markov h. Petrov	Elena
Kiro Kostadinov Arnaudov	Chirpan I
Dr. Ivan Kirov Vazov	Stara Zagora I
Dr. Georgi Rafailov Popov	Nova Zagora II
Dr. Ivan Beshkov Dunov	Pleven III
Nikola Ivanov Gradev	Popovo II
Hristo Stoianov Taukchiev	Nova Zagora I
Rusi Ivanov Marinov	Stara Zagora II
Panaiot Todorov Stankov	Vidin III
Dr. Nikola Ivanov Durov	Devina

Dr. Petko Stoianov Stainov (Kazanluk I) attached a note to the protest giving it his full support, but did not sign it properly because, despite the presence of signatures of some prominent members of the opposition, he regarded it as a document of the government faction.

Bulgarian Cabinets from October 23, 1939, to September 9, 1944

Formed October 23, 1939

Prime Minister and Foreign Affairs	Georgi K'oseivanov
Internal Affairs	Ned'o Nedev
War	Teodosi Daskalov
Finance	Dobri Bozhilov
Agriculture	Ivan Bagrianov
Justice	Vasili Mitakov
Education	Bogdan Filov
Trade	Slavcho Zagorov
Railroads	Petur Gabrovski
Public Works	Dimitur Vasilev

Formed February 15, 1940

Prime Minister and Education	Bogdan Filov
Foreign Affairs	Ivan Popov
Internal Affairs	Petur Gabrovski
War	Teodosi Daskalov
Finance	Dobri Bozhilov
Agriculture	Ivan Bagrianov
Justice	Vasili Mitakov
Trade	Slavcho Zagorov
Railroads	Ivan Gorianov
Public Works	Dimitur Vasilev

On February 4, 1941, Bagrianov resigned and Dimitur Kushev replaced him.

Formed April 11, 1942

Prime Minister and Foreign Affairs	Bogdan Filov
Internal Affairs	Petur Gabrovski
War	Nikola Mihov
Finance	Dobri Bozhilov
Agriculture	Hristo Petrov
Justice	Konstantin Partov
Education	Boris Iotsov
Trade	Nikola Zahariev
Railroads	Vasil Radoslavov
Public Works	Dimitur Vasilcv

Formed September 14, 1943

Prime Minister and Finance	Dobri Bozhilov
Foreign Affairs	Sava Kirov
Internal Affairs	Docho Hristov
War	Rusi Rusev (of Gabrovo)
Agriculture	Ivan Beshkov
Justice	Konstantin Partov
Education	Boris Iotsov
Trade	Ivan Vazov
Railroads	Hristo Petrov
Public Works	Dimitur Vasilev

On October 13, 1943, Kirov resigned and Dimitur Shishmanov replaced him.

Formed June 1, 1944

Prime Minister (without portfolio)	Ivan Bagrianov
Foreign Affairs	Purvan Draganov (From June 12)
Internal Affairs	Aleksandur Stanishev
War	Rusi Rusev (of Gabrovo)
Finance	Dimitur Savov
Agriculture	Doncho Kostov
Justice	Rusi Rusev (of Kotel)

Education	Mihail Arnaudov
Trade	Hristo Vasilev
Railroads	Boris Kolchev
Public Works	Slaveiko Vasilev
	(From June 12)

On June 12, 1944, Aleksandur Staliiski replaced Rusev as minister of justice. Rusev of Kotel replaced Kostov as minister of agriculture.

Formed September 2, 1944

Prime Minister and Foreign Affairs	Konstantin Muraviev
Internal Affairs (in charge of railroads)	Vergil Dimov
War	Ivan Marinov
Finance (in charge of Trade)	Aleksandur Girginov
Agriculture	Hristo Popov
Justice (in charge of Education)	Boris Pavlov
Public works	Stefan Daskalov
Ministers without portfolio	Nikola Mushanov
	Dimitur Gichev
	Atanas Burov

Formed September 9, 1944*

Prime Minister (without portfolio)	Kimon Georgiev (Zveno)
Foreign Affairs	Petko Stainov (Zveno)
Internal Affairs	Anton Iugov (BKP)
War	Damian Velchev (Zveno)
Finance	Petko Stoianov (independent)
Agriculture	Asen Pavlov (BZNS)
Justice	Mincho Neichev (BKP)
Education	Stanko Cholakov (Zveno)
Trade	Dimitur Neikov (BRSDP)

* The cabinet of September 9, 1944, was the first since May 19, 1934, to be formed according to political parties.

Railroads	Angel Durzhanski (BZNS)
Public Works	Boris Bumbarov (BZNS)
Health	Racho Angelov (BKP)
Social Welfare	Grigor Cheshmedzhiev (BRSDP)
Propaganda	Dimo Kazasov (independent)
Ministers without Portfolio	Dorbi Terpeshev (BKP)
	Nikola Petkov (BZNS)

Abbreviations Used in Text

AIU	Alliance Israélite Universelle
BAN	Bulgarska akademiia na naukite (Bulgarian Academy of Sciences)
BDZh	Bulgarski durzhavni zhelezultsi (Bulgarian State Railway)
BKP	Bulgarska komunisticheska partiia (Bulgarian Communist party
BNB	Bulgarska narodna banka (Bulgarian National Bank)
BRSDP	Bulgarska rabotnicheska sotsial-demokraticheska partiia (Bulgarian Workers' Social Democratic party)
Bulgarian Jewish Organization	General Cultural-Educational Organization of the Jews in the People's Republic of Bulgaria
BZNS	Bulgarski zemedelski naroden suiuz (Bulgarian National Agrarian Union)
CDIA	Tsentralen durzhaven istoricheski arhiv (Central State Historical Archives)
DV	*Durzhaven Vestnik* (*State Gazette*)
EAM	Ethniko Apeleftherotiko Metopo (National Liberation Front)
ELAS	Ethnikos Laikos Apeleftherotikos Stratos (National Popular Liberation Army)
IMRO	Internal Macedonian Revolutionary Organization
JTA	Jewish Telegraph Agency
KEV	Komisarstvo za evreiskite vuprosi (Commissariat for Jewish Questions)
MHI-Yad WaShem	Belgrade, Military Historical Institute, archives, copies of documents in Yad WaShem
OF	Otechestven front (Fatherland Front)
OKW	Oberkommando der Wehrmacht
ONS	Obiknoveno Narodno Subranie (Ordinary National Assembly)
RAM	Reichsaussenminister

RM	Reichsmark
RSHA	Reichssicherheitshauptamt
SAMS	State Archives of the People's Republic of Macedonia
SS	Schutzstaffel
T120	German Records Microfilmed at Alexandria, Va. (now located in the National Archives, Washington, D.C.), Microcopy No. T120
Yad WaShem	Yad WaShem Martyrs' and Heroes' Memorial Authority (Jerusalem)
YIVO	YIVO Institute for Jewish Research (New York)
ZZN	Zakon za zashtitata na natsiiata (Law for the Defense of the Nation)

Bibliographical Essay

The major sources for this work are found in archives in Sofia, Bulgaria; Israel; and Washington, D.C.; but supplementary material can be located elsewhere. The captured German records in the National Archives (Washington, D.C., the National Archives and Records Service General Services Administration, German Records Microfilmed at Alexandria, Va.) are a great boon to the historian of World War II. These are the only records of a European power, except Italy, open for that period. I relied heavily on these documents not only for the German view of the Bulgarian Final Solution, but also for general information on international diplomacy and the internal state of affairs in Bulgaria. The archives of the foreign office (microcopy no. T120), particularly those from the Inland II geheim files, are, of course, the most pertinent. Kent's directory to the foreign office documents (George O. Kent, comp. and ed., *A Catalog of Files and Microfilms of the German Foreign Ministry Archives, 1920–1943*, 3 vols. [Stanford, Calif.: Hoover Institution, Stanford University, 1962–1966]) is invaluable for finding relevant material. Records of the Department of State, also in the National Archives, supplement the German information, but since the Americans were not represented in Sofia during most of the war, the latter is far more useful. State Department documents filed under classification 874.4016 concern the Bulgarian Jews.

I was unable to use the collection of the Central State Historical Archives (CDIA) in Sofia for the research for this book, but fortunately documents from the archives' files pertaining to the Jews have been copied and photostated for deposit in various archives throughout the world. Seven volumes of such copies are located in the archives of the General Cultural-Educational Organization of the Jews in the People's Republic of Bulgaria. Although some commissariat reports and other

223

classified material are included, most of the items copied are public documents.

Documents of the KEV pertaining to the deportation of Jews from the occupied territories and attempts to deport them from Bulgaria were published shortly after the war in Natan Grinberg's *Dokumenti* [Documents] (Sofia: Central Consistory of Jews in Bulgaria, 1945). The archives of the Hebrew Studies section (*Ebroistika sektsiia*) of the Bulgarian Academy of Sciences' Institute for Balkan Studies contain many copies of German and Bulgarian documents concerning the Jews during the war. They also hold depositions of survivors and participants, press clippings and other items of general interest such as revenue stamps from the KEV and special markings for Jewish persons, homes, and businesses. The library has many volumes about the Jews in Bulgaria during all periods.

In Israel the archives of the Yad WaShem Martyrs' and Heroes' Memorial Authority include depositions of survivors, copies of German documents, copies of documents from the Military Historical Institute at Belgrade, and an incomplete copy of the Protocols of People's Court No. 7, 6 vols. (Sofia: n.p., 1945)—also found in BAN, Ebroistika. Several other archives in Israel contain interesting and vital documents. The HaShomer HaTzier kibbutz "Moreshet" at Givat Harira has copies of CDIA items as well as material relevant to rescue operations organized by the Jewish agency and HaShomer HaTzier. The Ghetto Fighters' House (Kibbutz Lohamei HaGhetaoth), Haifa, has copies and originals of Bulgarian documents including a copy of the Peshev protest letter of March 1943. The archives of the Ichud Olei Bulgariyah (Union of Bulgarian Immigrants) contain depositions of survivors and volumes about Bulgarian Zionism.

Several important documents, in particular commissariat reports, are in the possession of Mr. Benjamin Arditi of Holon, Israel. His library contains many examples of Bulgarian anti-Semitic literature and books and brochures written in defense of the Jews. Mr. Arditi kindly allowed me to see some of these reports, but before I finished surveying them, he informed me that I could no longer use them. He planned to sell them to a private institution, and one of the conditions of the sale was that the documents were not to be used before the transaction. I have been unable to learn from Mr. Arditi whether or not the transaction has taken place or the name of the archives.

In Yugoslavia the archives of the Military Historical Institute and the Organization of the Jewish Religious Communities of Yugoslavia, both in Belgrade, have documents concerning the Jews under Bulgarian occupation in that country. The State Archives of the People's Republic of Macedonia at Skopje contain documents from the Commissariat for Jewish Questions concerning their activities in Macedonia and records from the Jewish Religious Community of Skopje.

Finally, some additional useful material is located in the Wiener Library in London, Le Centre de Documentation Juive Contemporaine in Paris, and the YIVO Institute for Jewish Research in New York. The Wiener Library and YIVO have collections of press clippings and wire releases concerning the Bulgarian Jews. All three have copies of German documents and Le Centre de Documentation has some Bulgarian copies.

Published sources of great value include the Bulgarian *Durzhaven Vestnik* [State gazette], which contains laws, decrees, and orders enacted by the National Assembly, the Council of Ministers, and the Commissariat for Jewish Questions, and the *Stenografski Dnevnitsi* [Stenographic minutes] of the Bulgarian National Assembly (Sofia: Narodno Subranie, 1938-1944). Regenstein Library of the University of Chicago has most of the minutes for the 24th and 25th ordinary national assemblies.

There are a great number of memoirs of Bulgarians, Germans, Jews, and Allied leaders which shed light on the events of the period. Most of the more familiar memorialists of World War II have only scattered references to Bulgaria, but of great value are Floyd H. Black, *The American College of Sofia: A Chapter in American-Bulgarian Relations* (Boston: Trustees of Sofia American Schools, 1958); Dimo Kazasov, *Burni godini 1918-1944* [Turbulent years 1918-1944] (Sofia: Knigaizdatelstvo "Naroden pechat," 1949); George Rendel, *The Sword and the Olive: Recollections of Diplomacy and the Foreign Service, 1913-1954* (London: John Murray, 1957); and Rabbi Daniel Tsion, *Pet godini pod fashistki gnet (Spomeni)* [Five years under fascist terror (memoirs)] (Sofia: n.p., 1945). The statements of participants deposited in various archives are also extremely useful. I fould that written statements are more reliable than oral interviews, although I conducted many of the latter, including interviews with ambassadors Rendel and Beckerle, Dimo Kazasov, Petko Stainov, Josef Geron, Buko Levi, and Daniel Tsion.

I also surveyed many contemporary Bulgarian and foreign newspapers and news journals for political information. Quite often, I found more insight in the major Western dailies, e.g., the *New York Times* and the London *Times*, than in the government-controlled or censored Bulgarian press. Yet relying on the Western papers alone can be hazardous because they often contain errors of fact, omission, or interpretation. Of the Bulgarian news sources, the *Biuletin na Tsetralnata konsistoriia na evreite v Bulgariia* [Bulletin of the Central Consistory of Jews in Bulgaria] published in Sofia, 1920-1942, is of more than routine interest. The Library of Congress contains *La Parole Bulgare* and *Bulgarische Wochenschau*, two government papers which were published during the war. *Bulgarski periodichen pechat, 1844-1944: anotiren bibliografski ukazatel* [Bulgarian periodic press, 1844-1944: an annotated bibliographic directory] edited by Dimitur P. Ivanchev, 3 vols. (Sofia: "Nauka i izkustvo," 1962-1969) is a comprehensive study of Bulgarian periodic publications and extremely useful for the modern Bulgarian historian. The newspaper *Naroden Sud* [People's court] appeared in eight issues in Sofia in 1944 and 1945. It reported the results of the war crimes trials in Bulgaria and contained important documents such as excerpts from the diaries of Professor Filov and General Mihov. The newspaper *Otechestven Front* [Fatherland front] also had extracts from Filov's diary in 1944 and 1945.

There is no good modern history of Bulgaria. A number of monographs dealing with specific periods, persons, or events are useful for garnering information. Joseph Rothschild, *The Communist Party of Bulgaria 1883-1936: Origins and Development* (New York: Columbia University Press, 1959) is valuable for the political history of the entire period. The Bulgarian Academy of Sciences, *Istoriia na Bulgariia* [History of Bulgaria], edited by D. Kosev et al., 3 vols. (Sofia: "Nauka i izkustvo," 1962-1964) is the standard history in Bulgarian. On World War II Nikofor Gornenski, *Vuoruzhenata borba na bulgarskiia narod za osvobozhdenie ot hitleristkata okupatsiia i monarho-fashistkata diktatura—1914-1944 g.* [The armed struggle of the Bulgarian people for liberation from the Hitlerist occupation and the monarcho-fascist dictatorship—1941-1944] (Sofia: Natsionalen suvet na Otechestveniia front, 1958) and Mitka Grubcheva, *V imeto na naroda* [In the name of the people] (Sofia: BKP, 1962) are of particular interest.

I also found two unpublished Ph.D. dissertations very valuable: Nissan Oren, "The Bulgarian Communist Party, 1934-1944" (Columbia University, 1960) and Marin V. Pundeff, "Bulgaria's Place in Axis Policy" (University of Southern California, 1958). Early in 1972, Mr. Oren brought out an expanded monograph based on his work—too late to use in this study.

On the general question of the Jewish holocaust in Europe I have relied a great deal on Raul Hilberg, *The Destruction of the European Jews* (Chicago: Quadrangle Books, 1961), but have found Gerald Reitlinger, *The Final Solution: The Attempt to Exterminate the Jews of Europe 1939-1945* (New York: Beechhurst Press, 1953), also of use.

Books on the Bulgarian Jews before World War II are difficult to find, but more have been appearing, especially because of the work of the Hebrew Studies section of the Institute for Balkan Studies in Sofia. Since 1966 the Bulgarian Jewish Organization has published annually a yearbook which contains articles on Jewish history in the country up through the twentieth century. The Union of Bulgarian Immigrants in Tel Aviv has sponsored a study edited by A. Romano, Joseph Ben, and Nisim (Buko) Levy, *Yehudut Bulgariyah* [The Jews of Bulgaria] (Jerusalem: Encyclopedia of the Jewish Diaspora Co., 1968) which relates the Bulgarian Jews' history from earliest times. Saul Mezan, *Les Juifs Espagnols en Bulgarie* (Sofia: n.p., 1925) is still extremely valuable. N. M. Gelber, "Jewish Life in Bulgaria," *Jewish Social Studies*, 8 (1946), pp. 103-26, is the best account in English of the Jews in prewar Bulgaria. Peter Meyer's chapter on Bulgaria in the collection he edited, *The Jews in the Soviet Satellites* (Syracuse, N. Y.: Syracuse University Press, 1953) relies heavily on Gelber for the prewar account and is of limited value for the events during the war.

Most accounts of the Bulgarian Jews during the war are of a polemical or popular nature. Haim Keshales, "Tova se sluchi v onezi dni: Belezhki za zhivota na evreite v Bulgariia prez 1939-1950 godini" [It happened in those days: notes on the life of the Jews in Bulgaria during the period 1939-1950] is a sober account of the events by a participant. The unpublished Bulgarian original is located at Yad WaShem, but there is a Hebrew version in *Yehudut Bulgariyah*. Haim Oliver, *Nie, Spasenite, ili kak evreite v Bulgariia biahi iztrugnani ot lagerite na smurtta (hronika ot blizkoto minalo)* [We, the saved, or how the Jews in Bulgaria were snatched from the camps of death (a chronicle of the recent past)] (Sofia: Izdatelstvo za literatura na chuzhdi eziki, 1967) is a good popular account which the publishers have translated into several languages including English. Nissan Oren, "The Bulgarian Exception: A Reassessment of the Salvation of the Jewish Community," *Yad WaShem Studies on the European Jewish Catastrophe and Resistance*, 13 (1969), pp. 83-106, is an excellent scholarly summary.

Benjamin Arditi, *Roliata na tsar Boris III pri izselvaneto na evreite ot Bulgariia* [The role of King Boris III in the deportation of the Jews from

Bulgaria] (Tel Aviv: n.p., 1952) is of value, as the author was a participant, but it too often sinks to the level of a polemic on behalf of the king. Arditi's *Yehudi Bulgariyah Bishanot Hamishpat Hanatsi: 1940-1944* [The Jews of Bulgaria during the years of Nazi occupation: 1940-1944] (Tel Aviv: Israel Press, 1962), while still overemphasizing the importance of Boris on the outcome of events, is a more scholarly work. Natan Grinberg, *Hitleristkiiat natisk za unishtozhavane na evreite ot Bulgariia* [The Hitlerist pressure for destroying the Jews of Bulgaria] (Tel Aviv: Amal, 1961), is a polemical history of the events directed against the king. An account of this type in English emphasizing the role of the popular masses in determining the fate of the Jews is Matei Yulzari, "The Bulgarian Jews in the Resistance Movement," in *They Fought Back: The Story of the Jewish Resistance in Nazi Europe*, edited and translated by Yuri Suhl (New York: Crown Publishers, 1967), pp. 275-81. Another account on the role of public opinion is Vladislav Topalov, "L'opinion publique bulgare contre les persécutions des juifs (octobre 1940-9 septembre 1944)," in *Études Historiques à l'occasion du XXIIᵉ Congrès Internationale des Sciences Historiques—Vienne, août-septembre, 1965, II* (Sofia: BAN, 1965).

There are two important works which give accounts of the role of individuals and institutions in the events of the war years: Eli Baruh, *Iz istoriiata na bulgarskoto evreistvo* [From the history of the Bulgarian Jews] (Tel Aviv: n.p., 1960); and Misho Leviev, ed., *Nashata blagadarnost* [Our thanks] (Sofia: Sbornik "kadima" [1946])—a copy of this is in the New York Public Library. Buko Piti of Jaffa, Israel, had prepared a similar unpublished manuscript which he kindly allowed me to see. He later published this under the title *Te, spasitelite* [They, the rescuers] (Tel Aviv: n.p., 1969).

The Central Consistory of Jews in the People's Republic of Bulgaria has prepared a memorial tome, *Evrei-zaginali v anti-fashistkata borba* [Jews killed in the anti-Fascist battle] (Sofia: Nasionalen komitet na Otechestveniia front, 1958) which deals with Jewish partisans. David B. Koen, "Eksropriatsiata na evreiskite imushtestva prez perioda na hitleristkata okupatsiia" [Expropriation of Jewish property during the period of the Hitlerist occupation], in the *Godishnik* [Yearbook] of the Bulgarian Jewish Organization, 2 (1967), pp. 109-10, is an excellent account of the economic aspects of the Bulgarian Jewish policy. Aleksandar Matkovsky has written two valuable accounts of the Bulgarian Jewish policy in Macedonia: *Tragedijata na Evreite od Makedonija* [The tragedy of the Jews of Macedonia] (Skopje: "Kultura," 1962); and

"The Destruction of Macedonian Jewry," *Yad WaShem Studies on the European Jewish Catastrophe and Resistance*, 3 (1959), pp. 222-58. Rabbi Michael Molho has edited an account of the war years in Greece, including the Bulgarian occupied zones: *In Memoriam: Hommage aux victimes juives des Nazis en Grèce* (Salonika: Salonika Jewish Community, 1948).

Index

Action Juive, 156
Aegean Islands, 196
Africa, 49, 52, 198
Agrarians. *See* Bulgarian National Agrarian Union
Albania: World War II in, 21, 158; border of, 44-45; Macedonian Jews flee to, 122, 124, 125; Jews in, 124, 195-96
Alexander II, King of Yugoslavia, 4
Alexandroupolis. *See* Dede Agach
Alfasa, Avraham, 91
Alliance Israélite Universelle, 30-31
Allied Control Commission, 177
Allies: and rescue of Jews, xiv, 130-31, 135-37, 138, 154, 155-57, 174, 103, 198; and Eastern Europe, 11; and Balkans, 13, 20; and Germany, 14, 15, 154; Bulgarian attitudes toward, 15, 57, 129, 138, 158, 172, 175; and World War II, 52, 136-37, 139, 154, 157, 158, 177, 181; air raids over Bulgaria of, 75-76, 132, 139, 155, 169; Bulgarian peace overtures to, 160, 171, 172, 174-75; mentioned, 140. *See also* Bulgaria—Allies
Altenburg, Günther, 162n
Altunov, Victor, 102
American College of Sofia, 41-42
Amin el Husseini (Grand Mufti of Jerusalem), 137
Andreev, Dimitur, 153, 190
Angelov, Racho, 218
Ankara, 156, 160, 165, 170, 174
Anti-Comintern Pact, 14
Anti-Semitism: in Germany, 23-27, 33, 74, 121-22, 139, 199; in Poland, 28; in Austria, 33; in United States, 33; in Rumania, 33, 196, 197; and King Boris, 36-37, 96, 139, 184-85, 197-98; and fascism, 37-38, 43, 194; in Europe, 40, 194, 197, 199; in Greece, 101-02; in Macedonia, 140-41. *See also* Bulgaria—Jews: Bulgarian attitudes toward; Legislation: Bulgarian anti-Semitic

Antonescu, Ion, 156
Antonov (president of soldiers' association in Giumiurdzhina), 108n
Arabs, 132, 133, 137, 182
Arditi, Benjamin, 62, 145, 146
Argel (German military attaché in Sofia), 169n
Armenians, 153-54, 182-83
Ashkenazim, 27-28, 31, 59
Asseov, Jaques, 131
Atanasov, Hristo, 110
Atanasov, Zlato, 109n
Auschwitz, 27, 195
Austria: and Bulgaria, 12, 33, 71, 177; and Italy, 13; and Germany, 13, 26-27; Jews in, 26-27, 78-79; anti-Semitism in, 33
Auswärtige Amt. *See* German foreign office
Axis: and World War II, 44-45, 139, 157; and Jews, 87, 104, 137, 156, 186; and Rumania, 196; mentioned, 133. *See also* Bulgaria—Axis; Bulgaria—Relationship with Germany; Germany; Italy

Babalekov (president of Drama workingman's association), 108n

231